iMac®

FOR

DUMMIES®

6TH EDITION

iMac® FOR DUMMIES® 6TH EDITION

by Mark L. Chambers

John Wiley & Sons, Inc.

iMac® For Dummies®, 6th Edition

Published by
John Wiley & Sons, Inc.
111 River Street
Hoboken, NJ 07030-5774

www.wiley.com

WILEY

About the Author

Mark L. Chambers has been an author, computer consultant, BBS sysop, programmer, and hardware technician for more than 25 years — pushing computers and their uses far beyond "normal" performance limits for decades now. His first love affair with a computer peripheral blossomed in 1984 when he bought his lightning-fast 300 BPS modem for his Atari 400. Now he spends entirely too much time on the Internet and drinks far too much caffeine-laden soda.

With a degree in journalism and creative writing from Louisiana State University, Mark took the logical career choice: programming computers. However, after five years as a COBOL programmer for a hospital system, he decided there must be a better way to earn a living, and he became the Documentation Manager for Datastorm Technologies, a well-known communications software developer. Somewhere in between writing software manuals, Mark began writing computer how-to books. His first book, *Running a Perfect BBS*, was published in 1994 —and after a short fifteen years of fun (disguised as hard work), Mark is one of the most productive and best-selling technology authors on the planet.

His favorite pastimes include collecting gargoyles, watching St. Louis Cardinals baseball, playing his three pinball machines and the latest computer games, supercharging computers, and rendering 3D flights of fancy — and during all that, he listens to just about every type of music imaginable. Mark's worldwide Internet radio station, *MLC Radio* (at www.mlcbooks.com), plays only CD-quality classics from 1970 to 1979, including everything from Rush to Billy Joel to the *Rocky Horror Picture Show*.

Mark's rapidly expanding list of books includes *MacBook All-in-One For Dummies; MacBook For Dummies,* 2nd Edition*; Mac OS X Snow Leopard All-in-One For Dummies; Macs for Seniors For Dummies; Build Your Own PC Do-It-Yourself For Dummies; Building a PC For Dummies,* 5th Edition*; Scanners For Dummies,* 2nd Edition*; CD & DVD Recording For Dummies,* 2nd Edition*; PCs All-in-One Desk Reference For Dummies,* 4th Edition*; Mac OS X Tiger: Top 100 Simplified Tips & Tricks; Microsoft Office v. X Power User's Guide; BURN IT! Creating Your Own Great DVDs and CDs; The Hewlett-Packard Official Printer Handbook; The Hewlett-Packard Official Recordable CD Handbook; The Hewlett-Packard Official Digital Photography Handbook; Computer Gamer's Bible; Recordable CD Bible; Teach Yourself the iMac Visually; Running a Perfect BBS; Official Netscape Guide to Web Animation;* and *Windows 98 Troubleshooting and Optimizing Little Black Book*.

His books have been translated into 15 different languages so far — his favorites are German, Polish, Dutch, and French. Although he can't read them, he enjoys the pictures a great deal.

Mark welcomes all comments about his books. You can reach him at mark@mlcbooks.com, or visit MLC Books Online, his Web site, at www.mlcbooks.com.

Dedication

This book is dedicated to my youngest daughter, Rose Chambers — she of the Cleo Beast and Major Tom — with all the love and happiness I can give her.

Author's Acknowledgments

A guide to Apple's iMac should be as elegantly designed and straightforward as the computer itself . . . and luckily, I had just the right mix of folks to make sure that it turned out that way!

First, my thanks are due to my technical editor, Dennis Cohen, who kept watch on the accuracy of my facts, comments, and step-by-step procedures concerning both the Apple iMac and Mac OS X Snow Leopard.

I've often said that Wiley's Production team is the best in the business, and the layout and composition of this book is proof positive — my appreciation to everyone who lent a hand with the graphics, proofing, and cover work for *iMac For Dummies,* 6th Edition.

As with all my books, I'd like to thank my wife, Anne; and my children, Erin, Chelsea, and Rose; for their support and love — and for letting me follow my dream!

Lastly, I'd like to thank the two editorial professionals who made this book happen: my good friend Bob Woerner, the Wiley acquisitions editor who has guided my way through the jungle of technology yet again; and Nicole Haims, my hard-working project editor, who somehow fit several chapters of new material into the same page count. It's folks like the two of you who make this the greatest career on the planet — my heartfelt thanks to you both from a very grateful Mac owner!

Publisher's Acknowledgments

We're proud of this book; please send us your comments at http://dummies.custhelp.com. For other comments, please contact our Customer Care Department within the U.S. at 877-762-2974, outside the U.S. at 317-572-3993, or fax 317-572-4002.

Some of the people who helped bring this book to market include the following:

Acquisitions, Editorial, and Vertical Websites

Project Editor: Nicole Haims
   (Previous Edition: Paul Levesque)

Senior Acquisitions Editor: Bob Woerner

Copy Editor: Nicole Haims

Technical Editor: Dennis Cohen

Editorial Manager: Jodi Jensen

Vertical Websites Project Manager:
   Laura Moss-Hollister

Vertical Websites Assistant Project Manager:
   Jenny Swisher

Vertical Websites Associate Producers: Josh
   Frank, Marilyn Hummel,
   Douglas Kuhn, Shawn Patrick

Editorial Assistant: Amanda Graham

Sr. Editorial Assistant: Cherie Case

Cartoons: Rich Tennant
   (www.the5thwave.com)

Composition Services

Project Coordinator: Patrick Redmond

Layout and Graphics: Timothy C. Detrick,
   Joyce Haughey, Kelly Kijovsky

Proofreaders: Rebecca Denoncour,
   John Greenough, Sossity R. Smith

Indexer: Becky Hornyak

Publishing and Editorial for Technology Dummies

   Richard Swadley, Vice President and Executive Group Publisher

   Andy Cummings, Vice President and Publisher

   Mary Bednarek, Executive Acquisitions Director

   Mary C. Corder, Editorial Director

Publishing for Consumer Dummies

   Kathleen Nebenhaus, Vice President and Executive Publisher

Composition Services

   Debbie Stailey, Director of Composition Services

Contents at a Glance

Table of Contents

Introduction

Skeptical about your new anodized aluminum iMac, with that super-charged Intel dual-core or quad-core processor? Perhaps you're thinking it's too doggone thin, or you're wondering where all the buttons are. Shouldn't there be places to plug cables? And where the heck is the DVD drive you paid for? (Oh, there it is, on the side, at the top right.)

Ladies and gentlemen, I have great news for you: Not only did you make The Right Decision about which computer to buy — you shot a hole in one! The aluminum iMac has everything a computer power user could want: speed, the latest in hardware and standards, a top-of-the-line LED screen, and all the connectors you need to add just about any device meant for today's computers.

I wrote this book especially for the proud Intel iMac owner who wants to make the most of this new stunning aluminum computer, so this book is a guide to both the iMac hardware and *Snow Leopard,* the latest version of Apple's superb Mac OS X (operating system). I start by describing the basics that every iMac owner should know and then move on to chapters devoted to the software that comes with your iMac. Along the way, you come across a generous sprinkling of power user tips and tricks that save you time, effort, and money.

Like my half-dozen other *For Dummies* titles, I respect and use the same English language you do, avoiding jargon, ridiculous computer acronyms, and confusing techno-babble whenever possible.

What's Really (Not) Required

Here's a reasonably complete list of what's not required to use this book:

- ✔ I make no assumptions about your previous knowledge of computers and software.

- ✔ Heck, you don't even need the computer! If you're evaluating whether the new iMac is right for you, this book is a great choice.

- ✔ Upgrading from the monster that is a PC running the Windows operating system? I've got tips, tricks, and entire sections devoted to those hardy pioneers called *Switchers!* You can see all about the similarities and differences between the iMac running Snow Leopard and the PC running Windows. I also show you how to make the switch as easy and quick as possible.

✔ If your friends and family told you that you're going to spend half your life savings on software — or that no "decent" software is available for Mac computers — just smile quietly to yourself! The iMac comes complete with about a ton more software than any Windows box, and the iLife '09 suite of applications is better than anything available on a PC! (Note, however, that the iWork '09 applications provided with a new iMac are time-limited, so if you decide to use iWork '09 you'll have to buy a license code.)

So what is required? Only your desire to become a *power user* (someone who produces the best work in the least amount of time, and has the most fun doing it)!

This book was written using the latest Intel dual-core iMac computer, so owners of older iMac computers might not be able to follow along with everything I cover. If you upgraded an older Intel iMac with Mac OS X Snow Leopard and the iLife '09 application suite, you should be able to use most of the book with no problem!

About This Book

Each chapter in this book is written as a reference on a specific hardware or software topic. You can begin reading anywhere you like because each chapter is self-contained. However, I recommend that you read the book from front to back because the order of this book makes a great deal of sense.

Conventions Used in This Book

Even with a minimum of techno-speak, this book needs to cover the special keys that you have to press or menu commands that you have to choose in order to make things work — hence this short list of conventions. (Note that you usually have to press the Return key before anything happens when entering a manual command.)

✔ **Stuff you type.** If I ask you to type (or enter) something, like in a text box or field, that text appears in bold, like this:

Type me.

If I ask you to type a command within Mac OS X, that text appears like this:

```
Type me.
```

✔ **Menu commands.** I list menu paths and commands using another format. For example, this instruction indicates that you should click the Edit menu and then choose the Copy menu item:

Edit⇨Copy

✔ **Web addresses.** No up-to-date book on a computer would be complete without a bag full of Web addresses for you to check out. When you see these in the text, they look like this: `www.mlcbooks.com`.

✔ **For the technically curious.** Tangential techy stuff is presented in sidebars, and you don't have to read them unless you want to know what makes things tick.

How This Book Is Organized

After careful thought (read that *flipping a coin*), I divided this book into seven major parts — plus an index, just because you deserve one! For your convenience, cross-references to additional coverage of many topics are also sprinkled liberally throughout the book.

Part 1: Know Your iMac

This part introduces you to the important features of your iMac — like where all the cables connect (or don't) — and helps you set up your system. I also introduce *Mac OS X Snow Leopard,* the Apple operating system that comes preinstalled on your aluminum iMac.

Part II: Shaking Hands with Mac OS X

Time to familiarize you with Snow Leopard — how to take care of mundane chores (like moving your stuff) as well as how to customize and personalize your system until it fits like the proverbial glove! Switchers from the PC world will be especially interested in mastering the ins and outs of Mac OS X.

Part III: Connecting and Communicating

Time to jump into the one application you're likely to use every single day: your Safari Web browser! You can also read here about Apple's MobileMe Internet subscriber service and how to connect your iMac for printing, scanning, videoconferencing, and faxing. (I told you this thing was powerful, didn't I?)

Part IV: Living the iLife

Ah, readers, you can begin humming happily to yourself right this second! Yep, this part provides coverage of the latest iLife '09 release, with the names that are the envy of the Windows crowd: iPhoto, iMovie, iDVD, iWeb and GarageBand (along with iTunes, which is available for Windows). You see how to turn your iMac into the hub for all your digital media. Whether you listen to it, display it, compose it, offer it online or direct it, this part of the book explains it!

Part V: Getting Productive with iWork and Other Tools

Part V is dedicated to the iWork '09 productivity suite. You'll learn how to produce works of office art: spreadsheets, presentations and printed documents that deliver your message with aplomb. I also discuss how to share your iMac among a group of people or how to connect your iMac to a network. (Wired or wireless, makes no difference to me!)

Part VI: The Necessary Evils: Troubleshooting, Upgrading, Maintaining

So you want to upgrade your iMac with more memory or new hardware? If you need to troubleshoot a problem with your hardware or software, my should-be-patented troubleshooting guide resides in this part. Finally, I describe what you can do to help keep your iMac running as fast and as trouble free as the day you took it out of the box!

Part VII: The Part of Tens

The two chapters that make up the famous "Part of Tens" section are served in classic Late Night style: Each chapter contains a quick reference of tips and advice on a specific iMac topic. Each list has ten concise tips, and one or two readers have told me that they make excellent tattoos. (Personally, I'm not *that* much of a Mac guru.)

If you're dying to find out how to share data among wireless devices via Bluetooth technology and iSync — or how to broadcast your music around your house like Wolfman Jack — check out the handy Bluetooth and Wireless bonus chapter at the MLC Books Online Web Site (www.mlcbooks.com).

Icons Used in This Book

Like other technology authors, I firmly believe that important nuggets of wisdom should **stand out on the page!** With that in mind, this *For Dummies* book includes a number of margin icons for certain situations:

This is the most popular icon in the book, and you find these parked next to suggestions that I make to save you time and effort (and even cash!).

You don't have to know this stuff, but the technologically curious love high-tech details. (Of course, we're great fun at parties, too.)

Always **read the information for this icon first!** I'm discussing something that could actually harm your hardware or throw a plumber's helper into your software.

Consider these nuggets as highlighter stuff — not quite as universally accepted (or as important to the author) as a Mark's Maxim but good reminders nonetheless. I use these icons to reinforce what you should remember.

These nuggets are easily spotted; just look for the likeness of my rugged, iMac-lovin' mug. These are My Favorite Recommendations. In fact, I'll bet just about any iMac power user would tell you the same. Follow my Maxims to avoid the quicksand and pitfalls that I've encountered with all sorts of Macs for well over a decade!

Where to Go from Here

My recommendations on how to proceed? You know, I just happen to have three:

- ✔ If you're thinking about buying a new iMac, the box is still unopened in your living room, or you'd like help setting things up, I would start with Part I.

- ✔ If your iMac is already running but you'd like guidance with running Mac OS X — Windows Switchers, take note — start with Part II.

- ✔ For all other concerns, use the index or jump straight to the chapter you need. (You can always return later, at your leisure.)

A Final Word

I'd like to thank you for buying this book, and I hope that you find *iMac For Dummies,* 6th Edition, valuable! With this book in hand, I believe that you and your aluminum iMac supercomputer will bond together as I have with mine. (That sounds somewhat wrong, but it's *really* not.)

Part I
Know Your iMac

The 5th Wave   By Rich Tennant

"Phillip just got a new redesigned iMac
and gave me his old one to use."

In this part . . .

Your iMac odyssey begins with a description of the computer itself, as well as the details you need to know when unpacking and setting up your newest family member. You also find an introduction to Mac OS X Snow Leopard, the latest version of Apple's super-popular operating system.

Chapter 1

Okay, This Machine Looks Really, Really Weird

· ·

In This Chapter

▶ Identifying the important parts of your iMac

▶ Locating the right home for your computer

▶ Plugging stuff in and getting hooked up

▶ Playing with your bundled software

▶ Buying additional stuff that you might need

· ·

*Y*ou bought a brand-new iMac, and there it sits, in the box. Waiting. Waiting for you.

If you're a little nervous about unpacking that shiny aluminum-and-glass rectangle, I completely understand. Face it: The latest iMac follows in the footsteps of many revolutionary iMac designs that have come before it. (In other words, it doesn't *look* like a computer at all, and that can be a bit disconcerting.) And if you're switching from a Windows PC to the Apple universe, you might find yourself floating weightlessly in your office or your living room without a familiar bulky beige box to anchor yourself. Hence the reluctance you might be feeling.

However, dear reader, let me assure you that you've indeed made The Right Choice. I commend you! The aluminum Intel iMac is the fastest, leanest, and easiest-to-use self-contained all-in-one computer ever built. Practically everything's in one shining panel (except for your keyboard and mouse). You've got one of the best backlit LED screens on the planet, a super-fast processor, room for a ton of RAM (memory), and a regular laundry list of the latest technology. Best of all, you don't have to be a techno-nerd to use all that power!

In this chapter, I introduce you to your new dream machine, giving you an overview of the more important locations within iMac City. I show you how to unpack your new computer, what wires go where, and where your iMac should set up housekeeping. I preview the awesome software that's waiting within that powerful panel. Finally, I list the accessories that help keep both you *and* your new iMac computing smoothly.

An Introduction to the Beast

The Intel iMac might look like a sculpture straight out of your local museum of modern art, but it still sports everything that it needs to function as a computer. In this section, I identify the important stuff that you need to live your life — you know, write a term paper in Pages, hear the music you downloaded, or manage the affairs of those lazy Sims.

Major parts of your major appliance

Every computer requires some of the same gizmos. Figure 1-1 helps you track them down. Of course, as you'd expect, a computer has a "body" of sorts in which all the innards and brains are stored (the screen, in this case), a display screen, a keyboard, a mouse/pointing device, and ports for powering and exchanging data with peripherals.

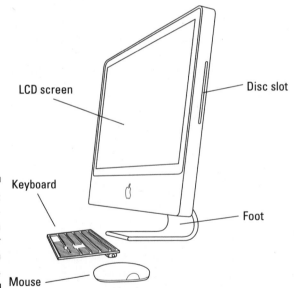

LCD screen

Disc slot

Keyboard

Figure 1-1:
The charismatic form of your aluminum Intel iMac.

Foot

Mouse

That magnificent screen

What a view you've got! An aluminum iMac is graced with either a 21.5" or 27" LED display.

LED screens use far less electricity than their antique CRT ancestors, and they emit practically no radiation (less, in fact, than even the LCD screens Apple recently used).

Both sizes of iMac screens offer a *widescreen* aspect ratio (the screen is considerably wider than it is tall), which augurs well for those who enjoy watching DVD movies. (A favorite editor of mine loves it when I use the antique word *augur,* meaning *to predict or foretell.*) For example, the 27" screen boasts a whopping 2560 x 1440 resolution.

That reminds me: Throw away your printed dictionary! You won't need it because Mac OS X Snow Leopard includes the fantastic Dictionary widget that uses the Internet to retrieve definitions from Dictionary.com. More on the widgets in Chapter 5 . . . and yes, the Dictionary widget does contain *augur*.

The keyboard and mouse

Hey, here's something novel for the Intel iMac — something *external* (outside the computer's case). Gotta have a keyboard and mouse, right? And you gotta love the options with iMac: You'll go nomadic . . . um, that is, wireless and free.

The iMac comes standard with a truly 21st century combo of an Apple wireless keyboard and Magic Mouse! This dynamic duo lets you sit back and relax with your keyboard in your lap, without being tied down by a cord. (Say it with me: "Death to cords, death to cords.") Just stay within about 30 feet of your iMac screen, and sweet freedom is yours. You can also feel safe using these wireless peripherals because they offer secure 128-bit, over-the-air encryption, which helps keep sensitive information safe while you type and click away. One downside about the wireless keyboard, though: Unlike the previous wired keyboard, the wireless model doesn't include any USB ports, and you will need a supply of batteries. (Go rechargeable!)

The keyboard is a particular favorite of mine because from here

- You can either control the sound volume (using the volume control buttons F11 and F12) or mute all that noise completely (using the Mute button F10).

- A handy-dandy Media Eject key lets you eject a CD or DVD.

The wireless Magic Mouse needs a flat surface, but that's what TV trays are for, right?

The disc slot

You'll notice a long groove on the right edge of your iMac. No, it's not for your credit card. (If you order online often enough, you'll memorize your card number.) This slot accepts standard-size CDs and DVDs into your optical drive (don't try using mini-CD or DVD discs in your iMac — they can get stuck and Ruin Your Day). If the drive is empty, loading a disc is as simple as sliding it in an inch or so; the drive sucks in the disc automatically. (And we don't need no stinkin' floppy drive. Macs haven't had floppy drives for years now, and the PC types are just beginning to follow.)

"Luke, the printed label side of the disc should always be *facing you* when you load a disc. Always."

Yes, your computer has a foot . . . just one

You and I — normal human beings — would say that the iMac is supported by a sturdy aluminum stand, but Apple calls it a *foot*. The foot lets you tilt the iMac panel up and down for the best viewing angle. Most importantly, though, the foot minimizes the computer's desk space requirements (or its *footprint*). (Engineers . . . sheesh.) And yes, that foot is perfectly balanced and quite stable, so there's no danger of your treasured iMac taking a dive.

If you decide to get really snazzy and mount your 27-inch iMac to the wall, you can remove the foot and install the VESA mounting adapter (available separately for about $30). You can use any VESA standard mounting bracket on your wall, too. You can be positioned within 30 yards or so of your wall-mounted iMac with a wireless Apple keyboard and mouse.

Hey, Hewlett-Packard or Dell, can you mount one of those monolithic PCs to the wall? *I think not.*

Food for your ears

A machine this nice had better have great sound, and the iMac doesn't disappoint. You have a couple of options for iMac audio:

- ✔ **The iMac sports built-in stereo speakers (and a microphone to boot)**
- ✔ **Built-in ports connect your iMac audio to either**
  - • More powerful (and more expensive) external speaker systems
  - • A set of headphones
  - • A home stereo system

The power cable

Sorry, but you can't get a wireless power system . . . yet. (Apple's working hard on that one.) With the wireless keyboard and mouse setup, the power cable is actually the only required cable that you need to run your computer! Now that's *sassy*.

The power button

Yep, you've got one of these, too. It's on the back of the case.

Those holes are called ports

Our next stop on your tour of Planet iMac is Port Central — that row of holes on the back of your computer (see Figure 1-2). Each port connects a different type of cable or device, allowing you to easily add all sorts of extra functionality to your computer.

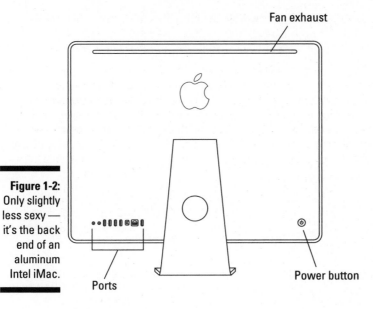

Fan exhaust

Figure 1-2:
Only slightly
less sexy —
it's the back
end of an
aluminum
Intel iMac.

Ports

Power button

Each of these stellar holes is identified by an icon to help you identify it.
Here's a list of what you'll find as well as a quick rundown on what these
ports do.

 ✔ **FireWire:** These ports are the standard in the Apple universe for connecting external hard drives and DVD recorders, but they do double
duty as the connector of choice for most digital video (DV) camcorders. (A *peripheral* is another silly techno-nerd term, meaning a separate
device that you connect to your computer.) Note that the iMac offers a
FireWire 800 port, which is twice as fast as the older FireWire 400 port —
the ports are shaped differently, so you can't plug a FireWire 400 device
into a FireWire 800 port in error. (Converter cables are available that
allow you to plug a FireWire 400 device into your FireWire 800 port.)

 ✔ **USB:** Short for *Universal Serial Bus,* the familiar USB port is the jack-of-
all-trades in today's world of computer add-ons. Most external devices
(such as portable hard drives, scanners, or digital cameras) that you
want to connect to your iMac use a USB port. The iMac sports four USB
2.0 ports on its back. USB 2.0 connections are much faster than the old
USB 1.1 standard.

For the specs on connecting your keyboard and mouse, see the upcoming section, "Absolutely essential connections."

For more on FireWire and USB ports, get the lowdown in Chapter 23.

 ✔ **Ethernet:** The iMac includes a standard 10/100/1000 Ethernet port, so
it's ready to join your existing wired Ethernet network. (Alternatively,
you can go wireless for your network connection; find more on that in
the next section and in Chapter 21.)

Apple doesn't include a built-in modem on the iMac, so if you need a dialup connection to the Internet, you need an external 56K v.92 USB modem. (Apple sells a USB modem, which can send and receive faxes, too.)

 ✔ **Mini DisplayPort:** In case that splendid screen isn't quite big enough, you can add an adapter to this port and send the video signal from your iMac to an LCD monitor or flatscreen TV with a DVI port. (Apple also offers different adapters that can connect your iMac to standard VGA monitors and projectors.)

Connections for external audio

Your Intel iMac comes equipped with two pretty powerful stereo speakers on the bottom of the case, but you're certainly not limited to them. Apple provides a number of connectors to add a wide range of audiophile equipment to your system.

 ✔ **Headphone/Optical Output:** You can send the high-quality audio from your rectangular beast to a set of standard headphones or to an optical digital audio device, such as a high-end, home theater system.

✔ **Line In:** Last (but certainly not least) is the audio Line In jack, which allows you to pipe the signal from another audio device into your iMac. This one comes in particularly handy when you record MP3 files from your old vinyl albums or when you want to record loops within GarageBand, which you can read more about in Chapter 15. This jack supports both analog and digital input.

Important Hidden Stuff

When you bought your new digital pride and joy, you probably noticed a number of subtle differences between the low-end iMac and the uber-expensive top-end model. I call these differences the *Important Hidden Stuff* (or IHS, if you're addicted to acronyms), and they're just as important as the parts and ports that you can see.

 ✔ **Hard drive:** The aluminum iMac uses *serial ATA* hard drives.

As I type these words, the iMac product line offers three different hard drive sizes, depending on the processor speed and screen size you choose: 500GB, 1TB or an immense 2TB (yes, friends and neighbors, that TB means *terabyte*, or 1000GB). The bigger, the better.

✔ **Optical drive:** Okay, I'm cheating a little here. I mention the optical drive in an earlier section, but all you can see is the slot, so it qualifies as an IHS item. All new iMac models include a DVD-R SuperDrive (which can play and record both CDs and DVDs).

✔ **Wireless Ethernet:** "Look, Ma, no wires!" As I mention earlier, your iMac can join an existing wireless Ethernet network with its built-in AirPort Extreme card. With wireless connectivity, you can share documents with another computer in another room, share a single high-speed Internet connection betwixt several computers, or enjoy wireless printing. Truly *sassy!*

Although Apple would want you to build your wireless wonderland with an Apple AirPort Extreme Base Station — go figure — you can actually use your iMac with any standard 802.11g or 802.11n wireless network. And yes, PCs and Macs can intermingle on the same wireless network without a hitch. (Scandalous, ain't it?)

✔ **Bluetooth:** Let's get the old "digital pirate" joke out of the way: "Arrgg, matey, I needs me a wireless parrot." (Engineers again . . . sheesh.) Although strangely named, Bluetooth is actually another form of wireless connectivity. This time, however, the standard was designed for accessories like your keyboard and mouse, and devices like your personal digital assistant (PDA) and cellphone. Bluetooth is now built in to every aluminum iMac.

✔ **SD Card slot:** This slot allows you to directly read photos and video from standard SD memory cards — photographers and video junkies, rejoice!

✔ **iSight camera:** The iMac's built-in video and still camera appears as a tiny lens and activity light at the top of your computer.

✔ **Video card:** If your applications rely heavily on high-speed 3-D graphics, you'll be pleased as punch to find that your iMac comes equipped with an NVIDIA GeForce 9400M, ATI Radeon HD 4670 or (for the more expensive models) an ATI Radeon HD 4850 card. All three cards are well suited to 3-D modeling, video editing, and well, honestly, blasting the enemy into small smoking pieces with aplomb.

Choosing a Home for Your New Pet

If you pick the wrong spot to park your new iMac, I can guarantee that you'll regret it later. Some domiciles and office cubicles obviously don't offer a choice — you've got one desk at work, for example, and nobody's going to hand over another one — but if you can select a home for your iMac, consider the important placement points in this section.

Picking the right location

You know the mantra: Location, location, location.

✔ **There's always the wall.** Your iMac can disguise itself as a particularly interesting digital picture frame. With the right mounting adapter, you can hang your computer right on the wall and snub your desk altogether.

This wall-mounted solution has two big problems:

- Your VESA mounting plate must be installed safely and correctly (for example, using the studs within your walls).

  The iMac is slim and trim, but it's no lightweight, and it doesn't bounce well. You don't want it to take a high dive!

- External peripherals aren't happy campers — that includes any FireWire and USB devices, which must either camp out on the floor or on a nearby (and conspicuous) shelf. (Personally, I think the cables for external devices tend to spoil the appearance of a wall-mounted computer.)

Your iMac must be mounted at the proper height on the wall. It's not good ergonomic practice to sit more than two feet away from your iMac's screen, and the screen should be placed at (or slightly below) eye level.

My solution? Don't plan on using any external devices. Instead, opt for a wireless network with a remote printer and remote backup storage space, like a Time Capsule unit on your network.

✔ **Keep things cool.** Your new iMac is nearly silent, but that super-fast Intel dual or quad-core processor generates quite a bit of heat. Fans inside the case draw the heat away. (Nothing like an overheated processor to spoil an evening of Civilization 4.)

Follow these three rules to keep your cool. Make sure that

- The location you choose is far from heating vents.

- The location you choose is shielded from direct sunlight.

- Allow plenty of room below the machine (where the air enters the case) and above the machine (where heated air escapes from the slot at the top of the case).

Hot air from a wall-mounted iMac can discolor the wall.

Considering the convenience factor

Technology is nothing if you can't make it convenient:

- ✓ **Outlets, outlets, outlets!** Your computer needs a minimum of at least one nearby outlet, and perhaps as many as three or four:

  - A standard AC outlet (I'll discuss surge protectors and uninterruptible power supplies at the end of this chapter)

  - A telephone jack (if you use an external USB modem for connecting to the Internet or sending and receiving faxes)

  - A nearby Ethernet jack (if you use the iMac's built-in Ethernet port for connecting to a wired Ethernet network)

    If you prefer to send your data over the airwaves, consider wireless networking for your iMac. I discuss everything you need to know in Chapter 21.

- ✓ **Don't forget the lighting.** Let me act as your Mom. (I know that's a stretch, but bear with me.) She'd say, "You can't possibly expect to work without decent lighting! You'll go blind!" She's right, you know. At a minimum, you need a desk or floor lamp.

- ✓ **Plan to expand.** If your iMac hangs out on a desk, allow an additional foot of space on each side. That way, you have space for external peripherals, more powerful speakers, and that wired keyboard and mouse.

Unpacking and Connecting

You are going to love this section — it's short and sweet because the installation of an aluminum iMac on your desktop is a piece of cake. (Sorry about the cliché overload, but this really *is* easy.)

Unpacking your iMac For Dummies

Follow these guidelines when unpacking your system:

- ✓ **Check for damage.** I've never had a box arrive from Apple with shipping damage, but I've heard horror stories from others (who claim that King Kong must have been working for That Shipping Company). Check all sides of your box before you open it.

Take a photograph of any significant damage (just in case).

✓ **Search for all the parts.** When you're removing those chunks o' Styrofoam, make certain that you check all sides of each foam block for parts that are snuggled therein or taped for shipment.

✓ **Keep all those packing materials.** Do *not* head for the trash can with that box and those packing materials. Keep your box intact and also keep all packing materials for at least a year until your standard Apple warranty runs out. If you have to ship it to an Apple service center, the box and the original packing is the only way for your iMac to fly.

And now, a dramatic Mark's Maxim about cardboard containers:

Smart computer owners keep their boxes far longer than a year.

For example, if you sell your iMac or move across the country, you'll want that box. *Trust me on this one.*

✓ **Store the invoice for safekeeping.** Your invoice is a valuable piece of paper, indeed.

Save your original invoice in a plastic bag, along with your computer's manuals and original software, manuals, and other assorted hoo-hah. Keep the bag on your shelf or stored safely in your desk, and enjoy a little peace of mind.

✓ **Read the iMac's manual.** "Hey, wait a minute, Mark — why do I have to read the manual from Apple along with this tome?" Good question, and here's the answer: There might be new and updated instructions in the documentation from Apple that override what I tell you in this book. (For example, *"Never* cut the red wire. Cut the blue wire instead." Or something to that effect.)

Besides, Apple manuals are rarely thicker than a restaurant menu.

Connecting cables like a true nerd

The iMac makes all its connections really simple, but your computer depends on you to get the outside wires and thingamabobs where they go.

Absolutely essential connections

After your new iMac is resting comfortably in its assigned spot (I assume that's a desktop), you need to make a minimum of one connection: the power cable. Plug the cable into the corresponding socket on the iMac first; then plug 'er in to that handy AC outlet.

Your batteries will need to be installed in your wireless keyboard and mouse. After the batteries are in, you're set to go.

Adding the Internet to the mix

If you have Internet access or a local computer network, you need to make at least one of the following connections.

If you don't already have *any* Internet service, you'll probably want to start with local dialup Internet access (if you have an external USB modem for your iMac). If you decide to investigate your high-speed options immediately, your local cable and telephone companies can provide you with more information on DSL or cable Internet service.

Dialup Internet access

If you get on the Internet by dialing a standard phone number, you'll need an external USB modem to connect your iMac. Follow these steps:

1. **Plug your external USB modem into one of the USB ports on the back of your iMac.**

2. **Plug one of the telephone cable's connectors into your modem's line port.**

3. **Plug the other telephone cable connector into your telephone line's wall jack.**

Networks and high-speed Internet access

If you have high-speed Internet service or if you're in an office or school with a local computer network, you can probably connect through the iMac's built-in Ethernet port. You make two connections:

1. **Plug one end of the Ethernet cable into the Ethernet port on the iMac.**

2. **Plug the other end of the Ethernet cable into the Ethernet port from your network. It's probably one of the following:**

   • An Ethernet wall jack

   • An Ethernet hub or switch

   • A cable or DSL Internet router (or sharing device)

Will you be joining a wireless network? If so, you find all the details you need in Chapter 21 to configure Snow Leopard for wireless networking.

Discovering All the Cool Things You Can Do

This section answers the most common of all novice computer questions: "What the heck will I *do* with this thing?" You find additional details and exciting factoids about the software that you get for free, software you'll want to buy, and stuff you can do on the Internet.

What software do I get?

Currently, all iMac computers ship with these major software applications installed and ready to use:

- **The iLife suite:** You know you want these applications! They turn your iMac into a digital hub for practically every kind of high-tech device on the planet, including DV camcorders, digital cameras, portable music players, PDAs, and even cellphones.

  Chapters 11–16 of this book focus on the five major applications that make up iLife: iMovie, iDVD, iTunes, iPhoto, iWeb and GarageBand.

- **The iWork suite:** A *demo* version of Apple's powerful office productivity suite is included with your iMac. You can create documents, spreadsheets, and presentations within Pages, Numbers, and Keynote. It's much like that Other Office Suite (the one that costs a bundle) from those guys in Redmond.

  Figure 1-3 illustrates a flyer under construction in Pages.

- **Front Row:** This onscreen menu system makes it easy to watch movies, listen to your music, and display your favorite photos on that gorgeous iMac screen . . . all remotely, if you invest in an Apple Remote! I go into the details of Front Row in Chapter 10.

The installed software on your iMac might change as new programs become available.

Looking forward to fun on the Internet

What is a modern computer without the Internet? Apple gives you great tools to take full advantage of every road sign and offramp on the Information Superhighway, right out of the box:

✔ **Web surfing:** I use Snow Leopard's Safari Web browser every single day. It's faster and better designed than other browsers (although I might be biased). Safari includes tabbed browsing and has built-in RSS feeds.

If *tabbed browsing* and *RSS feeds* sound like ancient Aztec to you, don't worry. Chapter 8 is devoted entirely to Safari.

✔ **Web searches:** Your Dashboard widgets can search the entire Internet for stocks, movie listings, business locations, and dictionaries.

✔ **Chat:** *iChat* lets you use your iMac to chat with others around the world for free via the Internet — by keyboard, voice, or (with your built-in iSight Web camera) full-color video. This is awesome stuff straight out of Dick Tracy and Buck Rogers. If you've never seen a video chat, you'll be surprised by just how good your friends and family look!

Always wear a shirt when videoconferencing.

✔ **E-mail:** Soldier, Apple's got you covered. The Mail application is a full-featured e-mail system, complete with defenses against the torrent of junk mail awaiting you. (Imagine a hungry, digital, saber-toothed tiger with an appetite for spam.) Send pictures and attached files to everyone else on the planet, and look doggone good doing it.

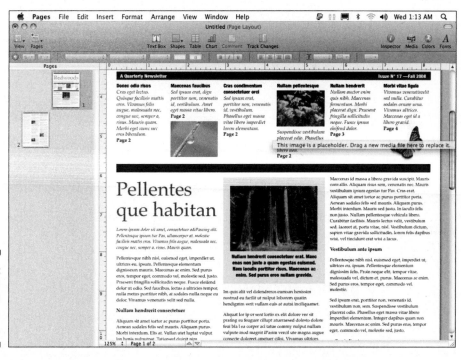

Figure 1-3: Pages is a great tool for home and office.

Applications that rock

Dozens of small applications are built into Mac OS X. I mention them in later chapters, but here are three good examples to whet your appetite:

- ✔ **iCal:** Keep track of your schedule and upcoming events, and even share your calendar online with others in your company or your circle of friends. See how to keep your life in order in Figure 1-4.

- ✔ **DVD Player:** Put all that widescreen beauty to work and watch your favorite DVD movies with DVD Player! You have all the features of today's most expensive standalone DVD players, too, including a spiffy onscreen control that looks like a remote.

- ✔ **Address Book:** Throw away that well-thumbed collection of fading addresses. Snow Leopard's Address Book can store, search, and recall just about any piece of information on your friends, family, and acquaintances.

You can use the data you store in your Address Book in other Apple applications that are included with Snow Leopard, such as Apple Mail and iChat.

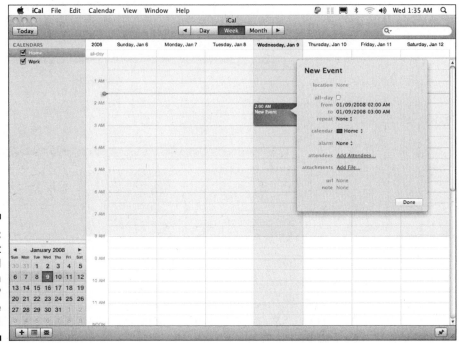

Figure 1-4:
Hey, isn't that iCal running on your iMac? You are iTogether!

Would you like to play a game?

"All productivity and no play. . . ." Hey, Steve Jobs likes a good challenging game as much as the next guy, so you can look forward to playing Chess on your iMac right out of the box — ah, but this isn't the chessboard your Dad used! Play the game of kings against a tough (and configurable) opponent — your iMac — on a beautiful 3-D board. Heck, your iMac even narrates the game by speaking the moves!

Stuff You Oughta Buy Right Now

No man is an island, and no computer is either. I always recommend the same set of stuff for new PC and Mac owners. These extras help keep your new computer clean and healthy (and some make sure you're happy as well):

✔ **Surge suppressor or UPS (uninterruptible power supply):** Even an all-in-one computer like your iMac can fall prey to a power surge. I recommend one of these:

- A *basic surge suppressor* with a fuse can help protect your iMac from an overload.

- A *UPS* costs a little more, but it does a better job of filtering your AC line voltage to prevent brownouts or line interference from

- A UPS provides a few minutes of battery power during a blackout so you can save your documents and safely shut down your iMac.

✔ **Screen wipes:** Invest in a box of premoistened screen wipes. Your iMac's screen can pick up dirt, fingerprints, and other unmentionables faster than you think.

Make sure your wipes are especially meant for flat-panel monitors or laptop computer screens.

✔ **Blank CDs and DVDs:** Depending on the type of media you're recording — like computer data CDs, DVD movies, or audio CDs — you'll want blank discs for

- CD-R (record once)

- CD-RW (record multiple times)

- DVD-R (record once)

- DVD-RW (record multiple times)

✔ **Cables:** Depending on the external devices and wired network connectivity you'll be using, these are

  • A standard Ethernet cable (for wired networks or high-speed Internet)

  • FireWire or USB cables for devices you already have

    Most hardware manufacturers are nice enough to include a cable with their products, but there are exceptions, especially USB printers. *Shame on those cheapskates!*

✔ **A wrist rest for both your keyboard and mouse:** You might have many reasons to buy a new iMac, but I know that a bad case of carpal tunnel syndrome is *not* one of them. Take care of your wrists by adding a keyboard and mouse rest (even for a wireless keyboard/mouse combo, even on a TV tray).

Chapter 2

Life! Give My iMac Life!

*I*f you've already been through Chapter 1, you got as far as unpacking your iMac and connecting at least one cable to it. And unless you solely bought this computer as a work of modern art, it's time to actually turn on your iMac and begin living The Good Life. (Plus, you still get to admire that Apple design whilst using iTunes.) After you get your new beauty powered on, I help you here with an initial checkup on your iMac's health.

I also familiarize you with the initial chores that you need to complete — such as using Mac OS X Setup as well as moving the data and settings from your existing computer to your iMac — before you settle in with your favorite applications.

In this chapter, I assume that Mac OS X Snow Leopard (version 10.6) was preinstalled on your iMac or that you just completed an upgrade to Snow Leopard from an earlier version of Mac OS X. (If you're upgrading, your iMac is already turned on — and you can skip the next section!)

Throwing the Big Leaf Switch

Your iMac's power switch is located on the back of the computer, at the lower-left corner of the case (as you look at the screen). Press it now to turn on your iMac, and you hear the pleasant startup tone that's been a hallmark of Apple computers for many years now. Don't be alarmed if you don't imme-diately see anything onscreen, because it takes a few seconds for the initial Apple logo to appear.

In my experience, a simple quick press of the power button on some iMacs sometimes just doesn't do it. Instead, you actually have to hold down the button for a count of two or so before the computer turns on.

While the Apple logo appears, you see a twirling, circular high-tech progress indicator appear that looks like something from a *Star Wars* movie. That's the sign that your iMac is loading Snow Leopard and checking your internal drive for problems. Sometimes the twirling circle can take a bit longer to disappear. As long as it's twirling, though, something good is happening.

Next, Snow Leopard displays the soon-to-be-quite-familiar Aqua Blue (yup, that's its name) background while it loads file sharing, networking, and printing components (and such).

At last, your patience of a whole 10–15 seconds is rewarded, and after a short (but neat) video, you see the Snow Leopard Setup Assistant appear.

Mark's Favorite Signs of a Healthy iMac

Before you jump into the fun stuff, don't forget an important step — a quick prelim check of the signs that your iMac survived shipment intact and happy. (Although the shipping box that Apple uses for the aluminum iMac series is one of the best I've ever encountered in 20-plus years of swapping computer hardware, your computer could still have met with foul play.)

If you can answer Yes to each of these questions, your iMac likely made the trip without serious damage:

1. **Does the computer's chassis appear undamaged?**

   It's pretty easy to spot damage to your iMac's svelte metal and glass design. Look for scratches, puncture damage, and misalignment of the screen.

2. **Does the LED screen work, and is it undamaged?**

   I'm talking about obvious scratches or puncture damage to your screen. Additionally, you should also check whether any individual dots (or *pixels*) on your LED monitor are obviously malfunctioning. Bad pixels either appear black or in a different color than everything surrounding them.

   Techs call these irritating anarchists *dead pixels*. Unfortunately, many new LED screens include one or two. After all, a 21.5" iMac screen sports literally more than one million pixels.

3. **Can you feel a flow of air from the vent on top?**

Your iMac's Intel processor generates quite a bit of heat, so the fan system never turns off completely. If you don't feel warm air from the fan system after your iMac has been on for a minute or two, you might have a problem.

4. **Do the keyboard and mouse work?**

Check your iMac's Bluetooth connection by moving the mouse; the cursor should move on your screen. To check the keyboard, press the Caps Lock key and observe whether the green Caps Lock light turns on and off.

If you do notice a problem with your iMac (and you can still use your Safari browser and reach the Web), you can make the connection to an Apple support technician at www.apple.com. If your iMac is lying on its back with its foot in the air and you can't get to the Internet, you can check your phone book for a local Apple service center, or call the AppleCare toll-free number at 1-800-275-2273. Chapter 22 also offers troubleshooting information.

Harriet, It's Already Asking Me Questions!

After your iMac is running and you've given it the once-over for obvious shipping damage, your next chore is to set up your iMac. Unlike other tasks in this book, I won't cover the setup process step by step. Apple "tweaks" the questions that you see during setup on a regular basis, and the questions are really very easy to answer. Everything is explained onscreen, complete with onscreen Help if you need it.

However, I do want you to know what to expect as well as what information you need to have at hand. I also want you to know about support opportunities, such as the AppleCare Protection Plan and the Apple MobileMe Internet services. Hence this section. Consider it a study guide for whatever your iMac's setup procedure has to throw at you.

Setting up Mac OS X Snow Leopard

After you start your iMac for the first time — or if you just upgraded from an earlier version of Mac OS X — your iMac will likely automatically launch the Snow Leopard set-up procedure. (Note that some custom install options, like the Archive and Install option, might not launch the Setup procedure.) The set-up process takes care of a number of different tasks:

✔ **Setup provides Snow Leopard with your personal information.**

As I mention in Chapter 1, your iMac ships with a bathtub full of applications, and many of those use your personal data (like your address and telephone number) to automatically fill out your documents.

If that personal stored information starts you worrying about identity theft, I congratulate you. If you're using your common sense, it *should*. However, Apple doesn't disseminate this information anywhere else, and the applications that use your personal data won't send it anywhere, either. And the Safari Web browser fills out forms on a Web page automatically only if you give your permission.

✔ **Setup configures your language and keyboard choices.**

Mac OS X Snow Leopard is a truly international operating system, so Setup offers you a chance to configure your iMac to use a specific language and keyboard layout.

✔ **Setup configures your e-mail accounts within Apple Mail.**

If you already have an e-mail account set up with your Internet service provider (ISP), keep that e-mail account information that the ISP provided handy to answer these questions. (The list should include the incoming POP3/IMAP and outgoing SMTP mail servers you'll be using, your e-mail address, and your login name and password. Don't worry about those crazy acronyms — your ISP will know exactly what you mean when you ask for this information.) Snow Leopard can even automatically configure many Web-based e-mail accounts for you (including Google Mail, Yahoo! Mail, and AOL Mail) if you supply your account ID and password. *Sweet.*

✔ **Setup allows you to open a trial subscription with Apple's MobileMe service.**

A MobileMe subscription service provides you with online file storage, iSync capability across multiple computers, backups to your online storage, Apple e-mail accounts (through both Web mail and the Apple Mail application), and your own acre of Web site on the Internet. I go into all these in detail in Chapter 9. For now, just sign up and take the opportunity to feel smug about owning an Apple computer.

✔ **Setup sends your registration information to Apple.**

As a proud owner of an iMac, take advantage of the year of hardware warranty support and the free 90 days of telephone support. You have to register to use 'em, but rest assured that all this info is confidential.

✔ **Setup launches Migration Assistant.**

This assistant guides you through the process of *migrating* (an engineer's term for *moving*) your existing user data from your old Mac or PC to your new iMac. Naturally, if your iMac is your first computer, you can skip this step with a song in your heart! (Read more on Migration Assistant in the section, "Importing Documents and Data from Your Old Mac.")

Registering your iMac

I'll be honest here: I know that many of us, myself included, don't register every piece of computer hardware we buy. However, your iMac is a different kettle of fish altogether, and I *strongly* recommend that you register your purchase with Apple during the setup process. You spent a fair amount of moolah on your computer, and it's an investment with a significant number of moving parts.

Even the hardiest of techno-wizards would agree with this important Mark's Maxim:

If you don't register your iMac, you can't receive support.

And rest assured that Apple is not one of those companies that constantly pesters you with e-mail advertisements and near-spam. I've registered every Apple computer I've owned, and I've never felt pestered. (And I have an extremely low tolerance for pester.)

Importing Documents and Data from Your Old Mac

If you're upgrading from an older Mac running Mac OS X to your new iMac, I have great news for you: Apple includes the Migration Assistant utility application that can help you copy (whoops, I mean, *migrate*) all sorts of data from your old Mac to your new machine. The list of stuff that gets copied over includes

- ✔ **User accounts:** If you set up multiple user accounts (so that more than one person can share the computer), the utility ports them all to your new iMac.

- ✔ **Network settings:** Boy, howdy, this is a real treat for those with manual network settings provided by an ISP or network administrator! Migration Assistant can re-create the entire network environment of your old Mac on your new iMac.

- ✔ **System Preferences settings:** If you're a fan of tweaking and customizing Mac OS X to fit you like a glove, then rejoice. The Assistant actually copies over all the changes that you've made within System Preferences on your old Mac! (Insert sound of angelic chorus of cherubim and seraphim: *Hallelujah!*)

- ✔ **Documents:** The files in your Documents folder(s) are copied to your new iMac.

 ✔ **Applications:** Migration Assistant tries its best to copy over the third-party applications that you've installed in your Applications folder on the older Mac. I say *tries its best* because you might have to reinstall some applications, anyway. Some developers create applications that spread out all sorts of files across your hard drive, and the Assistant just can't keep track of those nomadic files. Too, some other applications make the trek just fine, but you might have to reenter their serial numbers.

Setup launches its Migration Assistant automatically if you indicate that you need to transfer stuff during the Setup process, but you can always launch Migration Assistant manually at any time. You'll find it in the Utilities folder inside your Applications folder; just double-click the Migration Assistant icon.

To use Migration Assistant to copy your system from your older Mac, you need either:

 ✔ a FireWire cable (compatible with most Macs made within the last five years or so) to connect the computers. If you don't already have one, you can pick up a standard FireWire cable at your local Maze o' Wires electronics store or at your computer store. (This cable will probably come in handy in the future as well, so it's not a one-use wonder.)

 The latest crop of iMacs includes only a FireWire 800 port! If you're upgrading from an older Mac that has only FireWire 400 ports, you'll need a FireWire 800 cable and a 400-to-800 adapter, which you can typically get at any large computer store (or through Amazon, or through eBay).

 ✔ a wired or wireless network connection between the computers. If you've already hooked up your new iMac to your wired or wireless Ethernet network while using the Setup Assistant, then eschew the FireWire cable and click Use Network instead!

Follow these steps to use Migration Assistant:

1. Click Continue on the opening screen.

 Migration Assistant prompts you for your account name and password that you create during the Setup procedure, as shown in Figure 2-1. Your account is an *admin account,* meaning that you have a higher security level that allows you to change things within Snow Leopard. (Much more detail on user accounts is covered in Chapter 20.)

2. Type your account name and password and then click OK.

 Characters in your password are displayed as bullet characters for security. After you've successfully entered your admin account name and password, this dialog disappears and you get to play in the real Migration Assistant dialog.

Introduction

You can use Migration Assistant to transfer your important

Migration Assistant requires that you type your password.

Name: Mark Chambers

Password:

▶ Details

Cancel   OK

password or an administrator user.

Go Back   Continue

Figure 2-1:
Enter your
admin pass-
word to use
Migration
Assistant.

3. Select the From Another Mac radio button and then click Continue.

You can also restore your iMac's data from a Time Machine backup drive, using Migration Assistant.

4. To use a FireWire connection, click Use FireWire and connect a FireWire cable between the two computers — to use a network connection to transfer the data, click Use Network.

5. Click Continue.

If you're using a network connection, you can gleefully skip steps 6 and 7.

6. Restart your older Mac while holding down the T key.

This restarts your older computer in *FireWire Target Disk mode,* in which your older Mac essentially becomes a huge external FireWire hard drive. (Neat trick.)

You must hold down the T key until you see the FireWire symbol (which looks like a stylized Y) appear on your older machine.

7. Click Continue.

8. Select the check boxes next to the user accounts that you want to transfer from your older machine (as shown in Figure 2-2) and then click Continue.

The Assistant displays how much space is required to hold the selected accounts on your iMac's hard drive.

9. Select the check boxes next to the applications and files that you want to copy (see how in Figure 2-3) and then click Continue.

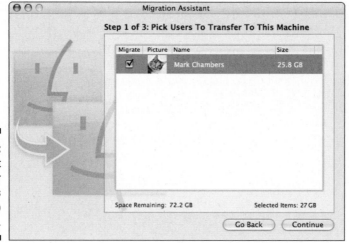

Figure 2-2:
Select
the user
accounts
you want to
migrate.

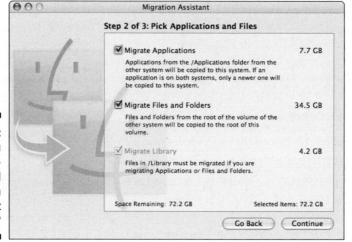

Figure 2-3:
Would you
like applica-
tions and
files with
that
migration?

10. **Select the check boxes next to the settings that you want to transfer (as shown in Figure 2-4).**

    Typically, you want to migrate all three of these settings groups: Network Settings, Time Zone, and Sharing Settings.

11. **Click the Migrate button.**

12. **After everything is copied, click the Apple icon on the Finder menu and choose Shutdown to turn off your older Mac. If you used a FireWire connection, it's safe to disconnect the FireWire cable.**

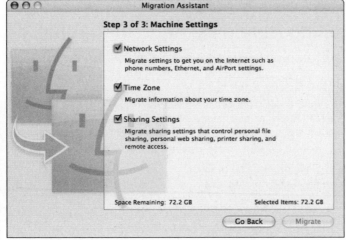

Figure 2-4:
Copy
your Mac
OS X set-
tings with
Migration
Assistant.

Importing Documents and Data from Windows

If you're a classic Windows-to-Mac *Switcher,* you made a wise choice, especially if you're interested in the creative applications within the iLife '09 suite!
Although you can choose to start your Apple computing life anew, you probably want to migrate some of your existing documents and files from that
tired PC to your bright, shiny, new iMac.

Unfortunately, no Windows Migration Assistant exists within Mac OS X.
However, if you're moving from a Windows PC to an iMac, you can copy your
files manually from a CD or DVD, from a USB Flash drive, or over a network.
(Note, however, that the iMac doesn't come with a floppy drive. And trust
me, you wouldn't want to use one to move anything that matters, anyway.)

The Mac OS X Help system contains an entire subsection on specific tricks
that you can use when switching from Windows to Mac, including how to connect to a Windows network and how to directly connect the two computers.

Because Snow Leopard can't run Windows programs directly (at least, not
without extra software), moving applications like Paint Shop Pro won't
do you any good. In general, however, you can move documents, movies,
photos, and music without a problem. Table 2-1 illustrates what can be
moved between Windows and Mac OS X as well as the application that you
use in Snow Leopard to open those files and documents.

Switching from a PC to . . . an Apple PC?

With the Snow Leopard Boot Camp feature, you can actually create a full Windows XP, Vista or Windows 7 system on your Intel iMac. Yup, Windows and Snow Leopard coexist peacefully *on the same computer*. However, you have to reboot your computer to use your iMac as a Windows system.

This brings a whole new meaning to the term *Switcher* because some iMac owners are moving their stuff from Windows (running on their old PC) to . . . well, Windows (running on their new iMac) rather than Snow Leopard. If you do decide to create a Windows system on your iMac by using Boot Camp, the files and folders on your existing PC can be copied directly by using a good, old-fashioned Windows wizard.

Table 2-1   Moving Media and Documents betwixt Computers

File Type	Windows Location	Mac OS X Location	Mac Application
Music files	My Music folder	Music folder	iTunes
Video and movie files	My Videos folder	Movies folder	QuickTime/DVD Player
Digital photos	My Pictures folder	Pictures folder	iPhoto
Office documents	My Documents folder	Documents folder	Mac Office/iWork

If you don't mind investing around $40, try using the Move2Mac software utility, which does most of the work of Migration Assistant for those switching from a Windows PC. From Detto Technologies (www.detto.com/move-2-mac-overview.php), Move2Mac comes complete with a special USB-to-USB cable that connects your two computers for high-speed copying. With Move2Mac, you can choose what you want to transfer to your new iMac (use Table 2-1 as a guide), and the copying is done automatically for you. Plus, Move2Mac also transfers goodies like your home page and bookmarks from Internet Explorer, desktop backgrounds, and even your Address Book contacts and account settings from Outlook Express. Move2Mac makes switching much easier, and I can highly recommend it.

Chapter 3

Introducing the Apple of Your iMac

In This Chapter

▶ Introducing Mac OS X Snow Leopard

▶ Appreciating the Unix core underneath Snow Leopard

▶ Recognizing similarities between Windows and Snow Leopard

▶ Getting help while exploring Snow Leopard

*I*n the other books that I've written about Mac OS X Snow Leopard, I use all sorts of somewhat understated phrases to describe my operating system of choice, such as *elegantly reliable, purely powerful,* and *supremely user friendly.*

But *why* is Snow Leopard such a standout? To be specific, why do creative professionals and computer techno-wizards across the globe hunger for the very same Mac OS X that runs your iMac? Why is Snow Leopard so far ahead of Windows 7 in features and performance? Good questions, all!

In this chapter, I answer those queries and satisfy your curiosity about your new big cat. I introduce the main elements of the Snow Leopard Desktop, and I show you the fearless Unix heart that beats underneath Snow Leopard's sleek exterior. I also point out the most important similarities between Snow Leopard and Windows 7, and I outline the resources available if you need help with Mac OS X.

Oh, and I promise to use honest-to-goodness English in my explanations, with a minimum of engineer-speak and indecipherable acronyms. (Hey, you've got to boast about Snow Leopard in turn to your family and friends. Aunt Harriet might not be as technologically savvy as we are.)

A Quick Tour of the Premises

Snow Leopard is a special type of software called an *operating system*. You know, *OS,* as in *Mac OS X?* That means that Snow Leopard essentially runs your iMac and also allows you to run all your other applications, such as iTunes or Photoshop. It's the most important computer application — or *software* — that you run.

Think of a pyramid, with Snow Leopard as the foundation and other applications running on top of it.

You're using the OS when you aren't running a specific application, such as these actions:

- ✔ Copying files from a CD to your hard drive
- ✔ Choosing a different screensaver

Sometimes, Snow Leopard even peeks through an application while it's running. For example, actions like these are also controlled by Snow Leopard:

- ✔ The Open and Save As dialogs that you see when working with files in Photoshop
- ✔ The Print dialog that appears when you print a document in Microsoft Word

In this section, I escort you personally around the most important hotspots in Snow Leopard, and you meet the most interesting onscreen thingamabobs that you use to control your iMac. (I told you I wasn't going to talk like an engineer!)

The Snow Leopard Desktop

This particular desktop isn't made of wood, and you can't stick your gum underneath. However, your Snow Leopard Desktop does indeed work much like the surface of a traditional desk. You can store things there, organize things into folders, and take care of important tasks like running other applications. Heck, you've even got a clock and a trash can.

Gaze upon Figure 3-1 and follow along as you venture to your Desktop and beyond.

Finder menu

Figure 3-1:
Everything
Snow
Leopard
starts
here — the
Mac OS X
Desktop.

Dock

Meet me at the Dock

The Dock is the closest thing to the dashboard of a car that you're likely to find on a Macintosh. It's a pretty versatile combination — it's one part organizer, one part application launcher, and one part system monitor. From here, you can launch applications, see what's running, and display or hide the application windows.

Each icon in the Dock represents one of the following:

- An application that you can run (or that is running)
- An application window that's *minimized* (shrunk)
- A Web page
- A document or folder on your system
- A network server or shared folder
- Your Trash

I cover the Dock in more detail in Chapter 5.

The Dock is highly configurable:

- ✔ It can appear at different sides of the screen.
- ✔ It can disappear until you move your mouse pointer to the edge to call it forth.
- ✔ You can resize it larger or smaller.

Dig those crazy icons

By default, Snow Leopard always displays at least one icon on your Desktop: your iMac's internal hard drive. To open the hard drive and view or use the contents, you double-click the icon. Other icons that might appear on your Desktop can include

- ✔ CDs and DVDs
- ✔ An iPod
- ✔ External hard drives or USB Flash drives
- ✔ Applications, folders, and documents
- ✔ Files you downloaded from the Internet
- ✔ Network servers you access

Chapter 4 provides the good stuff on icons and their uses within Snow Leopard.

There's no food on this menu

The Finder menu isn't found in a restaurant. You find it at the top of the Desktop, where you can use it to control your applications. Virtually every application that you run on your iMac has a menu.

To use a menu command, follow these steps:

1. **Click the menu title (like File or Edit).**

2. **Choose the desired command from the list that appears.**

Virtually every Macintosh application has some menu titles, such as File, Edit, and Window. You're likely to find similar commands under these titles. However, only two menu titles are in *every* Mac OS X application that displays a menu bar:

- ✔ The *Apple menu* (which is identified with that jaunty Apple Corporation icon,).

✔ The *application menu* (which always bears the name of the active application). For instance, the DVD Player menu title appears when you run the Snow Leopard DVD Player, and the Word menu group appears when you launch Microsoft Word.

I cover these two common titles in more detail in Chapters 4 and 5.

You can also display a contextual menu — regular human beings call it a *right-click menu* or shortcut menu — by right-clicking your Snow Leopard Desktop, or on an application, folder, or file icon. I discuss right-click menus in detail in Chapter 4.

There's always room for one more window

You're probably already familiar with the ubiquitous window itself. Both Snow Leopard and the applications that you run use windows to display things like

✔ The documents that you create

✔ The contents of your hard drive

Snow Leopard gives you access to the applications, documents, and folders on your system through Finder windows.

Windows are surprisingly configurable. I cover them at length in Chapter 4.

What's going on underneath?

How the core is designed makes more of a difference than all the visual bells and whistles, which tend to be similar between Windows and Mac OS X Snow Leopard (and Linux as well, for that matter). Time for a Mark's Maxim:

Sure, Snow Leopard's elegant exterior is a joy to use, but Mac OS X is a better OS than Windows because of the unique Unix muscle that lies underneath!

So what should you and I look for in an OS? Keep in mind that today's computer techno-wizard demands three requirements for a truly high-powered software wonderland — and Mac OS X Snow Leopard easily meets all three:

✔ **Reliability:** Your OS has to stay up and running reliably for as long as necessary — I'm talking *months* here — without lockups or error messages. If an application crashes, the rest of your work should remain safe, and you should be able to shut down the offending software.

Isn't Windows 7 the latest thing?

You've seen highly customized "pocket rocket" compact cars with the flashy paint jobs, huge noisy mufflers, and aerodynamic fiberglass stuff. You might think that these cars are real road racers, but what's underneath is different. The 4-cylinder engine that you *don't* see is completely stock. These cars don't perform any better than a mundane model straight from the factory.

The same holds true for Microsoft Windows 7 — another attempt by the folks at Redmond to put a modern face on an antique OS. Forget the flashy colors and the visual effects: Windows 7 is simply more of the same (at least it's newer than Windows Vista, which was beginning to creak). Sure, it's more reliable and faster than older versions of Windows, but there's not a boatload of revolutionary features in 7 — instead, Microsoft focused on making Windows 7 simpler to use. (Unfortunately, if you're running PC hardware, the only other practical choice for a computing novice is Linux, which is still regarded as too complex by major manufacturers like Dell and Hewlett-Packard. Therefore, with a PC, you're usually stuck with Windows Vista or Windows 7 — or you've picked up a very expensive paperweight.)

 ✔ **Performance:** If your computer has advanced hardware, your OS must be able to use those resources to speed things up big-time. The OS has to be highly configurable, and it has to be updated often to keep up with the latest in computer hardware.

"Mark, what do you mean by advanced hardware?" Well, if you're already knowledgeable about state-of-the-art hardware, examples include

- True 64-bit computing

- Multiple processors (like more than one Intel chip in your computer)

- A huge amount of RAM (16GB on the iMac, or far more on today's Power Mac computers)

- Multiple hard drives used as a RAID array

If all that sounds like ancient Sumerian, gleefully ignore this technical drabble and keep reading.

 ✔ **Ease of use:** All the speed and reliability in the world won't help an OS if it's difficult to use.

DOS was the PC OS of choice before the arrival of Windows. It was doomed because it wasn't intuitive or easy to master, requiring a PC owner to remember all sorts of commands that looked like hieroglyphics. (This is one of the reasons why the Macintosh was so incredibly popular in the days of DOS-based PCs. Macs had a mouse, and they were a snap to master and use.)

Similarities with that Windows behemoth

You might have heard of the *Windows Switcher:* a uniquely intelligent species that's becoming more and more common these days. Switchers are former PC owners who have abandoned Windows and bought a Macintosh, thereby joining the Apple faithful running Mac OS X. (Apple loves to document this migration on its Web site.) Because today's Macintosh computers are significantly faster than their PC counterparts — and you get neat software, such as Snow Leopard and the iLife suite when you buy a new Mac — switching makes perfect sense.

Switchers aren't moving to totally unfamiliar waters. Windows Vista, Windows 7, and Snow Leopard share a number of important concepts. Familiarizing yourself with Snow Leopard takes far less time than you might think.

TECHNICAL STUFF

It's Apple to the rescue!

Unix is the established, super-reliable OS that powers most of the high-performance servers that make up the Internet. Unix has built-in support for virtually every hardware device ever wrought by the hand of Man (including all the cool stuff that came with your iMac), and Unix is well designed and highly efficient.

Unfortunately, standard Unix looks as hideous as DOS, complete with a confusing command line, so ease-of-use for normal human beings like you and me goes out the door. Enter the genius types at Apple, who understood several years ago that all Unix needed was a state-of-the-art, novice-friendly interface! To wit: Mac OS X was developed with a Unix foundation (or *core*), so it shares the same reliability and performance as Unix. However, the software engineers at Apple (who know a thing or two about ease-of-use) made it good-looking and easy to use.

This is the secret to the worldwide fever over Mac OS X: It blends the best of Unix with the best of earlier Macintosh operating systems like Mac OS 9. Mac OS X is not only easy to use, but it also runs tight, concentric *sassy* rings around anything that Microsoft has to offer today.

That's as far as I delve into the foundation of Snow Leopard in this volume — understandably. If you're interested in all the details about what makes Mac OS X tick, as well as its settings and features, I can heartily recommend another of my books, the bestselling (and extremely heavy) *Mac OS X Snow Leopard All-in-One For Dummies* (Wiley). It comprehensively covers everything Snow Leopard — over 700 pages devoted entirely to Mac OS X and its companion applications!

Here's an overview of the basic similarities between the two operating systems:

- ✔ **The Desktop:** The Snow Leopard Desktop is a neat representation of a real physical desktop, and Windows uses the same idea:

  - You can arrange files, folders, and applications on your Desktop to help keep things handy.

  - Application windows appear on the Desktop.

- ✔ **Drives, files, and folders:** Data is stored in files on your hard drive(s), and those files can be organized in folders. Both Snow Leopard and Windows use the same file/folder concept.

- ✔ **Specific locations:** Both Windows and Snow Leopard provide every user with a set of folders to help keep various types of files organized. For example, the My Videos folder that you can use in Windows XP corresponds to the Movies folder that you find in your Home folder within Snow Leopard.

- ✔ **Running programs:** Both Snow Leopard and Windows run programs (or applications) in the same manner:

  - Double-clicking an application icon launches that application.

  - Double-clicking a document runs the corresponding application and then automatically loads the document.

- ✔ **Window control:** Yep, both operating systems use windows, and those windows can be resized, hidden (or minimized), and closed in similar fashions. (Are you starting to see the connections here?)

- ✔ **Drag-and-drop:** One of the basics behind a GUI (a ridiculous acronym that stands for *graphical user interface*) like Windows and Snow Leopard is the ability to drag documents and folders around to move, delete, copy, and open them. Drag-and-drop is one of the primary advantages of both of these operating systems because copying a file by dragging it from one window to another is intuitive and easy enough for a kid to accomplish.

- ✔ **Editing:** Along the same lines as drag-and-drop, both Snow Leopard and Windows offer similar cut-and-paste editing features. You've likely used Cut, Copy, and Paste for years, so this is familiar stuff.

Calling for Help

You can call on these resources if you need additional help while you're discovering how to tame the Snow Leopard.

Some of the help resources are located on the Internet, so your Web browser will come in handy.

The Snow Leopard built-in Help system

Sometimes the help you need is as close as the Help title on the menu. You can get help for either

- ✔ **A specific application:** Just click Help. Then, click in the Search box and type a short phrase that sums up your query (such as *startup keys*). You'll see a list of help topics appear on the menu. Just click a topic to display more information.

- ✔ **Actions and functions (topics):** Click a Finder window and then click Help on the menubar. Again, you'll see the Search box, and you can enter a word or phrase to find within the Help system. To display the Help viewer window, click the Mac Help item under the Search box.

The Apple Web-based support center

Apple has online product support areas for every hardware and software product that it manufactures. Visit `www.apple.com` and click the Support tab at the top of the Web page.

The Search box works just like the Mac OS Help system, but the Knowledge Base that Apple provides online has a *lot* more answers.

Magazines

Many magazines (both in print and online) offer tips and tricks on using and maintaining Mac OS X Snow Leopard.

My personal online favorites are Macworld (`www.macworld.com`) and MacAddict (`www.maclife.com`).

Mac support Web sites

A number of private individuals and groups offer support forums on the Web, and you can often find help from other Mac owners on these sites within a few hours of posting a question.

I'm very fond of the CNET forum MacFixIt (www.macfixit.com), Mac OS X Hints (http://forums.macosxhints.com), and MacTech (http://forums.mactech.com).

Mac newsgroups on Usenet

If you're familiar with Usenet newsgroups, you can find lots of help (typically dispensed with a healthy dose of opinion) in newsgroups like comp.sys.mac.system. Simply post a message and then check back within a few hours to read the replies.

Local Mac user groups

I'd be remiss if I didn't mention your local Mac user group. Often, a user group maintains its own Web site and discussion forum. If you can wait until the next meeting, you can even ask your question and receive a reply from a real-live human being . . . quite a thrill in today's Web-riffic world!

Part II
Shaking Hands with Mac OS X

In this part . . .

*I*n this part, you delve deeper into the works of Mac OS X Snow Leopard. I show you how to perform all sorts of common tasks as well as how to customize your system, how to change settings in System Preferences, where your personal files are stored, and how to use the latest Spotlight search technology to find virtually *anything* you've stored on your iMac!

Chapter 4

Opening and Closing and Clicking and Such

*A*h, the Finder — many admire its scenic beauty, but don't ignore its unsurpassed power nor its many moods. And send a postcard while you're there.

Okay, so Snow Leopard's Finder might not be *quite* as majestic as the mighty Mississippi River, but it's the basic toolbox that you use every single day while piloting your iMac. The Finder includes the most common elements of Mac OS X: window controls, common menu commands, icon fun (everything from launching applications to copying files), network connections, keyboard shortcuts, and even emptying the Trash. In fact, one could say that if you master the Finder and find how to use it efficiently, you're on your way to becoming a power user! (My editor calls this the Finder "window of opportunity." She's a hoot.)

That's what this chapter is designed to do: This is your Finder tour guide, and we're ready to roll.

Working within the Finder

This is a hands-on tour, with none of that, "On your right, you'll see the historic Go menu" for you! Time to get off the bus and start the tour with Figure 4-1, in which I show you around the most important elements of the Finder. (In the upcoming section, "Performing Tricks with Finder Windows," I give you a close-up view of window controls.)

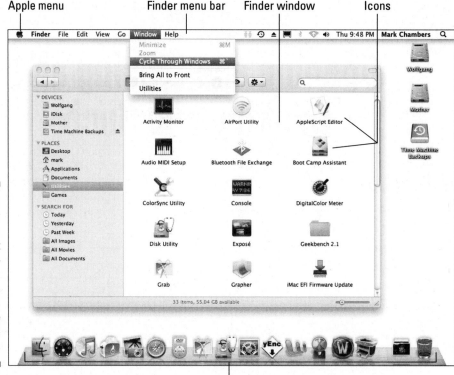

Apple menu   Finder menu bar   Finder window   Icons

Dock

Figure 4-1:
Snow
Leopard's
friendliest
face —
the Finder,
complete
with a win-
dow, window
bar and
menu bar.

The popular attractions include

✔ **The Apple menu (🍎):** This is a special menu because it appears both in the Finder and within every application menu that you run. It doesn't matter whether you're in iTunes or Photoshop or Word: If you can see a menu bar, the Apple menu is there. The Apple menu contains common commands to use no matter where you are in Snow Leopard, such as Restart, Shut Down, and System Preferences.

✔ **The Finder menu bar:** Whenever the Finder is ready to use (or, in Mac-speak, whenever the Finder is the *active* application, rather than another application), the Finder menu bar appears at the top of your screen. You know the Finder is active and ready when the word *Finder* appears at the left of the menu bar.

If you're brand new to computers, a *menu* is simply a list of commands. For example, you click the File menu and then choose Save to save a document. When you click a menu, it extends down so that you can see the commands it includes. While the menu is extended, you can choose any enabled menu item (just click it) to perform that action. You can tell that an item is enabled if its name appears in black. Conversely, a menu command is disabled if it is grayed out — clicking it does nothing.

When you see a menu path, like this example — File⇨Save — it's just a visual shortcut that tells you to click the File menu and then choose Save from the drop-down menu that appears.

✔ **The Desktop:** Your Desktop serves the same purpose as your physical desktop: You can store stuff here (files, alias icons, and so on), and it's a solid, stable surface where you can work comfortably. Application windows appear on the Desktop, for example, as do other applications, such as your Stickies notes and your DVD player. Just double-click an application there to launch it.

You can easily customize your Desktop. For example, you can use your own images to decorate the Desktop, organize it to store new folders and documents, arrange icons how you like, or put the Dock in another location. Don't worry — I cover all this in other areas of the book — I just want you to know that you don't have to settle for what Apple gives you as a default Desktop.

✔ **All sorts of icons:** This is a Macintosh computer, after all, replete with tons of make-your-life-easier tools. Check out the plethora of icons on your Desktop as well as icons within the Finder window itself. Each icon is a shortcut to a file, folder, network connection, or device in your system, including applications that you run and documents that you create. Refer to Figure 4-1 to see the icon for my iMac's hard drive icon, labeled Wolfgang. (I'm a huge Mozart fan.) Sometimes you click an icon to watch it do its thing (like icons in the Dock, which I cover next), but usually you double-click an icon to make something happen.

✔ **The Dock:** The Dock is a launching pad for your favorite applications, documents, folders, network connections, and Web sites. You can also refer to it to see what applications are running. Click an icon there to open the item. For example, the postage stamp icon represents the Apple Mail application, and clicking the spiffy compass icon launches your Safari Web browser.

✔ **The Finder window:** Finally! The basic Finder window in Figure 4-1 displays the contents of my Utilities folder. You use Finder windows to launch applications; perform disk chores, such as copying and moving files; and navigate your hard drive.

Mousing in a Mac World

Snow Leopard takes a visual approach to everything, and what you see in Figure 4-1 is designed for point-and-click convenience. You click an item, it opens, you do your thing, and life is good. If you've grazed on the other side of the fence — one of Those Who Were Once Windows Users — you're probably accustomed to using a mouse with at least two buttons. This brings up the nagging question: "Hey, Mark! Where the heck are my mouse buttons?"

In a nutshell, the buttons on your iMac's Magic Mouse are the entire top of the mouse! Although you won't see any separate buttons for right or left click, your Magic Mouse can tell when you tap with one finger (single-click) or two fingers (right-click).

To configure everything Magic Mouse — including all your buttons and your double-click/tracking/scrolling speeds — visit the Keyboard & Mouse pane within System Preferences. You can also configure your wireless mouse from here as well. (More on the System Preferences window in the next section.)

Clicking the right mouse button performs the same default function in Snow Leopard that it does in Windows. Namely, when you click the right mouse button on most items — icons, documents, even your Desktop — you get a *contextual menu* of things. That is, you get more commands specific to that item. (Boy, howdy, I hate that word *contextual,* but that's what engineers call it. I call it the right-click menu, and I promise to refer to it as such for the rest of the book.)

Figure 4-2 illustrates a typical convenient right-click menu within a Finder window.

Figure 4-2: Well-adjusted folks call this a right-click menu.

Other mouse actions include

- ✔ **Double-clicking.** Tap twice with one finger to double-click.
- ✔ **Scrolling.** To move in any direction within a document window, just swipe your finger across the top of the mouse in that direction.
- ✔ **Browse.** Swipe two fingers across the top of the mouse to move backwards and forwards through pages in many applications (like Web pages in Safari or photos in your iPhoto library).

> ✔ **Zooming.** Hold down the Control key and scroll with one finger to zoom in within applications.

Launching and Quitting for the Lazy iMac Owner

Now it's time for you to pair your newly found mouse acumen with Snow Leopard's Finder window. Follow along this simple exercise. Move your mouse cursor over the iTunes icon in the Dock (this icon looks like an audio CD with green musical notes on it) and click once. Whoosh! Snow Leopard *launches* (or starts) the iTunes application, and you see a window much like the one in Figure 4-3.

If an application icon is already selected (which I discuss in the next section), you can simply press ⌘+O to launch it. The same key shortcut works with documents, too.

Named (iTunes) menu

Close window button

Figure 4-3: Click a Dock icon to launch that application.

Besides the Dock, you have several other ways to launch an application or open a document in Snow Leopard:

- ✔ **From the Apple menu (🍎):** A number of different applications can always be launched anywhere within Snow Leopard from the Apple menu:

  - *System Preferences:* This is where you change all sorts of settings, such as your display background and how icons appear.

  - *Software Update:* This uses the Internet to see whether update patches are available for your Apple software, as I discuss in Chapter 24.

  - *Mac OS X Software:* This launches the Safari browser and displays software that you can download for your iMac.

- ✔ **From the Desktop:** If you have a document that you created or an application icon on your Desktop, you can launch or open it here by *double-clicking* that icon (tapping the mouse with one finger twice in rapid succession when the mouse cursor is on top of the icon).

Double-clicking a device or network connection on your Desktop opens the contents in a Finder window. This trick works for CDs and DVDs that you've loaded as well as for external hard drives and USB Flash drives. Applications and documents launch from a CD, a DVD, or an external drive just like they launch from your internal drive (the one that's named Macintosh HD), so you don't have to copy stuff from the external drive just to use it. (You can't change the contents of most CDs and DVDs; they're read-only, so you can't write to them.)

- ✔ **From the Recent Items selection:** When you click the Apple menu and hover your mouse over the Recent Items menu item, the Finder displays all the applications and documents that you used over the past few computing sessions. Click an item in this list to launch or open it.

- ✔ **From the Login Items list:** Login Items are applications that Snow Leopard launches automatically each time you log in to your user account.

  I cover Login Items in detail in Chapter 20.

- ✔ **From the Finder window:** You can also double-click an icon within the confines of a Finder window to open it (for documents), launch it (for applications), or display the contents (for a folder).

The Quick Look feature can display the contents of just about any document or file — without actually opening the corresponding application! *Sweet.* To use Quick Look from a Finder window, click a file to select it and then click the Quick Look button (which bears an eye icon) on the Finder window toolbar, or just press the spacebar.

After you finish using an application, you can quit that application to close its window and return to the Desktop. Here are a number of different ways to quit an application:

✓ **Press ⌘+Q.** This keyboard shortcut quits virtually every Macintosh application on the planet. Just first make sure that the application that you want to quit is active!

✓ **Choose the Quit command from the application's menu.** To display the Quit command, click the application's name — its menu — from the menu bar. This menu is always to the immediate right of the Apple (🍎) menu. For example, Safari displays a Safari menu, and that same spot in the menu is taken up by iCal when iCal is the active application. In Figure 4-3, look for the iTunes menu, right next to 🍎.

✓ **Choose Quit from the Dock.** You can Control-click (or right-click) an application's icon on the Dock and then choose Quit from the right-click menu that appears.

A running application displays a small black triangle under its icons on the Dock.

✓ **Click the Close button on the application window (refer to Figure 4-3).** Some applications quit entirely when you close their window, like the System Preferences window or the Apple DVD Player. Other applications might continue running without any window, like Safari or iTunes; to close these applications, you have to use another method in this list.

✓ **Choose Force Quit from the Apple menu.** *This is a last-resort measure!* Use this only if an application has frozen and you can't use another method in this list to quit. Force-quitting an application doesn't save any changes to any open documents within that application!

Juggling Folders and Icons

Finder windows aren't just for launching applications and opening the files and documents that you create. You can also use the icons within a Finder window to select one or more specific items or to copy and move items from place to place within your system.

A field observer's guide to icons

Not all icons are created equal. Earlier in this chapter, I introduce you to your iMac's hard drive icon on the Desktop, but here is a little background on the other types of icons that you might encounter during your iMac travels:

✔ **Hardware:** These are your storage devices (such as your hard drive and DVD drive) as well as external peripherals (such as your iPod and printer).

✔ **Applications:** These icons represent the applications (or programs) that you can launch. Most applications have a custom icon that incorporates the company's logo or the specific application logo, so they're very easy to recognize, as you can see in Figure 4-4. Double-clicking an application usually doesn't load a document automatically; you typically get a new blank document, or an Open dialog from which you can choose the existing file you want to open.

Figure 4-4:
A collection of some of my favorite application icons.

✔ **Documents:** Many of the files on your hard drive are documents that can be opened within the corresponding application, and the icon usually looks similar to the application's icon. Double-clicking a document automatically launches the required application (that is, as long as Mac OS X recognizes the file format).

✔ **Files:** Most of the file icons on your system are mundane things (such as preference and settings files, text files, log files, and miscellaneous data files), yet most are identified with at least some type of recognizable icon that lets you guess what purpose the file serves. You also come across generic file icons that look like a blank sheet of paper (used when Snow Leopard has no earthly idea what the file format is).

✔ **Aliases:** An *alias* acts as a link to another item elsewhere on your system. For example, to launch Adobe Acrobat, you can click an Adobe Acrobat alias icon that you can create on your Desktop rather than clicking the actual Acrobat application icon. The alias essentially acts the same way as the original icon, but it doesn't take up the same space — only a few bytes for the icon itself, compared with the size of the actual application. Plus, you don't have to go digging through folders galore to find the original application icon. (Windows Switchers know an alias as a *shortcut,* and the idea is the same although Macs had it first. Harrumph.) You can always identify an alias by the small curved arrow at the base of the icon, and the icon might also sport the tag alias at the end of its name.

You have three ways to create an alias. Here's one:

a. *Select the item.* The following section has details about selecting icons.

b. *Choose File➪Make Alias, or press ⌘+L.*

Figure 4-5 illustrates a number of aliases, arranged next to their linked files.

Figure 4-5: No, not the famous girl-spy TV show. These are alias icons in Snow Leopard.

Here's another way to create an alias:

a. *Hold down ⌘+Option.*

b. *Drag the original icon to the location where you want the alias.*

Note that this funky method doesn't add the `alias` tag to the end of the alias icon name (unless you drag it to another location in the same directory)!

Another option for creating an alias is to right-click the original icon and choose Make Alias.

So why bother to use an alias? Two good reasons:

- ✔ **Launch an application or open a document from anywhere on your drive.** For example, you can start Pages directly from the folder where you store the documents for your current Pages project. Speed, organization, and convenience . . . life is good.

- ✔ **Send an alias to the Trash without affecting the original item.** When that Pages project is finished, you can safely delete the alias without worrying about deleting the actual application icon.

If you move or rename the original file, Snow Leopard is actually smart enough to update the alias, too! However, if the original file is deleted (or if the original is moved to a different volume, such as an external hard drive), the alias no longer works. (Go figure.)

Selecting items

Often, the menu commands or keyboard commands that you perform in the Finder need to be performed on something: Perhaps you're moving an item to the Trash, or getting more information on the item, or creating an alias for that item. In order to identify the target of your action to the Finder, you need to select one or more items on your Desktop or in a Finder window. In this section, I show you just how to do that.

Selecting one thing

Snow Leopard gives you a couple of options when selecting just one item for an upcoming action:

- ✔ **Move your mouse pointer over the item and click.** A dark border (or *highlight*) appears around the icon, indicating that it's selected.

- ✔ **If an icon is already highlighted on your Desktop or within a window, move the selection highlight to another icon in the same location by using the arrow keys.** To shift the selection highlight alphabetically, press Tab (to move in order) or press Shift+Tab (to move in reverse order).

REMEMBER

Selecting items in the Finder doesn't actually *do* anything to them by itself. You have to perform an action on the selected items to make something happen.

Selecting a whole bunch of things

You can also select multiple items with aplomb by using one of these methods:

✓ **Adjacent items**

- *Drag a box around them.* If that sounds like ancient Sumerian, here's the explanation: Click a spot above and to the left of the first item; then hold down your finger on the surface of the mouse and drag the mouse down and to the right. (This is *dragging* in Mac-speak.) A box outline like the one in Figure 4-6 appears, indicating what you're selecting. Any icons that touch or appear within the box outline are selected when you release the mouse button.

- *Click the first item to select it and then hold down the Shift key while you click the last item.* Snow Leopard selects both items and every-thing between them.

✓ **Nonadjacent items:** Select these by holding down the ⌘ key while you click each item.

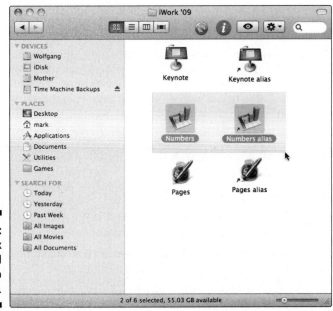

Figure 4-6:
Drag a box around icons to select them.

Check out the status line at the bottom of a Finder window. It tells you how much space is available on the drive you're working in as well as how many items are displayed in the current Finder window. When you select items, it shows you how many you highlighted.

Copying items

Want to copy items from one Finder window to another, or from one location (like a CD) to another (like your Desktop)? *Très* easy. Just use one of these methods:

✔ **On the same drive**

- *To copy one item to another location:* Hold down the Option key (you don't have to select the icon first) and then click and drag the item from its current home to the new location.

  To put a copy of an item within a folder, just drop the item on top of the receiving folder. If you hold the item that you're dragging over the destination folder for a second or two, Snow Leopard opens up a new window so you can see the contents of the target.

- *To copy multiple items to another location:* Select them all first (see the earlier section, "Selecting a whole bunch of things"), hold down the Option key and then drag and drop one of the selected items where you want it. All the items that you selected follow the item you drag. (Rather like lemmings. Nice touch, don't you think?)

  To help indicate your target when you're copying files, Snow Leopard highlights the location to show you where the items will end up. (This works whether the target location is a folder or a drive icon.) If the target location is a window, Snow Leopard adds a highlight to the window border.

✔ **On a different drive**

- *To copy one or multiple items:* Click and drag the icon (or the selected items if you have more than one) from the original window to a window you open on the target drive. (No need to hold down the Option key whilst moving.) You can also drag one item (or a selected group of items) and simply drop the items on top of the drive icon on your Desktop.

  The items are copied to the top level, or *root,* of the target drive.

If you try to move or copy something to a location that already has an item with the same name, Figure 4-7 illustrates the answer: You get a dialog that prompts you to decide whether to replace the file or to stop the copy/move procedure and leave the existing file alone. Good insurance, indeed.

Moving things from place to place

Moving things from one location to another location on the same drive is the easiest action you can take. Just drag the item (or selected items) to the new location. The item disappears from the original spot and reappears in the new spot.

Duplicating in a jiffy

If you need more than one copy of the same item within a folder, use the Snow Leopard Duplicate command. I use Duplicate often when I want to edit a document but ensure that the original document stays pristine, no matter what. I just create a duplicate and edit that file instead.

To use Duplicate, you can

- ✔ **Click an item to select it and then choose File➪Duplicate.**
- ✔ **Right-click the item and choose Duplicate from the menu.**
- ✔ **Hold down the Option key and drag the original item to another spot in the same window.** When you release the mouse button, the duplicate file appears like magic!

The duplicate item has the word copy appended to its name. A second copy is named copy2, a third is copy3, and so on.

Duplicating a folder also duplicates all the contents of that folder, so creating a duplicate folder can take some time to create if the original folder was stuffed full. The duplicate folder has copy appended to its name, but the contents of the duplicate folder keep their original names.

Keys and Keyboard Shortcuts to Fame and Fortune

Your iMac keyboard might not be as glamorous as your mouse, but any Macintosh power user will tell you that using keyboard shortcuts is usually the fastest method of performing certain tasks in the Finder, such as saving or closing a file. I recommend committing these shortcuts to memory and putting them to work as soon as you begin using your iMac so that they become second nature to you as quickly as possible.

Special keys on the keyboard

The Apple standard keyboard has a number of special keys that you might not recognize — especially if you've made the smart move and decided to migrate from the chaos that is Windows to Mac OS X! Table 4-1 lists the keys that bear strange hieroglyphics on the Apple keyboard as well as whatĺ they do.

Table 4-1	Too-Cool Key Symbols	
Action	Symbol	Purpose
Media Eject	⏏	Ejects a CD or DVD from your optical drive
Audio Mute	◀	Mutes (and restores) all sound produced by your iMac
Volume Up	🔊	Increases the sound volume
Volume Down	🔉	Decreases the sound volume
Command	⌘	Primary modifier for menus and keyboard shortcuts
Option	⌥	Modifier for shortcuts

Using Finder and application keyboard shortcuts

The Finder is chock-full of keyboard shortcuts that you can use to take care of common tasks. Some of the handiest shortcuts are included in the online Cheat Sheet for this book, which you'll find at

> http://www.dummies.com/how-to/content/imac-for-dummies-
> cheat-sheet.html

But wait, there's more! Most of your applications also provide their own set of keyboard shortcuts. While you're working with a new application, display the application's Help file and print out a copy of the keyboard shortcuts as a handy cheat sheet.

If you've used a PC before, you're certainly familiar with three-key shortcuts — the most infamous being Ctrl+Alt+Delete, the beloved shut-down shortcut nicknamed the Windows Three-Finger Salute. Three-key shortcuts work the same way in Snow Leopard (but you'll be thrilled to know you won't need to reboot your iMac using that notorious Windows shortcut)! If you're new to computing, just hold down the first two keys simultaneously and then press the third key.

You're not limited to just the keyboard shortcuts listed previously, either. Within System Preferences, visit the Keyboard pane and click on the Keyboard Shortcuts button to change an existing shortcut or add another.

Performing Tricks with Finder Windows

In this section of your introduction to Mac OS X, I describe basic windows management within Snow Leopard: how to move things around, how to close windows, and how to make 'em disappear and reappear like magic.

Scrolling in and resizing windows

Can you imagine what life would be like if you couldn't see more than a single window's worth of stuff? Shopping would be curtailed quite a bit — and so would the contents of the folders on your hard drives!

That's why Snow Leopard adds *scroll bars* that you can click and drag to move through the contents of the window. You can either

✔ Click the scroll bar and drag it.

✔ Click anywhere in the empty area above or below the bar to scroll pages one at a time.

✔ Hold down the Option key and click anywhere in the empty area above or below the bar to scroll to that spot in the window.

Of course, you can also scroll by moving one finger on your Magic Mouse in the desired direction (both vertically and horizontally). To set the scroll wheel's behavior, open System Preferences and click the Mouse pane.

Figure 4-8 illustrates both vertical and horizontal scroll bars in a typical Finder window.

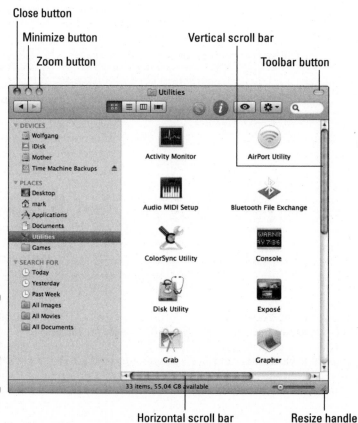

Figure 4-8: A plethora of helpful window controls.

Only one can be active at once

Yes, here's a very special Mark's Maxim in the Mac OS X universe.

Only one application window can be active in Snow Leopard at any time.

You can always tell which window is active:

✔ **The active window is on top of other windows.**

Tip: You can still use a window's Close, Minimize, and Zoom buttons when it's inactive.

✔ **Any input you make by typing or by moving your mouse appears in the active window.**

✔ **Mac OS X *dims* inactive windows that you haven't minimized.**

Often, pressing your Page Up and Page Down keys moves you through a document one page at a time. Also, pressing your arrow keys moves your insertion cursor one line or one character in the four compass directions.

You can also resize most Finder and application windows by enlarging or reducing the window frame itself. Move your mouse pointer over the Resize handle in the lower-right corner of the window (which smartly bears a number of slashed lines to help it stand out) and then drag the handle in any direction until the window is the precise size you need.

Minimizing and restoring windows

Resizing a window is indeed helpful, but maybe you simply want to banish the doggone thing until you need it again. That's a situation for the Minimize button, which also appears in Figure 4-8. A *minimized* window disappears from the Desktop but isn't closed: It simply reappears in the Dock as a miniature icon. Minimizing a window is easy: Move your mouse pointer over the Minimize button at the top-left corner of the window — a minus sign appears in the button to tell you that you're on target — and then click.

Hold down the Shift key whilst you minimize, and prepare to be amazed when the window shrinks in slow motion like Alice in Wonderland!

To restore the window to its full size again (and its original position on the Desktop), just click its window icon on the Dock.

Moving and zooming windows

Perhaps you want to move a window to another location on the Desktop so you can see the contents of multiple windows at the same time. Click the window's *title bar* (that's the top frame of the window, which usually includes a document or application name) and drag the window anywhere you like. Then release the mouse button. (Don't click the icon in the center of the title bar, though. You won't move the window, just the icon itself.)

Many applications can automatically arrange multiple windows for you. Choose Window↪Arrange All menu item (if it appears).

To see all that a window can show you, use the Zoom feature to expand any Finder or application window to its maximum practical size. Note that a zoomed window can fill the entire screen, or (if that extra space isn't applicable for the application) the window might expand only to a larger part of the Desktop. To zoom a window, move your mouse pointer over the button (as shown in the earlier Figure 4-8) at the top-left corner of the window. When the plus sign appears in the Zoom button, click to claim the additional territory on your Desktop. (You can click the Zoom button again to automatically return the same window to its original dimensions.)

Closing windows

When you're finished with an application or no longer need a window open, move your mouse pointer over the Close button at the top-left corner of the window. When the X appears in the button, click it. (And yes, I can get one more reference out of Figure 4-8, which I'm thinking of nominating as Figure of the Year.)

If you have more than one window open in the same application and you want to close 'em all in one swoop, hold down the Option key whilst you click the Close button in any of the windows.

If you haven't saved a document and you try to close that application's window, Snow Leopard gets downright surly and prompts you for confirmation. "Hey, human, you don't really want to do this, do you?" If you answer in the affirmative — "Why, yes, machine. Yes, indeed, I do want to throw this away and not save it." — the application discards the document that you were working on. If you decide to keep your document (thereby saving your posterior from harm), you can either save the document under the same filename or under a new name.

Toggling toolbars the Snow Leopard way

Time to define a window control that's actually *inside* the window for a change. A *toolbar* is a strip of icons that appears under the window's title bar. These icons typically perform the most common actions within an application; the effect is the same as if you use a menu or press a keyboard shortcut. Toolbars are very popular these days. You see 'em within everything from the Finder window to most application windows.

You can banish a window's toolbar to make extra room for icons, documents, or whatever it happens to be holding. Just click the little lozenge-shaped button at the right corner of the window. (You guessed it — the Toolbar button is also shown in Figure 4-8.) *Note:* If you toggle the Finder toolbar off, you also lose the Finder window Sidebar.

Chapter 5

A Plethora of Powerful Fun

*W*hen you're no longer a novice to Snow Leopard and the basics of the Finder, turn your attention to a number of more advanced topics 'n tricks to turn you into an iMac power user — which, after all, is the goal of every civilized consciousness on Planet Earth.

Consider this chapter a grab bag of Snow Leopard knowledge. Sure, I jump around a little, but these topics are indeed connected by a common thread: They're all surefire problem-solvers and speeder-uppers. (I can't believe the latter is really a word, but evidently it is. My editors told me so.)

Home, Sweet Home Folder

Each user account that you create within Snow Leopard is actually a self-contained universe. For example, each user has a number of unique characteristics and folders devoted just to that person, and Snow Leopard keeps track of everything that a user changes or creates. (In Chapter 20, I describe the innate loveliness of multiple users living in peace and harmony on your iMac.)

This unique universe includes a different system of folders for each user account on your system. The top-level folder uses the short name that Snow Leopard assigns when that user account is created. Naturally, the actual folder name is different for each person, so Mac techno-types typically refer to this folder as your *Home folder*.

Each account's Home folder contains a set of subfolders, including

- Movies
- Music
- Pictures
- Downloads (for files you download via Safari)
- Sites (for Web pages created by the user)
- Documents (created by the user)

Although you can store your stuff at the *root* (top level) of your hard drive, that gaggle of files, folders, and aliases can get very crowded and confusing very quickly. Here's a Mark's Maxim to live by:

Your Home folder is where you hang out and where you store your stuff. Use it to make your computing life *much* easier!

Create subfolders within your Documents folder to organize your files and folders even further. For example, I always create a subfolder in my Documents folder for every book that I write so that I can quickly and easily locate all the documents and files associated with that book project.

I discuss security within your Home folder and what gets stored where in Chapter 20. For now, Figure 5-1 shows how convenient your Home folder is to reach because it appears in the Finder window Sidebar. One click of your Home folder and all your stuff is in easy reach.

In addition to the Finder window Sidebar, you can also reach your Home folder in other convenient ways:

- **From the Go menu:** Choose Go➪Home to display your Home folder immediately from the Finder window. Alternatively, you can press ⌘+Shift+H to accomplish the same thing.

- **From within Open and Save dialogs:** Snow Leopard's standard File Open and File Save dialogs also include the same Home folder (and sub-folder) icons as the Finder window Sidebar.

- **Within any new Finder window you open:** If you like, you can set every Finder window that you open to open automatically within your Home folder.

    a. *Choose Finder➪Preferences to display the dialog that you see in Figure 5-2.*

    b. *Click the arrow button at the right side of the New Finder Windows Open pop-up menu.*

    A menu pops up (hence, the name).

Home folder

Figure 5-1:
Your Home folder is the central location for all your stuff on your iMac.

Sidebar

Figure 5-2:
Set Snow Leopard to open your Home folder within new Finder windows.

> c. *Click the Home entry in the menu.*
>
> d. *Click the Close button at the top-left corner of the dialog.*
>
> You're set to go. From now on, every Finder window you open displays your Home folder as the starting location!

Here's another reason to use your Home folder to store your stuff: Snow Leopard expects your stuff to be there when you migrate your files from an older Mac to a new Mac.

Arranging Your Desktop

Most folks put all their documents, pictures, and videos on their Snow Leopard Desktop because the file icons are easy to locate! Your computing stuff is right in front of you . . . or *is* it?

Call me a finicky, stubborn fussbudget — go ahead, I don't mind — but I prefer a clean Snow Leopard Desktop without all the iconic clutter. In fact, my Desktop usually has just three or four icons even though I use my iMac several hours every day. It's an organizational thing; I work with literally hundreds of applications, documents, and assorted knickknacks daily. Sooner or later, you'll find that you're using that many, too. When you keep your stuff crammed on your Desktop, you end up having to scan your screen for one particular file, an alias, or a particular type of icon, which ends up taking you more time to locate it on your Desktop than in your Documents folder!

Plus, you'll likely find yourself looking at old icons that no longer mean anything to you or stuff that's covered in cobwebs that you haven't used in years. Stale icons . . . *yuck.*

I recommend that you arrange your Desktop so you see only a couple of icons for the files or documents that you use the most. Leave the rest of the Desktop for that cool image of your favorite actor or actress.

Besides keeping things clean, I can recommend a number of other favorite tweaks that you can make to your Desktop:

✔ **Keep Desktop icons arranged as you like.**

> a. *From the Finder menu, choose View⇨Show View Options.*
>
> b. *Select the Arrange By check box.*
>
> c. *From the pop-up menu, choose the criteria that Snow Leopard uses to automatically arrange your Desktop icons, including the item name, the last modification date, or the size of the items.*
>
> I personally like things organized by name.

✔ **Choose a favorite background.**

    a. Tap two fingers on the surface of your Magic Mouse over any open spot on your Desktop. (Or, if you use an older pointing thing with a right mouse button, click that instead.)

    b. From the right-click menu that appears, choose Change Desktop Background.

    You see the Desktop & Screen Saver pane appear, as shown in Figure 5-3. Browse through the various folders of background images that Apple provides or use an image from your iPhoto library.

✔ **Display all the peripherals and network connections on your system.**

    a. Choose Finder⇨Preferences.

    b. Make sure that all four of the top check boxes (Hard Disks; External Disks; CDs, DVDs, and iPods; and Connected Servers) are enabled.

    Any external networks, hard drives, or devices to which you're connected show up on your Desktop. You can double-click the Desktop icon to view your external stuff.

Figure 5-3:
Choose a
Desktop
background
of more
interest.

Putting the Dock to the Test

If the Dock seems like a nifty contraption to you, you're right again — it's like one of those big control rooms that NASA uses. From the *Dock* — that icon toolbar at the bottom of Snow Leopard's Desktop — you can launch an application, monitor what's running, and even use the pop-up menu commands to control the applications that you launch. (Hey, that NASA analogy is even better than I thought!)

By default, the Dock hangs out at the bottom of your screen, but you can move it to another edge, change the size of the icons, or even hide it until it's necessary. (You can find more details on customizing the Dock using System Preferences in Chapter 6.)

When you launch an application — either by clicking an icon on the Dock or by double-clicking an icon in a Finder window or the Desktop — the icon begins to bounce hilariously on the Dock to indicate that the application is loading. (So much for my Mission Control analogy.) After an application is running, the application icon appears on the Dock with a shiny blue dot underneath. Thusly, you can easily see what's running at any time just by glancing at the Dock.

You can hide most applications by pressing ⌘+H. Although the application itself is still running, it might not appear on the Dock.

Some applications run in the *background* — that is, they don't show up on the Dock. You generally don't even know that these applications are working for you. However, if you need to see in detail what's going on, you can always use the Activity Monitor utility to view everything that's happening on your iMac. (For example, an Apple support technician might ask you to run Activity Monitor to help troubleshoot a problem.) To run the Activity Monitor

1. **Open a Finder window.**

2. **Click the Applications folder in the Sidebar.**

3. **Double-click the Utilities folder to open it.**

4. **Double-click the Activity Monitor icon.**

Adding Dock icons

Ah, but there's more: The Dock can offer more than just a set of default icons! You can add your own MIS (or *Most Important Stuff*) to the Dock, making it the most convenient method of taking care of business without cluttering up your Desktop. You can add

- **Applications:** Add any application to your Dock by dragging the application icon into the area to the left of the *separator line* (the vertical dotted line on the Dock which appears between applications and folders or documents). The existing Dock icons move aside so that you can place the new neighbor in a choice location.

  Do not try to add an application anywhere to the right of the separator line. You can't put applications there — and Snow Leopard might even think that you want the application dumped in the Trash!

- **Folders:** Here's where you want to add things to the area to the right of the separator line. A folder or volume icon that you drag to the Dock is called a *Stack* in Snow Leopard, and you can display the contents with a single click. (The contents of the folder "fan out" into a half-circle or grid arrangement, depending on the number of items in the folder. In fact, if you have enough items in the Stack, scroll bars will appear.) To open or launch an item, just click it in the Stack display.

  Snow Leopard already includes two Stacks in the Dock by default: your Documents folder and your Downloads folder.

- **Web URLs:** Sure, you can add your favorite Web site from Safari! Drag it right from the Safari Address bar into the area to the right of the separator line. When you click the URL icon, Safari opens the page automatically.

Removing Dock icons

You can remove an icon from the Dock at any time (as long as the application isn't running). In fact, I always recommend that every Snow Leopard user remove the default icons that never get used to make more room available for your favorite icons. The only two icons you can't remove are the Finder and the Trash icons. To remove an icon from the Dock, just click and drag it off the Dock. You're rewarded with a ridiculous puff of smoke straight out of a Warner Brothers cartoon! (One of the Mac OS X developers was in a fun mood, I guess.)

When you delete an icon from the Dock, all you delete is the Dock icon: The original application, folder, or volume is not deleted.

Using Dock icon menus

From the Dock menu, you can open documents, open the location in a Finder window, set an application as a Login Item, control the features in some applications, and other assorted fun, depending on the item.

To display the right-click Dock menu for an icon

1. **Move your mouse over the icon.**
2. **Right-click.**

   Note that you can also press the Control key and click the icon, or even hold down the left mouse button for a second or two.

I cover the Dock settings that you can change within System Preferences in Chapter 6. You can also change the same settings from the Apple menu if you hover your mouse over the Dock item, which displays a submenu with the settings.

What's with the Trash?

Another sign of an iMac power user is a well-maintained Trash bin. It's a breeze to empty the discarded items you no longer need, and you can even rescue something that you suddenly discover you still need!

The Snow Leopard Trash bin resides on the Dock, and it works just like the Trash has always worked in Mac OS X: Simply drag selected items to the Trash to delete them.

Note one very important exception: If you drag an external device or removable media drive icon on your Desktop to the Trash (such as an iPod, iPhone, DVD, or an external hard drive), the Trash bin icon automagically turns into a giant Eject icon, and the removable device or media is ejected or shut down — not erased. Repeat, *not erased*. (That's why the Trash icon changes to the Eject icon — to remind you that you're not doing anything destructive.)

Here are other methods of chunking items you select to go to the wastebasket:

- ↳ Choose File⇨Move to Trash.
- ↳ Click the Action button on the Finder toolbar and choose Move to Trash from the list that appears.
- ↳ Press ⌘+Delete.
- ↳ Right-click the item and choose Move to Trash from the right-click menu.

You can always tell when the Trash contains at least one item because the basket icon is full of crumpled paper! However, you don't have to unfold a wad of paper to see what the Trash holds: Just click the Trash icon on the

Dock to display the contents of the Trash. To rescue something from the Trash, drag the item(s) from the Trash folder to the Desktop or to any other folder in a Finder window. (If you're doing this for someone else who's not familiar with Snow Leopard, remember to act like it was a lot of work, and you'll earn big-time DRP, or *Data Rescue Points.*)

When you're sure that you want to permanently delete the contents of the Trash, use one of these methods to empty the Trash:

- **Choose Finder⇨Empty Trash.**
- **Choose Finder⇨Secure Empty Trash.**

    If security is an issue around your iMac and you want to make sure that no one can recover the files you've sent to the Trash, using the Secure Empty Trash command takes a little time but helps to ensure that no third-party hard drive repair or recovery program could resuscitate the items you discard.

- **Press ⌘+Shift+Delete.**
- **Right-click the Trash icon on the Dock and then choose Empty Trash from the right-click menu.**

Working Magic with Dashboard, Exposé, and Spaces

iMac power users tend to wax enthusiastic over the convenience features built into Snow Leopard. In fact, we show 'em off to our PC-saddled friends and family. Three of the features that I've demonstrated the most to others are Snow Leopard's Dashboard display, the Spaces Desktop manager, and the amazing convenience of Exposé. In this section, I show 'em off to you as well. (Then you can become the Snow Leopard evangelist on *your* block.)

Using Dashboard

The idea behind Dashboard is deceptively simple yet about as revolutionary as it gets for a mainstream personal computer operating system. *Dashboard* is an alternate Desktop that you can display at any time by using the keyboard or your mouse; the Dashboard desktop holds *widgets* (small applications that each provides a single function). Examples of default widgets that come with Snow Leopard include a calculator, a world clock, weather display, and a dictionary/thesaurus.

Oh, did I mention that you're not limited to the widgets that come with Snow Leopard? Simply click the plus button at the bottom of the Dashboard display and drag new widgets to your Dashboard from the menu at the bottom of the screen. To remove a widget while you're in this mode, click the X icon that appears next to each widget. When you're done with your widgets — that sounds a bit strange, but I mean no offense — press the Dashboard key again to return to your Desktop.

Widgets can also be rearranged any way you like by dragging them to a new location.

Simple applications like these are no big whoop. After all, Mac OS X has always had a calculator and a clock. What's revolutionary is how you access your widgets. You can display and use them anywhere in Snow Leopard, at any time, by simply pressing the Dashboard key. The default key is F4 although you can change the Dashboard key via the Exposé & Spaces pane within System Preferences (or even turn it into a key sequence, like Option+F4). You can also click the Dashboard icon on the Dock to summon your Dashboard widgets and then banish the Dashboard when you're done.

A WebClip widget can include text, graphics, and links, which Dashboard updates every time you display your widgets. Think about that for a second: Dynamic displays, such as weather maps, cartoons, and even the Free Music Download image from the iTunes Store are all good sources of WebClip widgets! (That last one is a real timesaver.)

Follow these steps to create a new WebClip Dashboard widget from your favorite Web site:

1. **Run Safari and navigate to the site you want to view as a widget.**

2. **Click the Open This Page in Dashboard button on the Safari Toolbar, which bears a pair of scissors and a dotted box.**

3. **Select the portion of the page you want to include in your widget.**

   Most Web pages use frames to organize and separate sections of a page, so this step allows you to choose the frame with the desired content.

4. **Drag the handles at the edges of the selection border to resize your widget frame to the right size and then click Add.**

   Bam! Snow Leopard displays your new WebClip widget within Dashboard.

When you click a link in a WebClip widget, Dashboard loads the full Web page in Safari, so you can even use WebClips for surfing chores with sites you visit often.

Switching between apps with Exposé

In Chapter 4, you can read about using the ⌘+Tab keyboard shortcut to switch between your open applications. If you've moved to the iMac from a PC running Windows, you might think this simple shortcut is all there is to it. Ah, dear reader, you're in Snow Leopard territory now!

Exposé is a rather racy-sounding feature, but (like Dashboard) it's really all about convenience. If you typically run a large number of applications at the same time, Exposé can be a real timesaver, allowing you to quickly switch among a forest of different application windows (or display your Desktop instantly without those very same windows in the way). The feature works in three ways:

✔ **Press the All Windows key (or key sequence) to display all your application windows on a single screen, as shown in the truly cool Figure 5-4. (By default, F3 is the All Windows key.)**

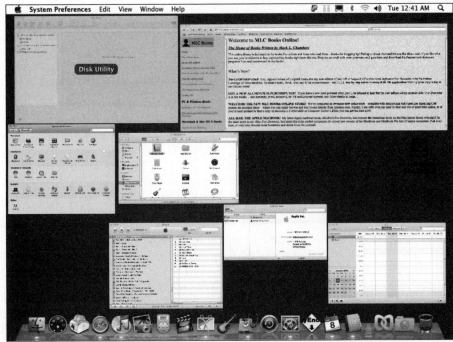

Figure 5-4: With Exposé, you can instantly see every open application window.

Then just click the window that you want to make active.

✔ **Press the Application Windows key (or key sequence) to display all the windows that have been opened by the active application. (By default, Ctrl+F3 is the Application Windows key sequence.)**

This comes in handy with those mega-applications, such as Photoshop Elements or FileMaker Pro, in which you often have three or four windows open at one time. Again, you can click the window that you want to make active.

✔ **Press the Desktop key (or key sequence) to move all your application and Finder windows to the sides of your Desktop so you can access your Desktop icons. (The default Desktop key sequence is ⌘+F3.)**

After you're done with your Desktop and you want to restore your windows to their original locations, press ⌘+F3 again to put things back.

Switching between desktops with Spaces

Ah, but what if you want to switch to an entirely different *set* of applications? For example, suppose that you're slaving away at your pixel-pushing job, designing a magazine cover with Pages. Your page design desktop also includes Photoshop and Aperture, which you switch between often using one of the techniques I just described. Suddenly, however, you realize you need to schedule a meeting with others in your office using iCal, and you also want to check your e-mail in Apple Mail. What to do?

Well, you could certainly launch those two applications on top of your graphics applications, and then minimize or close them. With Snow Leopard's *Spaces* feature, though, you can press the Control+← or Control+→ sequences to switch to a completely different "communications" desktop, with iCal and Apple Mail windows already open and in your favorite positions! Figure 5-5 illustrates the Spaces screen, showing two available desktops.

After you're done setting up your meeting and answering any important e-mail, simply press Control+← or Control+→ again to switch back to your "graphics" desktop, where all your work is exactly as you left it!

Now imagine that you've also created a custom "music" desktop for GarageBand and iTunes . . . or perhaps you joined iWeb, Safari, and iPhoto as a "Webmaster" desktop. See why everyone's so excited?

Unlike Exposé, Spaces has to be enabled and configured before you can use it. You can create new desktops, customize your desktops, and even choose a different set of key sequences to activate Spaces from within System Preferences. For the complete story on configuring Spaces, see Chapter 6.

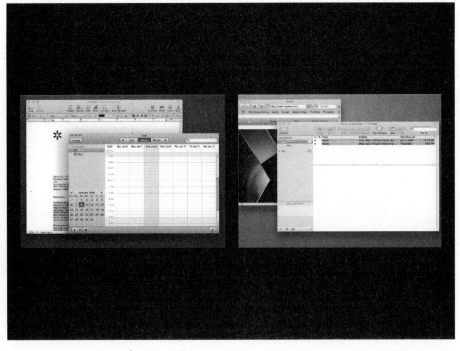

Figure 5-5:
With
Spaces,
you can
instantly
switch
between
multiple
desktops!

You can activate Exposé, Spaces, and Dashboard by using your mouse instead of the keyboard:

1. **Click the System Preferences icon on the Dock.**
2. **Click the Exposé & Spaces icon to display the settings.**
3. **Click the desired Screen Corner pop-up menu to choose what function that screen corner will trigger.**
4. **Press ⌘+Q to save your changes and then exit System Preferences.**

   When you move your mouse pointer to that corner, the feature you've specified automatically kicks in.

Printing within Mac OS X

Snow Leopard makes document printing a breeze. Because virtually all Mac printers use a Universal Serial Bus (USB) port, setting up printing couldn't be easier. Just turn on your printer and connect the USB cable between the printer and your iMac; Snow Leopard does the rest.

Printer manufacturers supply you with installation software that might add cool extra software or fonts to your system. Even if Snow Leopard recognizes your USB printer immediately, I recommend that you still launch the manufacturer's Mac OS X installation disc. For example, my new Epson printer came with new fonts and a CD/DVD label application, but I wouldn't have 'em if I hadn't installed the Epson software package.

After your printer is connected and installed, you can use the same procedure to print from within just about every Mac OS X application on the planet! To print with the default page layout settings — standard 8½-x-11" paper, portrait mode, no scaling — follow these steps:

1. **Within the active application, choose File⇨Print or press the ⌘+P shortcut.**

   Mac OS X displays the Print sheet.

2. **From this dialog, you can**

   • *Print from a different printer connected to your iMac or print over a network connection to a shared printer on another computer.*

     Click the Printer pop-up menu. In this pop-up menu, Snow Leopard displays all the printers that you can access.

   • *Check what the printed document will look like.*

     Click Preview to open it within the very same Preview application I discuss earlier in this chapter.

   If you have to make changes to the document or you need to change the default print settings, click Cancel to return to your document. (You have to repeat Step 1 again to display the Print dialog again.)

If everything looks good at this point and you don't need to change any settings (like multiple copies or to print only a portion of the document), click Print — you're done! If not, click the Expand button next to the Printer pop-up menu. (It bears a downward-pointing arrow.) Now you can proceed with these steps:

1. **(Optional) For more than one copy, click in the Copies field and type the number of copies that you need.**

   Collation (separating copies) is also available, and it doesn't cost a thing!

2. **(Optional) To print a range of selected pages, select the From radio button and then enter the starting and ending pages.**

To print the entire document, leave the default Pages option set to All.

3. **(Optional) If the application offers its own print settings, such as collating and grayscale printing, make any necessary changes to those settings.**

   To display these application-specific settings, click the pop-up menu in the Print dialog and choose the desired settings pane that you need to adjust. (You can blissfully ignore these settings and skip this step entirely if the defaults are fine.)

4. **When you're set to go, click Print.**

You can also save an electronic version of a document in the popular Adobe Acrobat PDF format from the Print dialog — without spending money on Adobe Acrobat. *(Slick.)*

1. **Click the PDF button to display the destination pop-up menu.**

2. **Click Save as PDF.**

   Snow Leopard prompts you with a Save As dialog, where you can type a name for the PDF document and specify a location on your hard drive where the file should be saved.

Heck, if you like, you can even fax a PDF (with an external USB modem or multifunction printer) or send it as an e-mail attachment! Just choose these options from the destination list rather than Save as PDF.

Chapter 6

A Nerd's Guide to System Preferences

*R*emember the old TV series *Voyage to the Bottom of the Sea?* You always knew you were on the bridge of the submarine Seaview because it had an entire wall made up of randomly blinking lights, crewmen darting about with clipboards, and all sorts of strange and exotic-looking controls on every available surface. You could fix just about anything by looking into the camera with grim determination and barking out an order. After all, you were On The Bridge. That's why virtually all the dialog and action inside the sub took place on that one (expensive) set: It was the nerve center of the ship, and a truly happenin' place to be.

I devote this entire chapter to the System Preferences window and all the settings within it. After all, if you want to change how Snow Leopard works or customize the features within our favorite operating system, this one window is the nerve center of Mac OS X, and a truly happenin' place to be. (Sorry, no built-in wall of randomly blinking lights — but there are exotic controls just about everywhere.)

A Not-So-Confusing Introduction

The System Preferences window (as shown in Figure 6-1) is a self-contained beast, and you can reach it in a number of ways:

✔ Click the Apple menu (⌘) and choose the System Preferences menu item.

✔ Click the System Preferences icon in the Dock.

✔ Click most of the Finder menu status icons and then choose the Open Preferences menu item. (This trick works with the Bluetooth, AirPort, Display, Modem, and Clock icons.)

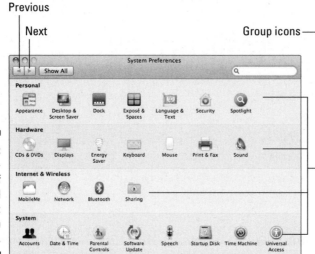

Previous

Next

Group icons

Figure 6-1:
The power-house of settings and switches: System Preferences.

When the System Preferences window is open, you can click any of the group icons to switch to that group's *pane;* the entire window morphs to display the settings for the selected pane. For example, Figure 6-2 illustrates the Sound pane, which allows you to set a system alert sound, configure your iMac's built-in microphone, and choose from several different output options.

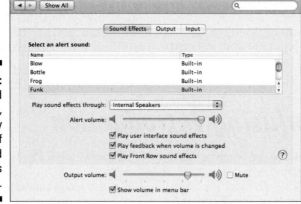

Figure 6-2:
The Sound pane, proudly showing off the Sound Effects panel.

Many panes also include a number of tabbed buttons at the top — in this case, Sound Effects, Output, and Input. You can click these tabs to switch to another *panel* within the same pane. Many panes within System Preferences have multiple panels. This design allows our friends at Apple to group a large number of related settings together in the same pane (without things getting too confusing).

To return to the top-level System Preferences panel from any pane, just click the Show All button (top left) or press ⌘+L. You can also click the familiar Previous and Next buttons to move backward through the panes you've already visited and then move forward again, in sequence. (Yep, these buttons work just like the browser controls in Safari. Sometimes life is funny that way.)

Your changes to the settings in a pane are automatically saved when you click Show All or when you click the Close button on the System Preferences window. You can also press ⌘+Q to exit the window and save all your changes automatically . . . a favorite shortcut of mine.

If you see an Apply button in a pane, you can click it to immediately apply any changes you make, without exiting the pane. This is perfect for some settings that you might want to try first before you accept them, like many of the controls on the Network pane. However, if you're sure about what you changed and how those changes will affect your system, you don't have to click Apply. Just exit the System Preferences window or click Show All as you normally would.

Searching for Settings

Hey, wouldn't it be great if you could search through all the different panes in System Preferences — with all those countless radio buttons, check boxes, and slider controls — from one place? Even when you're not quite sure exactly what it is you're looking for?

Figure 6-3 illustrates exactly that kind of activity taking place. Just click in the System Preferences Spotlight Search box (upper right, with the magnifying glass icon) and type in just about anything. For example, if you know part of the name of a particular setting you need to change, type that. Snow Leopard highlights the System Preferences panes that might contain matching settings. And if you're a *Switcher* from the Windows world, you can even type in what you might have called the same setting in Windows!

The System Preferences window dims and the group icons that might contain what you're looking for stay highlighted. *Slick.*

If you need to reset the Search box to try again, click the X icon that appears at the right side of the box to clear it.

Figure 6-3:
Searching
for specific
settings is a
breeze
with the
Search box.

Popular Preference Panes Explained

Time to get down to brass tacks. Open up the most-often-used panes in System Preferences to see what magic you can perform! I won't discuss every pane because I cover many of them in other chapters. (In fact, you might never need to open some System Preferences panes at all, like the MobileMe pane.) However, this chapter covers just about all the settings that you're likely to use on a regular basis.

The Displays pane

If you're a heavy-duty game player or you work with applications like video editing and 3-D modeling, you probably find yourself switching the characteristics of your monitor on a regular basis. To easily accomplish switching, visit the Displays pane (see Figure 6-4), which includes two panels:

✔ **Display:** Click a screen resolution to choose it from the Resolutions list on the left. Snow Leopard displays the number of colors (or *color depth*) allowed at that resolution, and you can pick a color depth from the Colors pop-up menu. (Typically, it's a good idea to use the highest resolution and the highest number of colors.) If you have an external monitor connected to your iMac, click the Detect Displays button to scan for that monitor. Drag the Brightness slider to change the brightness level of your display.

When you enable (mark) the Show Displays in Menu Bar check box, you can switch resolutions and color levels right from the Finder menu!

✔ **Color:** Your iMac can use a *color profile* file that controls the colors on your display. This setting comes in handy for graphic artists and illustrators who need color output from their printers that closely matches the colors displayed by the iMac. Click the Calibrate button to launch the Display Calibrator, which can create a custom ColorSync profile and calibrate the colors that you see on your monitor.

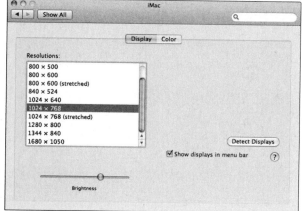

Figure 6-4: The Displays pane also comes in a handy Finder menu bar size!

The Desktop & Screen Saver pane

Hey, who doesn't want to choose their own background? And what about that nifty screen saver you just downloaded from the Apple Web site? You can change both your background and your screen saver by using these options on the Desktop & Screen Saver pane.

The settings on the Desktop panel (as shown in Figure 6-5) include

✔ **Current Desktop picture:** To change your Desktop background, click a thumbnail. You can also drag a picture from a Finder window or the desktop and drop it into the *well* (the fancy Apple word for the square box with the sunken look). Snow Leopard automatically updates your Desktop so you can see the results. To open another collection of images from Apple, click the desired collection folder in the list on the left of the panel. (I recommend the stunning images in the Nature folder.) If you want to open a different folder with your own images, click the Add button (which bears a plus sign) at the lower left of the panel and then navigate to that folder.

Figure 6-5:
Show
The Man
who's boss
and pick
your own
Desktop
background.

✔ **Arrangement:** You can automatically fit an image to your screen, *tile* your background image (repeat it across the Desktop), center it, and stretch it to fill the screen. Because the images from Apple are all sized correctly already, the Arrangement control appears only when you're using your own pictures.

✔ **Change Picture:** If you like a bit of automatic variety on your Desktop, select the Change Picture check box. You can click the pop-up menu to set the delay period. The images in the current collection or folder are then displayed in the sequence in which they appear in the thumbnail list.

✔ **Translucent Menu Bar:** When enabled, this feature turns your Finder and application menu bars semi-opaque, allowing them to blend in somewhat with your Desktop background. If you'd rather have a solid-color menu bar, deselect this check box.

✔ **Random Order:** Select this check box to throw caution utterly to the wind and display random screens from the current collection or folder!

The settings on the Screen Saver pane include

✔ **Screen Savers:** Click the screen saver that you want to display from the Screen Savers list. Snow Leopard displays an animated preview of the selected saver on the right. You can also click the Test button to try out the screen saver in full-screen mode. (Move your mouse a bit to end the test.)

If the selected screen saver has any settings you can change, the Options button displays them.

✔ **Start Screen Saver:** Drag this slider to choose the period of inactivity that triggers the screen saver. Choose Never if you want to disable the screen saver entirely.

✔ **Use Random Screen Saver:** Another chance to rebel against conformity! Enable this check box, and Snow Leopard picks a different screen saver each time.

✔ **Show With Clock:** Enable this check box, and Snow Leopard adds a smart clock display to your screen saver (a great help for those of us who spend many minutes on the phone).

✔ **Hot Corners:** Click this button to display a drop-down sheet, and then click any of the four pop-up menus at the four corners of the screen to select that corner as an *activating hot corner.* (Moving your mouse pointer to a hot corner immediately activates the screen saver.) You can also specify a corner as a *disabling hot corner* — as long as the mouse pointer stays in that corner, the screen saver is disabled. Note that you can also set the Dashboard, Spaces, and Exposé activation corners from here. (Read on for the entire lowdown.)

For additional security, check out the Security pane in System Preferences, where you'll find the Require Password to Wake This Computer from Sleep or Screen Saver check box and enable the check box.

The Exposé & Spaces pane

The pane you see in Figure 6-6 illustrates the settings that control Snow Leopard's Spaces, Dashboard, and Exposé features (features I discuss in more detail in Chapter 5). The settings on the Exposé tab include

✔ **Active Screen Corners:** The screen corners pop-up menus that I describe in the preceding section operate just like those in the Screen Savers panel. Click a corner's list box to set it as

- An Exposé *All Windows* corner (displays all windows on your Desktop).
- An Exposé *Application Windows* corner (displays only the windows from the active application).
- An Exposé *Desktop* corner (moves all windows to the outside of the screen to uncover your Desktop).
- A *Spaces* corner (activates the Spaces Desktop selection feature).

• A *Sleep Display* corner (immediately turns off your display, putting your screen in Sleep mode).

• A *Dashboard* corner (displays your Dashboard widgets). *Widgets* are small applications that each perform a single task; they appear when you invoke the awesome power of Dashboard.

These pop-up menus can also set the Screen Saver activate and disable hot corners.

✔ **Keyboard and mouse shortcuts:** Pretty straightforward stuff here. Click each pop-up menu to set the key sequences (and mouse button settings) for all three Exposé and Dashboard functions.

If you hold down a modifier key (Shift, Control, Option, or ⌘) while a shortcut pop-up menu is open, Snow Leopard adds that modifier key to the selections you can choose!

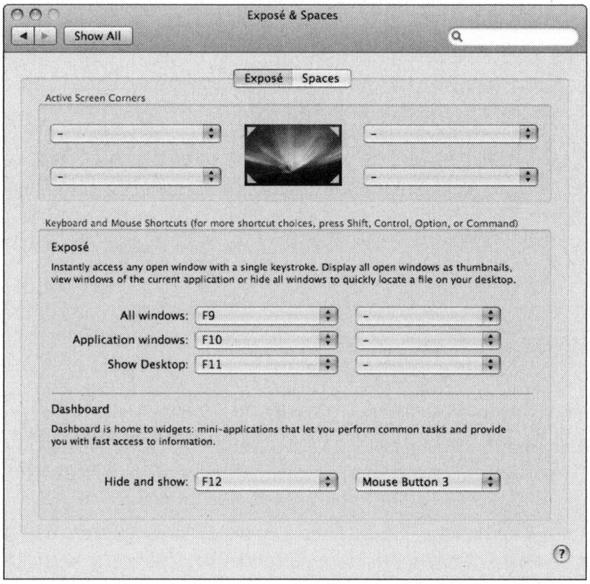

Figure 6-6:
The Exposé
& Spaces
pane in
System
Preferences.

One of Snow Leopard's hottest features is *Spaces,* which is the system you use to configure and control multiple "prefabricated" desktops that you can switch between at will! The settings on the Spaces tab include

✔ **Enable Spaces:** Enable this check box to use Spaces. (Go figure.)

✔ **Show Spaces in Menu Bar:** When this check box is enabled, Snow Leopard displays the Spaces desktop number you're currently using in the Finder menu bar. You can click the number in the menu bar to switch to another Spaces desktop or to open the Spaces Preferences pane.

✔ **Rows buttons:** To add a row of Spaces desktops to the Spaces grid, click the Add button with the plus sign. (By default, Spaces starts with two desktops enabled, so new rows and columns are numbered beginning with three.) To delete a row, click the Delete button (which bears a minus sign).

✔ **Columns buttons:** To add a column of Spaces desktops to the Spaces grid, click the Add (plus) button. Click the Delete (minus) button to remove a column from the grid.

If you choose to remove a column or row, Snow Leopard alerts you that the *bindings* (the specific applications linked to the deleted columns or rows) will be reassigned.

✔ **Add/Remove Application:** Click the Add Application button (the button with the plus sign under the Application Assignments list) to add an application to one of your Spaces desktops. You can select which desktop should include an application by clicking the up/down arrows next to the Space column for that application's entry — just click the desired desktop from the pop-up menu that appears. To remove an application, click it in the Application Bindings list to select it and then click the Remove Application button (which sports a minus sign).

Spaces can even add an application to all your desktops — choose Every Space from the pop-up menu.

✔ **Keyboard and mouse shortcuts:** Click each pop-up menu to set the key sequences (and mouse button settings) for all three Spaces functions.

Like with Dashboard and Exposé keyboard and mouse shortcuts, you can press Shift, Control, Option, and ⌘ keys while the box is open to display modified choices.

✔ **When Switching to an Application:** When selected, this check box allows you to switch applications between Spaces desktops using the ⌘+Tab shortcut. Snow Leopard will jump to the desktop that has an open window for the application you choose, even if that desktop is not currently active.

The Appearance pane

The talented Appearance pane (as shown in Figure 6-7) determines the look and operation of the controls that appear in application windows and Finder windows. It looks complex, but I cover each option here.

The settings include

- ✔ **Appearance:** Click this pop-up menu to specify the color Snow Leopard uses for buttons, menus, and windows.

- ✔ **Highlight Color:** Click this pop-up menu to choose the color that highlights selected text in fields, pop-up menus, and drop-down list boxes.

- ✔ **Place Scroll Arrows:** Select a radio button here to determine whether the arrows that control the scroll bar in a window appear together at the bottom of the scroll bar, or separately at the top and bottom of the scroll bar.

- ✔ **Click in the Scroll Bar To:** By default, Snow Leopard scrolls to the next or previous page when you click in an empty portion of the scroll bar. Select the Jump to Here radio button to scroll the document to the approximate position in relation to where you clicked. (Smooth scrolling slows down scrolling, which some people prefer.)

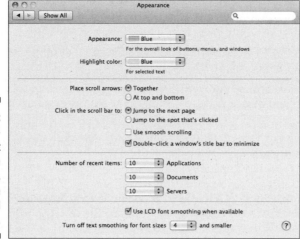

Figure 6-7:
Appear-
ances might
not be
everything,
but they're
easy to find
here.

You can minimize a Finder or application window by simply double-clicking the window's title bar. To enable this feature, mark the Minimize When Double Clicking a Window Title Bar check box.

- ✔ **Number of Recent Items:** By default, Snow Leopard displays ten recent applications, documents, and servers within Recent Items in the Apple menu. Need more? Just click the corresponding pop-up menu and specify up to 50 items.

- ✔ **Use LCD Font Smoothing:** By default, this check box is enabled, making the text on your iMac's LED display appear more like the printed page.

✔ **Turn Off Text Smoothing for Font Sizes:** Below a certain point size, text smoothing doesn't help fonts look any smoother onscreen. By default, any font displayed at 8 point or smaller isn't smoothed, which is a good choice for an iMac with a flat-panel LED screen.

The Energy Saver pane

I'm an environmentalist — it's surprising how many techno-types are colored green — so this pane (as shown in Figure 6-8) is pretty doggone important. When you use them correctly, you not only save electricity but also even invoke the Power of Snow Leopard to automatically start and shut down your iMac whenever you like!

To save electricity, drag the Computer Sleep slider to a delay period that triggers sleep mode when you're away from the keyboard for a significant period of time. (I prefer 30 minutes.) If your iMac must always remain alert and you want to disable sleep mode entirely, choose Never. You can set the delay period for blanking your monitor separately from the sleep setting with the Display Sleep slider.

To conserve the maximum juice and cut down on wear, enable the Put the Hard Disk(s) to Sleep When Possible check box to power-down your hard drives when they're not needed. (This might cause a delay of a second or two while loading or saving files because the drives must spin back up.)

You can set Snow Leopard to start or shut down your iMac at a scheduled time. Click the Schedule button and then select the desired schedule (the Start Up or Wake check box and the Shut Down/Sleep pop-up menu) to enable them. Set the trigger time by clicking the up and down arrows next to the time display for each schedule. Click OK to return to the Energy Saver pane.

Enable the Wake for Network Access check box to wake your iMac from sleep mode whenever your computer is accessed remotely across your network. If you prefer to send your iMac to sleep by pressing the Power button, enable the Allow Power Button to Put the Computer to Sleep check box. By default, your iMac's display will dim to indicate that sleep mode is approaching, but you can disable the Automatically Reduce the Brightness of the Display check box to maintain full brightness until sleep mode actually kicks in. Snow Leopard can also restart your iMac automatically after a power failure — a good feature for those running Apache Web server, because your Web site will automatically come back online after power is restored.

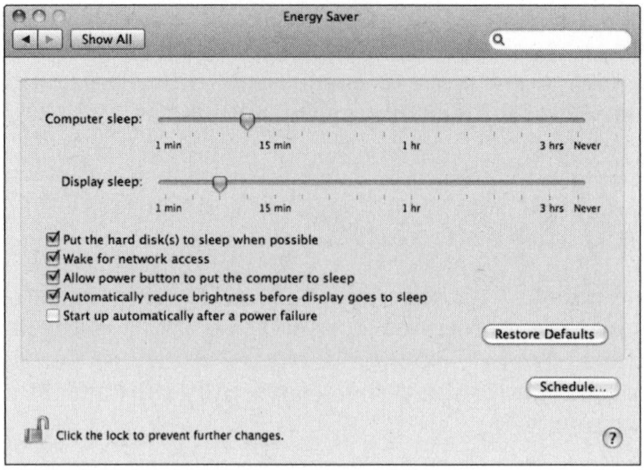

Figure 6-8:
Reduce
your iMac's
power
consump-
tion from
the Energy
Saver pane.

The Dock pane

You can use the settings, as shown in Figure 6-9, to configure the Dock's behavior until it fits your personality like a glove:

- **Size:** Pretty self-explanatory. Just drag the slider to change the scale of the Dock.

- **Magnification:** When you select this check box, each icon in your Dock swells like a puffer fish when you move your mouse cursor over it. (Just how much it magnifies is determined by the Magnification slider.) I really like this feature because I resize my Dock smaller, and I have a large number of Dock icons.

- **Position on Screen:** Select a radio button here to position the Dock on the left, bottom, or right edge of your iMac's Desktop.

- **Minimize Using:** Snow Leopard includes two cool animations that you can choose from when shrinking a window to the Dock (and expanding it back to the Desktop). Click the Minimize Using pop-up menu to specify the genie-in-a-bottle effect or a scale-up-or-down-incrementally effect.

- **Minimize windows into application icon:** By default, Snow Leopard minimizes a window as a thumbnail on the right side of the Dock. Select this check box to minimize a window into the icon for the parent application instead.

- **Animate Opening Applications:** Are you into aerobics? How about punk rock and slam dancing? Active souls who like animation likely get a kick out of the bouncing application icons in the Dock. They indicate that you've launched an application and that it's loading. You can turn off this bouncing behavior by disabling this check box.

✔ **Automatically Hide and Show the Dock:** Select this check box, and the Dock disappears until you need it. (Depending on the size of your Dock, the Desktop that you gain can be significant.) To display a hidden Dock, move your mouse pointer over the corresponding edge of the Desktop.

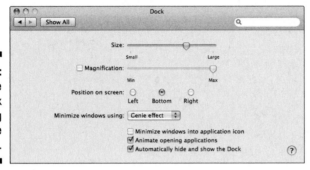

Figure 6-9:
Customize
your Dock
by using
these
controls.

The Sharing pane

So you're in a neighborly mood, and you want to share your toys with others on your local wired or wireless network. Perhaps you'd like to start your own Web site, or protect yourself against the Bad Guys on the Internet. All these fun diversions are available from the Sharing pane in System Preferences, as shown in Figure 6-10.

Click the Edit button to change the default network name assigned to your iMac during the installation process. Your current network name is listed in the Computer Name text field.

Each entry in the services list controls a specific type of sharing. To turn on any of these services, enable the On check box for that service. To turn off a service, click the corresponding On check box to disable it.

From a security standpoint, I highly recommend that you enable only those services that you actually use — each service you enable automatically opens your Snow Leopard firewall for that service. A Mark's Maxim to remember:

Poking too many holes in your firewall is *not* A Good Thing.

When you click one of the services in the list, the right side of the Sharing pane changes to display the settings you can specify for that particular service. To display all the details on these options, click the Help button at the lower-right corner of the System Preferences dialog.

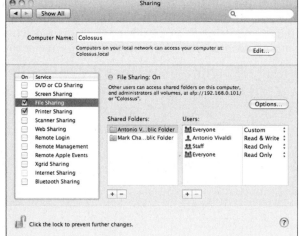

Figure 6-10:
Share your
toys with
others by
using the
controls on
the Sharing
pane.

The Time Machine pane

Mac users are excited about the Time Machine automatic backup feature.
You can easily configure how Time Machine handles your backups from the
pane shown in Figure 6-11. Of course, you'll need an external hard drive (or
a Time Capsule wireless backup station) for the best backup security. Note
that Time Machine won't work with your CD or DVD rewriteable drive . . . it's
got to be a hard drive.

To enable Time Machine, click the On switch and then click the Select Disk
button to choose a disk to hold your Time Machine backup data. Time
Machine backs up all the hard drives on your system; however, to save time
and hard drive space, Time Machine allows you to exclude specific drives
and folders from the backup process. Click the Options button; then click the
Add button (with the plus sign) to select the drives or folders you want to
exclude, and they appear in the Exclude list.

To remove an item you would like to exclude, select it in the list and click the
Delete button (with the minus sign); note the Estimated Size figure increases,
and Time Machine adds the item you deleted from the list to the next backup.

After you make your changes, you can elect to back up your Mac immediately
by clicking the Time Machine icon in the Finder menu and choosing the Back
Up Now item.

Figure 6-11:
Put Time
Machine to
work, and
your data
is always
backed up.

Chapter 7

Searching amidst iMac Chaos

● ●

● ●

*W*hat would you say if I told you that you could search your entire system for virtually every piece of data connected with a person — and in only the short time it takes to type that person's name? And I'm not just talking about files and folders that might include that person's name. I mean *every* e-mail message and *every* iCal calendar or event that references that person — and even that person's Address Book card to boot? Heck, how about if that search could dig up every occurrence of the person's name inside PDF documents? What if it could even search folders shared on other Macs across your network?

You'd probably say, "That makes for good future tech — I'll bet I can do that in five or ten years. It'll take Apple at least that long to do it . . . and just in time for me to buy a new iMac! (Harrumph.)"

Don't be so hasty: You can do all this, right now. The technology is the Mac OS X feature named *Spotlight,* built right into Snow Leopard. In this chapter, I show you how to use it like an iMac power guru.

Basic Searching 101

Figure 7-1 illustrates the Spotlight search field, which is always available from the Finder menu bar. Click the magnifying glass icon once (or press ⌘+Spacebar), and the Spotlight search box appears.

To run a search, simply click in the Spotlight box and begin typing. You see matching items appear as soon as you type, and the search results are continually refined while you type the rest of your search criteria. As with the Search box in earlier Finder window toolbars, you don't need to press Return to begin the search.

Figure 7-1:
A lot of
power is
behind
this single
Spotlight
search box.

The results of your Spotlight search are presented in the Spotlight menu, which is updated automatically in real time while you continue to type. The top 20 most-relevant items are grouped into categories right on the Spotlight menu. Categories include Messages, Definitions, Documents, Folders, Images, and Contacts. Spotlight takes a guess at the item that's the most likely match (based on your Search Results list in System Preferences, which I cover later in the chapter) and presents it in the special Top Hit category that always appears first.

To open the Top Hit item like a true Snow Leopard power user, just press Return. (My brothers and sisters, it just doesn't get any easier than that.)

Literally any text string is acceptable as a Spotlight search. However, here's a short list of the common search criteria I use every day:

✔ **Names and addresses:** Because Spotlight has access to Snow Leopard's Address Book, you can immediately display contact information using any portion of a name or address.

✔ **E-mail message text:** Need to open a specific e-mail message, but you'd rather not launch Mail and spend time digging through the message list? Enter the person's e-mail address or any text string contained in the message you're looking for.

✔ **File and folder names:** This is the classic search favorite. Spotlight searches your system for that one file or folder in the blink of an eye.

✔ **Events & To Do items:** Yep, Spotlight gives you access to your iCal calendars and those all-important To Do lists you've created.

✔ **System Preferences:** Now things start to get *really* interesting! Try typing the word **background** in the Spotlight field. Some of the results will actually be System Preference panes! That's right, every setting in System Preferences is referenced in Spotlight. (For example, the Software Update pane contains the word *background* while the desktop background setting is on the Desktop & Screen Saver pane in System Preferences.)

✔ **Web pages:** *Whoa.* Stand back, Google. You can use Spotlight to search the Web pages you've recently displayed in Safari! (Note, however, that this feature doesn't let you search through all the Internet as Google does . . . only the pages stored in your Safari Web cache and any HTML files you've saved to your iMac's hard drive.)

✔ **Metadata:** That's a pretty broad category, but it fits. For example, I like to locate Word documents on my system using the same metadata that's stored in the file, such as the contents of the Comments field in a Word document. Other supported applications include Photoshop images, Excel spreadsheets, Keynote presentations, and other third-party applications that offer a Spotlight plug-in.

To reset the Spotlight search and try another text string, click the X icon that appears on the right side of the Spotlight box. (Of course, you can also backspace to the beginning of the field, but that's a little less elegant.)

After you find the item that you're looking for, you can click it once to launch it (if the item is an application), open it in System Preferences (if it's a setting or description on a Preferences pane), open it within the associated application (if the item is a document or a data item) or display it within a Finder window (if the item is a folder).

Here's another favorite timesaver: You can display all the files of a particular type on your system by using the file type as the keyword. For example, to provide a list of all images on your system, just use *images* as your keyword — the same goes for *movies* and *audio,* too. You can use common extensions like JPG and DOC to search for certain types of files as well.

In fact, you can display the same search results from the Snow Leopard Sidebar, which includes a Search For heading! You can display All Images, All Movies, and All Documents with a single click of your mouse button, from any Finder window.

Is Spotlight Really That Cool?

Don't get fooled into simply using Spotlight as another file-'n-folder-name search tool. Sure, it can do that, but Spotlight can also search inside PDF, Word, Pages and HTML files, finding matching text that doesn't appear in the name of the file! To wit: A search for *Snow Leopard* on my system pulls up all sorts of items with Snow Leopard in their names, but also files with Snow Leopard *in* them, like a PowerPoint presentation including slides containing the text Snow Leopard, or an iCal event pointing to a conference call with my editor about upcoming Snow Leopard book projects. Notice that not one of these three examples actually has the words *Snow Leopard* occurring anywhere in the title or filename, yet Spotlight found them because they all contain the text *Snow Leopard* therein.

Heck, suppose that all you remember about a file is that you received it in your mail last week or last month. To find it, you can actually type in time periods, such as *yesterday, last week,* or *last month,* to see every item that you saved or received within that period. (Boy, howdy, I *love* writing about truly good ideas.)

Again, the Sidebar also allows you to search for files by time period, using the links under the Search For heading.

Be careful, however, when you're considering a search string. Don't forget that (by default) Spotlight matches only those items that have *all* the words you enter in the Spotlight box. To return the highest number of possible matches, use the fewest number of words to identify the item; for example, use *horse* rather than *horse image,* and you're certain to be rewarded with more hits. (On the other hand, if you're looking specifically for a picture of a knight on horseback, a series of keywords, such as *horse knight image,* shortens your search considerably. It all depends on what you're looking for and how widely you want to cast your Spotlight net.)

To allow greater flexibility in searches, Apple also includes those helpful Boolean friends that you may already be familiar with: AND, OR, and NOT. For example, you can perform Spotlight searches, such as

- *Horse* AND *cow* (which collects all references to both those barnyard animals into one search)

- *Batman* OR *Robin* (which returns all references to either Batman or Robin)

- *Apple* NOT *PC* (which displays all references to Apple that don't include any information on dastardly PCs)

Because Spotlight functions are a core technology of Mac OS X Snow Leopard — in other words, all sorts of applications can make use of Spotlight throughout the operating system, including the Finder — the Finder window's Search box now shares many of the capabilities of Spotlight. In fact, you can use the time period trick that I mention earlier (entering *yesterday* as a keyword) in the Finder window Search box.

Is Spotlight secure?

So how about all those files, folders, contacts, and events that you *don't* want to appear in Spotlight? What if you're sharing your iMac as a multiuser computer, or accessing other Macs remotely? Can others search for and access your personal information through Spotlight?

Definitely not! The results displayed by Spotlight are controlled by file and folder permissions as well as your account login, just as the applications that create and display your personal data are. For example, you can't access other users' calendars using iCal, and they can't see your Mail messages. Only *you*

have access to your data, and only after you've logged in with your username and password. Spotlight works the same way. If a user doesn't normally have access to an item, the item simply doesn't appear when that user performs a Spotlight search. (In other words, only you get to see your stuff.)

However, you can even hide certain folders and disks from your own Spotlight searches if necessary. Check out the final section of this chapter for details on setting private locations on your system.

Okay, parents, listen closely: Here's a (somewhat sneaky) tip that might help you monitor your kid's computer time as well as what your kids are typing/reading in iChat:

1. **Enable the iChat transcript feature.**

   a. *From within iChat, choose iChat⇨Preferences.*

   b. *Click Messages.*

   c. *Select the Save Chat Transcripts To check box and choose a destination folder in a location you can access.*

2. **Click OK to return to iChat.**

   Now you can use Spotlight to search for questionable words, phrases, and names within those iChat transcripts.

Expanding Your Search Horizons

I can just hear the announcer's voice now: "But wait, there's more! If you click the Show All menu item at the beginning of your search results, we'll expand your Spotlight menu into the Spotlight Results window!" (Fortunately, you don't have to buy some ridiculous household doodad.)

Keyboard mavens will appreciate the Spotlight window shortcut key, and I show you where to specify this shortcut in the final section of this chapter.

Figure 7-2 illustrates the Results window (which is actually a Finder window with extras). To further filter the search, click one of the buttons on the Spotlight Results window toolbar or create your own custom filter. Click the button with the plus sign to display the search criteria bar and then click the pop-up menus to choose from criteria, such as the type of file, the text content, or the location on your system (for example, your hard drive, your Home folder, or a network server). You can also filter your results listing by the date the items were created or last saved. To add or delete criteria, click the plus and minus buttons at the right side of the search criteria bar. To save a custom filter that you've created, click the Save button.

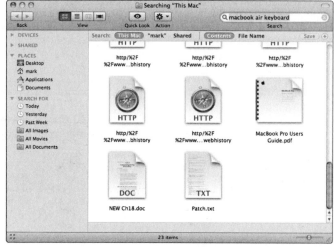

Figure 7-2: The spacious borders of the Spotlight Results window.

Images appear as thumbnail icons, so you can use that most sophisticated search tool — the human eye — to find the picture you're looking for. (If you don't see thumbnail images, click the Icon view button on the toolbar.) Don't forget that you can increase or decrease the size of the icons by dragging the slider at the bottom right of the window.

To display the contents item in the list (without leaving the comfortable confines of the Results window), click the icon to select it and click the Quick Look icon in the toolbar (or press the spacebar) for a better view.

Again, when you're ready to open an item, just double-click it in the Results window.

As I mention earlier, Spotlight can look for matching items on other Macs on your network — but only if those remote Macs are configured correctly. To allow another Mac running Mac OS X Tiger, Leopard, or Snow Leopard to be visible to Spotlight on your system, enable File Sharing on the other Mac. (Oh, and remember that you need an admin-level account on that Mac — or access to a good friend who has an admin-level account on that Mac.)

Follow these steps to enable File Sharing on the other Mac:

1. **Click the System Preferences icon in the Dock.**
2. **Click the Sharing pane.**
3. **Select the On check box next to the File Sharing item in the service list to enable it.**
4. **Click the Close button on the System Preferences window.**

Remember, you can search only items that you have rights and permissions to view on the remote Mac (such as the contents of the Public folders on that computer). I discuss more about these limitations earlier in this chapter, in the "Is Spotlight secure?" sidebar.

Customizing Spotlight to Your Taste

You might wonder whether such an awesome Mac OS X feature has its own pane within System Preferences — and you'd be right again. Figure 7-3 shows off the Spotlight pane within System Preferences: Click the System Preferences icon (look for the gears) in the Dock and then click the Spotlight icon (under Personal) to display these settings.

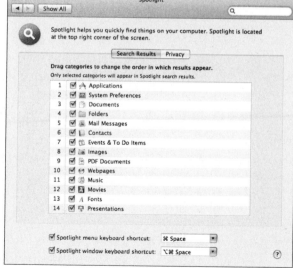

Figure 7-3: Fine-tune your Spotlight menu and Results window from within System Preferences.

Click the Search Results tab to

- ✔ **Determine which categories appear in the Spotlight menu and Results window.** For example, if you don't use any presentation software on your iMac, you can clear the check box next to Presentations to disable this category (thereby making more room for other categories that you *will* use).

- ✔ **Determine the order that categories appear in the Spotlight menu and Results window.** Drag the categories to the order in which you want them to appear in the Spotlight menu and window. For example, I like the Documents and System Preferences categories to appear higher in the list because I use them most often.

- ✔ **Specify the Spotlight menu and Spotlight Results window keyboard shortcuts.** You can enable or disable either keyboard shortcut and choose the key combination from the pop-up menu.

Click the Privacy tab (as shown in Figure 7-4) to specify disks and folders that should never be listed as results in a Spotlight search. I know, I know, I said earlier that Spotlight respected your security, and it does. However, the disks and folders that you add on this list won't appear even if *you* are the one performing the search. (This is a great idea for folders and removable hard drives that you use to store sensitive information, such as medical records.)

Figure 7-4: When certain folders and disks must remain private (even from you!), add them to this list.

To add locations that you want to keep private, click the Add button (bearing a plus sign) and navigate to the desired location. Click the location to select it and then click Choose. (Alternatively, you can drag folders or disks directly from a Finder window and drop them into the pane.)

Part III

Connecting and Communicating

The 5th Wave
By Rich Tennant

TROUBLE ON THE SET

©RICHTENNANT

All the software in the world won't make this a great film. Only you can, Rusty. Only you and the guts and determination to be the finest Frisbee catching dog in this dirty little town. Now come on Rusty- it's magic time.

We're losing the light, Dad.

In this part . . .

You want to do the Internet thing, don't you? Sure you do — and in this part, I describe and demonstrate your Safari Web browser. You also get to know all about Apple's MobileMe Internet subscription service, and how you can store and synchronize your data online. Finally, this part fills you in on connecting important stuff like printers and scanners.

Chapter 8

Let's Go on Safari!

1 proudly surf the Web via a lean, mean — and *very* fast — browser application. That's Safari, of course, and it just keeps getting better with each new version of Mac OS X. Safari delivers the Web the right way, without the wait. (Heck, if you like, you can even enlist your friends using PCs on this expedition — there's a version of Safari for Windows as well.)

If you need a guide to Safari, this is your chapter. Sure, you can start using it immediately, but wouldn't you rather read a few pages in order to surf like a power user?

Pretend You've Never Used This Thing

Figure 8-1 illustrates the Safari window. You can launch Safari directly from the Dock or you can click the Safari icon within your Applications folder. Major sections of the Safari window include

✔ **The toolbar:** You'll find the most often used commands on this toolbar — for tasks such as navigating, adding bookmarks, and searching Google. Plus, here you can type or paste the address for Web sites that you'd like to visit. The toolbar can be hidden to provide you with more real estate in your browser window for Web content. To toggle hidden mode on and off, press ⌘+| (the vertical bar right above the backslash) or choose View➪Hide/Show Toolbar.

Toolbar

Bookmarks bar

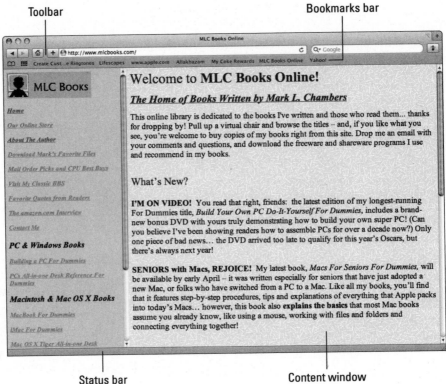

Figure 8-1:
Safari at a
glance.

Status bar

Content window

✔ **The Bookmarks bar:** Consider this a toolbar that allows you to jump directly to your favorite Web sites with a single click or two. I show you later, in the section "Adding and Using Bookmarks," how to add and remove sites from your Bookmarks bar. For now, remember that you can toggle the display of the Bookmarks bar by choosing View➪Hide/Show Bookmarks Bar or by pressing ⌘+Shift+B.

✔ **The Content window:** Congratulations! At last, you've waded through all the pregame show and you've reached the area where Web pages are actually displayed. As can any other window, the Content window can be scrolled; when you minimize Safari to the Dock, you get a *thumbnail* (minimized) image of the Content window.

The Content window often contains underlined text and graphical icons that transport you to other pages when you click them. These underlined words and icons are *links,* and they make it easy to move from one area of a site to another or to a completely different site.

✔ **The status bar:** The status bar displays information about what the cursor is currently resting upon, such as the address for a link or the name of an image; it also updates you on what's happening while a page is loading. To hide or display the status bar, press ⌘+/ (forward slash) or choose View➪Hide/Show Status Bar.

Visiting Web Sites

Here's the stuff that virtually everyone over the age of five knows how to do . . . but I get paid by the word, and some folks might not be aware of the myriad ways of visiting a site. You can load a Web page using any of the following methods:

✔ **Type (or paste) a Web site address into the Address box on the toolbar and then press Return.**

If you're typing in an address and Safari recognizes the site as one that you've visited in the past, it helps by completing the address for you. Press Return if you want to accept the suggested site. If this is a new site, just keep typing.

The latest versions of Safari include a *Smart Address* field that displays a new pop-up menu of sites that match the text you've entered. Safari does this by using sites taken from your History file and your bookmarks. If the site you want to visit appears in the list, click it to jump there immediately.

✔ **Click a Bookmarks entry within Safari.**

✔ **If the Home button appears on your toolbar, click it to return to the home page that you specify.**

More on this in the section "Setting Up Your Home Page," later in this chapter.

✔ **Click the Show Top Sites button on the toolbar.**

Safari displays a wall of preview thumbnail pages from your most frequently visited sites, and you can jump to a site just by clicking on the preview. Click the Edit button on the Top Sites screen to delete a preview thumbnail — click the X — or you can "anchor" a thumbnail to keep it on the screen permanently by clicking the pin icon next to the desired thumbnail. You can also choose the size of the preview thumbnails in Edit mode.

Because each thumbnail is updated with the most current content, the Top Sites wall makes a great time-saver — you can quickly make a visual check of all your favorite haunts from one screen!

✔ **Click a page link in Apple Mail or another Internet-savvy application.**

Some Mac applications require you to hold down ⌘ while clicking to open a Web page. (Note that if the link is in plain text, you can often select the text, right-click and choose Open URL from the menu that appears.)

✔ **Click a page link within another Web page.**

✔ **Use the Google box in the toolbar.**

Click in the Google box, type the contents that you want to find, and then press Return. Safari presents you with the search results page on Google for the text that you entered. (In case you've been living under the Internet equivalent of a rock for the last couple of years, *Google.com* is the preeminent search site on the Web — people use Google to find everything from used auto parts to ex-spouses.)

✔ **Click a Safari page icon in the Dock or a Finder window.**

For example, Mac OS X already has an icon in the Dock that takes you to the Mac OS X page on the Apple Web site. Drag a site from your Bookmarks bar and drop it on the right side of the Dock. Clicking the icon that you add launches Safari and automatically loads that site.

This trick works only on the side of the Dock to the right of the vertical line.

If you minimize Safari to the Dock, you'll see a thumbnail of the page with the Safari logo superimposed on it. Click this thumbnail in the Dock to restore the page to its full glory.

Navigating the Web

A typical Web surfing session is a linear experience — you bop from one page to the next, absorbing the information that you want and discarding the rest. However, after you visit a few sites, you might find that you need to return to where you've been or head to the familiar ground of your home page. Safari offers these default navigational controls on the toolbar:

✔ **Back:** Click the Back button (the left-facing arrow) on the toolbar to return to the last page you visited. Additional clicks take you to previous pages, in reverse order. The Back button is disabled if you haven't visited at least two sites.

✔ **Forward:** If you've clicked the Back button at least once, clicking the Forward button (the right-facing arrow) takes you to the next page (or through the pages) where you originally were, in forward order. The Forward button is disabled if you haven't used the Back button.

✔ **Home:** Not all these buttons and controls must appear on your toolbar. To display or hide toolbar controls, choose View⇨Customize Toolbar. The sheet that appears works just like the Customize Toolbar sheet within a Finder window: Drag the control you want from the sheet to your Safari toolbar or drag a control that you don't want from the toolbar to the sheet. (For example, I like to add the Home button to the default toolbar — a click on the Home button immediately returns you to your home page.)

✔ **AutoFill:** If you fill out a lot of forms online — when you're shopping at Web sites, for example — you can click the AutoFill button (which looks like a little text box and a pen) to complete these forms for you. You can set what information is used for AutoFill by choosing Safari⇨Preferences and clicking the AutoFill toolbar button.

To be honest, I'm not a big fan of releasing *any* of my personal information to *any* Web site, so I don't use AutoFill often. If you do decide to use this feature, make sure that the connection is secure (look for the padlock icon in the upper-right corner of the Safari window) and read the site's Privacy Agreement page first to see how your identity data will be treated.

✔ **Zoom:** Shrinks or expands the size of text on the page, offering smaller, space-saving characters (for the shrinking crowd) or larger, easier-to-read text (for the expanding crowd). Hence the button, which is labeled with a small and large letter *A*.

✔ **Stop/Reload:** Click Reload at the right side of the Address box (look for the circular arrow) to *refresh* (reload) the contents of the current page. Many pages change their content at regular intervals. Reload allows you to see what's changed on these pages. (I use Reload every hour or so with CNN.com, for example.) While a page is loading, the Reload button turns into the Stop button — with a little X mark — and you can click it to stop the loading of the content from the current page. This is a real boon when a download takes *foorrevverr.*

✔ **Open in Dashboard:** Click this button to create a Dashboard widget using the contents of the currently displayed Web page. Safari prompts you to choose which clickable section of the page to include within the widget's borders (such as the local radar map on your favorite weather Web site). Click Add, and Dashboard loads automatically with your new widget. (More on widgets in Chapter 5.)

✔ **Add Bookmark:** Click this toolbar button (which carries a plus sign) to add a page to your Bookmarks bar or Bookmarks menu. (More on this in a tad.)

✔ **Google Search:** As I mention earlier, you can click in this box and type text that you want to find on the Web via the Google search engine; press Return to display the results. To repeat a recent search, click the down arrow in the Google Search box and select it from the pop-up menu.

✔ **Print:** Click this convenient button to print the contents of the Safari window. (Dig that crazy printer icon!)

✔ **Report Bug:** When you click the Bug button, you'll see a sheet with the settings shown in Figure 8-2; take time to enter a short description of the problem. Click More Options to enable the Send Screen Shot of Current Page and the Send Source of Current Page check boxes, giving the Apple folks more to work with. Click the Submit button.

Figure 8-2:
Have
at thee,
troublesome
buggy page!

Setting Up Your Home Page

Choosing a home page is one of the easiest methods of speeding up your Web surfing, especially if you're using a dial-up modem. However, a large percentage of the Mac owners whom I've talked with have never set their own home page; instead, they simply use the default home page provided by their browser! With Safari running, take a moment to follow these steps to declare your own freedom to choose your own home page:

1. **If you want to use a specific Web page as your new home page, display it in Safari.**

    I recommend selecting a page with few graphics or a fast-loading popular site.

2. **Choose Safari⇨Preferences or press ⌘+, (comma).**

3. **Click the General button.**

    You see the settings shown in Figure 8-3.

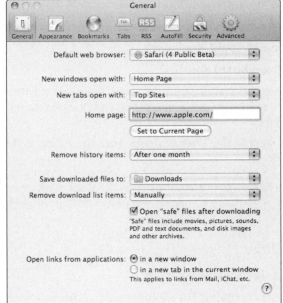

4. **Click the Set to Current Page button.**

5. **Alternatively, click the New Windows Open With pop-up menu and choose Empty Page if you want Safari to open a new window with a blank page.**

   This is the fastest choice of all for a home page.

   Choose Top Sites from the New Windows Open With pop-up menu to display the Top Sites screen I described earlier each time you open a new window.

6. **Click the Close button to exit the Preferences dialog.**

Visit your home page at any time by clicking the Home button on the toolbar.

Adding and Using Bookmarks

No doubt about it: Bookmarks make the Web a friendly place. As you collect bookmarks in Safari, you can immediately jump from one site to another with a single click of the Bookmarks menu or the buttons on the Bookmarks bar.

To add a bookmark, first navigate to the desired page and then do any of the following:

✔ **Choose Bookmarks⇨Add Bookmark.**

✔ **Press the ⌘+D keyboard shortcut.**

Safari displays a sheet where you can enter the name for the bookmark and also select where it appears (on the Bookmarks bar or the Bookmarks menu).

✔ **Drag the icon next to the Web address from the Address field to the Bookmarks bar.**

You can also drag a link on the current page to the Bookmarks bar, but note that doing this adds a bookmark only for the page corresponding to the link — not the current page.

To jump to a bookmark

✔ **Choose it from the Bookmarks menu.**

If the bookmark is contained in a folder, which I discuss later in this section, move your pointer over the folder name to show its contents and then click the bookmark.

✔ **Click the bookmark on the Bookmarks bar.**

If you've added a large number of items to the Bookmarks bar, click the More icon on the edge of the Bookmarks bar to display the rest of the buttons.

✔ **Click the Show All Bookmarks button (which looks like a small, opened book) on the Bookmarks bar and then click the desired bookmark.**

The Bookmarks window that you see in Figure 8-4 appears — complete with swank Cover Flow display — where you can review each collection of bookmarks at leisure. As you might expect, Safari's Cover Flow works just as the Cover Flow view does in a Finder window.

The more bookmarks you add, the more unwieldy the Bookmarks menu and the Bookmarks window become. To keep things organized, choose Bookmarks⇨Add Bookmark Folder and then type a name for the new folder. With folders, you can organize your bookmarks into *collections,* which appear in the column at the left of the Bookmarks window (or as separate submenus within the Bookmarks menu). You can drag bookmarks into the new folder to help reduce the clutter. To delete a bookmark or a folder from the Bookmarks window, click it and then press Delete.

Figure 8-4:
The
Bookmarks
window
puts all your
bookmarks
within easy
reach.

Downloading Files

A huge chunk of the fun that you'll find on the Web is the ability to download images and other files. If you've visited a site that offers files for downloading, typically you just click the Download button or the download file link, and Safari takes care of the rest. You'll see the Downloads status window, which keeps you updated as to the progress of the transfer. While the file is downloading, feel free to continue browsing or even download additional files; the status window helps you keep track of what's going on and when everything will be finished transferring. To display the Download status window from the keyboard, press ⌘+Option+L.

By default, Safari saves any downloaded files to the Downloads folder that appears in your Dock, which I like and use. To change the specified location where downloaded files are stored — for example, if you'd like to save them directly to the desktop — follow these steps:

1. **Choose Safari⇨Preferences or press ⌘+, (comma).**

2. **Click the General tab and then click the Save Downloaded Files To pop-up menu.**

3. **Choose Other.**

4. **Navigate to the location where you want the files stored.**

5. **Click the Select button.**

6. **Click the Close button to exit Preferences.**

To download a specific image that appears on a Web page, move your pointer over the image and right-click. Then choose Save Image As from the pop-up menu that appears. Safari prompts you for the location where you want to store the file.

You can choose to automatically open files that Safari considers safe — things like movies, text files, and PDF files that are **very** unlikely to store a virus or a damaging macro. By default, the Open "Safe" Files after Downloading check box is selected on the General pane. However, if you're interested in preventing *anything* you download from running until you've manually checked it with your antivirus application, you can deselect the check box and breathe easy.

Luckily, Safari has matured to the point that it can seamlessly handle virtually any multimedia file type that it encounters. However, if you've downloaded a multimedia file and Safari doesn't seem to be able to play or display it, try loading the file within QuickTime Player. QuickTime Player is the Swiss Army knife of multimedia players, and it can recognize a huge number of audio, video, and image formats.

Using Subscriptions and History

To keep track of where you've been, you can display the History list by clicking the History menu. To return to a page in the list, just choose it from the History menu. Note that Safari also arranges older history items by the date you visited the site, so you can easily jump back a couple of days to that page you forgot to bookmark!

In fact, Safari also searches the History list automatically, when it fills in an address that you're typing — that's the feature I mention in the earlier section "Visiting Web Sites."

To view your Top Sites thumbnail screen, press ⌘+Shift+1 or choose Show Top Sites from the History menu.

If you're worried about security and would rather not keep track of where you've been online, I show you how to clear the contents of the History file in the "Handling ancient history" section, later in this chapter.

Tabs Are Your Browsing Friends

Safari also offers *tabbed browsing,* which many folks use to display (and organize) multiple Web pages at the same time. For example, if you're doing a bit of comparison shopping for a new piece of hardware between different online stores, tabs are ideal.

When you hold down the ⌘ key and click a link or bookmark using tabs, a tab representing the new page appears at the top of the Safari window. Just click the tab to switch to that page. (If you don't hold down ⌘, things revert to business as usual, and Safari replaces the contents of the window with the new page.) If you hold down *both* Shift and ⌘ while you click, Safari opens a new tab and automatically switches to the new tab. Figure 8-5 illustrates a number of pages that I've opened in Safari using tabs.

You can also open a new tab by clicking the plus sign that appears at the upper-right corner of the Safari window. Done with a page? You can remove a tabbed page by clicking the X button next to the tab's title.

Figure 8-5: Hang on, Martha; we've struck tabs!

To fine-tune your tabbed browsing experience, choose Safari⇨Preferences to display the Preferences dialog; then click Tabs. From here, you can turn off the confirmation window that normally appears when you close Safari with multiple tabs or windows open. You can also specify whether a new tab or window automatically becomes the active window within Safari.

Saving Web Pages

If you've encountered a page that you'd like to load later, you can save it to disk in its entirety. (Just the text, mind you, not the images.) Follow these steps:

1. **Display the desired page.**

2. **Choose File⇨Save As or press ⌘+S.**

3. **In the Save As text field, type a name for the saved page.**

4. **From the Where pop-up menu, navigate to the location where you want to store the file on your system.**

   To expand the sheet to allow navigation to any location on your system, click the button with the downward arrow.

5. **Click the Format pop-up menu to choose the format for the saved page.**

   Usually, you'll want to choose a Web Archive, which saves the entire page and can be displayed just as you see it. However, if you want to save just the HTML source code, choose Page Source.

6. **Click Save to begin the download process.**

   After the Save file has been created, double-click it to load it in Safari.

A quick word about printing a page within Safari: Some combinations of background and text colors might conspire together to render your printed copy practically worthless. In a case like that, use your printer's grayscale setting (if it has one) or deselect the Print Backgrounds check box in the Print dialog. Alternatively, you can simply click and drag to select the text on the page, press ⌘+C to copy it, and then paste the text into Word or Pages, where you can print the page on a less offensive background (while still keeping the text formatting largely untouched). You can also save the contents of a page as plain text, as I just demonstrated.

If you'd rather mail the contents of a Web page to a friend — or just send the friend a link to the page, which is faster — choose either File⇨Mail Contents of This Page or File⇨Mail Link to This Page. (From the keyboard, press ⌘+I to send the contents in an e-mail message or press ⌘+Shift+I to send a link in e-mail.) Mail loads automatically, complete with a prepared e-mail message. Just address it to the recipients and then click Send!

Protecting Your Privacy

No chapter on Safari would be complete without a discussion of security, against both outside intrusion from the Internet and prying eyes around your iMac. Hence this last section, which covers protecting your privacy.

Although diminutive, the padlock icon that appears at the top of the Safari window when you're connected to a secure Web site means a great deal! A *secure site* encrypts the information that you send and receive, making it much harder for those of unscrupulous ideals to obtain things such as credit card numbers and personal information. You can click the padlock icon (next to the site name) to display the security certificate in use on that particular site.

Yes, there are such things as bad cookies

First, a definition of this ridiculous term: A *cookie,* a small file that a Web site automatically saves on your hard drive, contains information that the site will use on your future visits. For example, a site might save a cookie to preserve your site preferences for the next time or — in the case of a site such as Amazon.com — to identify you automatically and help customize the offerings that you see.

In and of themselves, cookies aren't bad things. Unlike a virus, a cookie file isn't going to replicate itself or wreak havoc on your system, and only the original site can read the cookie that it creates. However, many folks don't appreciate acting as a gracious host for a slew of little snippets of personal information. (Not to mention that some cookies have highly suggestive names, which could lead to all sorts of conclusions. End of story.)

You can choose to accept all cookies — the default — or you can opt to disable cookies altogether. You can also set Safari to accept cookies only from the sites you choose to visit. To change your *Cookie Acceptance Plan* (or CAP, for those who absolutely crave acronyms), follow these steps:

1. **Choose Safari⇨Preferences.**
2. **Click the Security toolbar button.**

   Safari displays the preference settings shown in Figure 8-6.

3. **Choose how to accept cookies via these radio button choices:**

   Never: Block cookies entirely.

   Always: Accept all cookies.

   Only from Sites You Navigate To: Personally, I use this option, which allows sites like Amazon.com to work correctly without allowing a barrage of illicit cookies.

4. **To view the cookies currently on your system, click the Show Cookies button.**

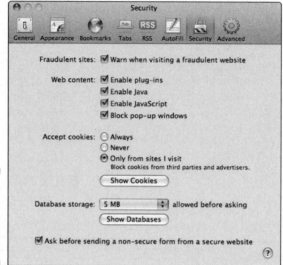

If a site's cookies are blocked, you might have to take care of things manually, such as by providing a password on the site that used to be read automatically from the cookie.

5. **Click the Close button to save your changes.**

Cleaning your cache

Safari speeds up the loading of Web sites by storing often-used images and multimedia files in a temporary storage, or *cache,* folder. Naturally, the files in your cache folder can be displayed (hint), which could lead to assumptions (hint, hint) about the sites you've been visiting (hint, hint, hint). (Tactful, ain't I?)

Luckily, Safari makes it easy to dump the contents of your cache file. Just choose Safari➪Empty Cache; then click Empty to confirm that you want to clean up your cache.

Handling ancient history

As you might imagine, your History file leaves a very clear set of footprints indicating where you've been on the Web. To delete the contents of the History menu, choose History⇨Clear History (at the very bottom of the History menu).

Safari also allows you to specify an amount of time to retain entries in your History file. Open the Safari Preferences dialog, click the General tab, and then click the Remove History Items pop-up menu to specify the desired amount of time. Items can be rolled off daily, weekly, biweekly, monthly, or yearly.

Avoiding those @*!^%$ pop-up ads

I hate pop-up ads, and I'm sure you do, too. To block most of those pop-up windows with advertisements for everything from low-rate mortgages to "sure-thing" Internet casinos, click the Safari menu and verify that Block Pop-Up Windows is selected. (If it's not selected, click the menu item to toggle the menu item on.)

If you need to temporarily deactivate pop-up blocking, press ⌘+Shift+K to toggle it off. Then press ⌘+Shift+K again to turn pop-up blocking back on after you've finished with the site.

Chapter 9

Moving to MobileMe

Readers often ask me to name my favorite reasons why they should switch — that is, why should a Windows user who *thinks* all is well move to the Apple universe? Of course, I always mention the superior hardware and how much better of a job Snow Leopard does as an operating system. Here's my favorite selling point: "Apple simply does things right the first time, and everyone else plays catch-up."

And then I pose this question: "What if you could reach a hard drive with your files over any Internet connection — anywhere in the world — and it just *showed up* on your Desktop automatically?" Usually, another person decides to find out more — about the Apple MobileMe online hosting service, that is. In fact, if you've used online storage — for example, through Google — you've already been introduced to *cloud computing*, where both data and applications are accessed through the Internet, wherever you are.

In this chapter, I save you the trouble of researching all the benefits of MobileMe. Heck, that's one of the reasons why you bought this book, right?

Grabbing Internet Storage for Your iMac

To set up iDisk — the online data storage provided by MobileMe that I mentioned earlier — on your Mac OS X system, you need a MobileMe account. You did create one during the installation of the Big X, right? These trial accounts are active for 60 days. To subscribe, visit www.me.com and follow the prompts to join from there. (At the time of this writing, the subscription fee for an individual account is $99 per year from Apple. However, Amazon.

com sells MobileMe subscriptions for significantly less. You need a credit card to create a MobileMe account, but you can cancel your trial account at any time.)

Here's a bit of good news: Other than the 60-day limit, there's almost no difference between a MobileMe trial account and a full, $99 yearly subscription, so if you're not sure you want to invest the dough, you can try out all the MobileMe features, exactly as though you were already paying for them. *Sweet!*

With an active MobileMe account, iDisk is available automatically. To see how much storage you're using and to configure access to your Public folder, open System Preferences, click the MobileMe icon, and then click the iDisk button to display the settings that you see in Figure 9-1. (You can also click the Upgrade Storage button on this pane to subscribe to MobileMe, or if you're already a MobileMe subscriber, add storage space.)

Figure 9-1:
Your iDisk settings are available from System Preferences.

The iDisk Disk Space bar graph illustrates how much of your current iDisk territory you're using.

You can specify the access privilege level for other MobileMe users from this pane as well. Select the Read Only radio button to prevent any other MobileMe user from copying files to your Public folder, or select the Read & Write radio button to allow others to save files there.

No matter which privilege level you choose, you can also set a password that other MobileMe users must type before they're allowed access to your Public folder. This is the very definition of *A Truly Good Idea*. (More on the Public folder in the next section.)

Pinning down your iDisk

So where exactly *are* your files kept when you use your iDisk? In earlier versions of Mac OS X, your acre of storage farmland always sat exclusively on one of Apple's iDisk *file servers* — perhaps in Cupertino, perhaps elsewhere. These server computers are especially designed to store terabytes (TB) of information (1TB equals 1,000GB), and they're connected to the Internet via high-speed trunk lines. (And yes, they do have a firewall.) Your Internet copy of your iDisk is still stored on an Apple file server.

However, you can elect to keep a local copy of your iDisk storage area — usually called a *mirror* — on your iMac's hard drive. Before you scratch your head wondering why you're duplicating your iDisk files on your computer, here's the reason: If you do decide to keep a local copy of your files, you can work on them even when you're not connected to the Internet! Snow Leopard automatically synchronizes any files that you've updated locally with your remote iDisk whenever you connect to the Internet. (If you use multiple Macs at different locations, think about being able to access the latest copies of your files from *any* of them, right from the Finder!)

This nifty mirror also greatly speeds up things when you're browsing the contents of your iDisk or perhaps loading and saving an iDisk document; that's because you're working with your local copy, and Mac OS X updates any changes that you make to the corresponding remote file on the iDisk server. You can tell that things are updating when that funky little yin-yang, circular doodad — the thing next to your iDisk in the Finder window — is rotating in its animated fashion. (And yes, I have it on good authority: That's what the Apple software developers call it, too.)

You're not required to use a mirror, however. To disable the mirroring feature and return to the remote-only operation of old, click the iDisk Syncing Stop button on the iDisk pane in System Preferences to turn it off. Remember, though, that with the mirroring feature turned off, you must have an Internet connection to use iDisk, and things will move more slowly because you're accessing everything across the Internet.

If you've already set a password, you can change it by clicking the Set Password button and typing the new word in the Password box. Retype the word in the Confirm box to verify it; then click OK to save the change and return to the MobileMe System Preferences pane.

Understanding What's on Your iDisk

In contrast to the physical hard drive in your iMac, your iDisk never needs formatting or defragmenting, and you never have to check it for errors. However, the structure of an iDisk is fixed, so you can't just go crazy creating your own folders. In fact, you can't create new folders at the *root* — the top level — of your iDisk at all. However, you can create new folders inside most of the root folders.

Now that you're thoroughly rooterized, here are the folders that you find hanging out in your iDisk:

- ✔ **Backup:** This is a read-only folder that contains the backup files created with the MobileMe Backup application. You can copy the files in this folder to a removable drive on your system for an additional level of safekeeping.

- ✔ **Documents:** This folder holds any application documents that you want to store — things like spreadsheets and letters. By default, no one but you can access these items; you can tag items in the Documents folder as *shared*, allowing individuals or groups to download them using an access code sent by MobileMe in an e-mail message. Sharing files is a great way to transfer files too big to send as e-mail attachments.

- ✔ **Groups:** This folder holds files that you want to share with others in any MobileMe Groups you might have joined.

- ✔ **Library:** Another read-only folder. This spot contains the configuration data and custom settings that you've created for other MobileMe features.

- ✔ **Movies:** QuickTime movies go here — again, you can add the movies stored here to your Web pages.

- ✔ **Music:** This is the repository for all your iTunes music and playlists, and the contents can be added to your Web pages. (iTunes is the star of Chapter 11.) My playlists are stuffed full of Mozart, Scarlatti, and that Bach fellow.

- ✔ **Pictures:** This folder is the vault for your JPEG and GIF images, including those that you want to use with your Web pages.

- ✔ **Public:** This is the spot to place files that you specifically want to share with others, either directly through iDisk or with your Web pages. If you've allowed write access, others can copy files to your Public folder as well.

- ✔ **Sites:** The Web pages that you store here can be created with iWeb, which I cover in Chapter 16. In fact, you can even use your own Web page design application and copy the completed site files here.

- ✔ **Software:** Apple provides this read-only folder as a service to MobileMe members; it contains a selection of the latest freeware, shareware, and commercial demos for you to enjoy. To try something out, open the Software folder and copy whatever you like to your Mac OS X Desktop. Then you can install and run the application from the local copy of the files.

- ✔ **Web:** This folder holds your MobileMe Galleries created from within iPhoto, as well as other media used by iWeb.

Opening and Using iDisk

When you're connected to the Internet, you can open your iDisk in one of the following ways:

- ✔ **From the Finder menu, choose Go⇨iDisk and then choose My iDisk from the submenu or use the ⌘+Shift+I keyboard shortcut.**
- ✔ **Click the iDisk icon in the Finder Sidebar.**
- ✔ **Add an iDisk button to your Finder window toolbar by choosing View⇨Customize Toolbar.**

    After you add the button, you can click it to connect to your iDisk from anywhere in the Finder.

Your iDisk opens in a new Finder window. After you use one of these methods in a Mac OS X session, your iDisk icon appears on the Mac OS X Desktop; Figure 9-2 shows the iDisk contents in a Finder window. The iDisk volume icon remains until you shut down or restart your iMac. (Alternatively, you can dismiss the iDisk volume icon from your Desktop using the same method by which you eject an external drive: Click the iDisk icon and press ⌘+E or click the Eject button next to the iDisk icon in the Finder window Sidebar.)

Figure 9-2:
The contents of your iDisk — pretty iNeat, I'm thinking.

If you're using a remote PC with an Internet connection, you can log in to the MobileMe page at www.me.com and use your Web browser to access the contents of your iDisk. (Hey, sometimes this is the only choice you have.)

However, you don't actually need to open your iDisk in a Finder window to use it, because you can also load and save files directly to your iDisk from within any application. Simply choose your iDisk as you would any of the hard drives on your system when using the application's Open, Save, or Save As commands.

You can also open an iDisk Public folder — either yours or the Public folder inside another person's iDisk — as if it were an Internet file server. As I explain earlier in the chapter, if that person has set a password, you need to enter that password to gain access to all of his or her iDisk folders. From the Finder menu, choose Go⇨iDisk⇨Other User's iDisk (or, to jump directly to their Public folder, choose Go⇨iDisk⇨Other User's Public Folder). If you choose the former, Snow Leopard prompts you for the other person's member name and password; if you pick the latter, you need only enter the other MobileMe member's account name.

After you enter a valid iDisk member name (and password, if required), you see the MobileMe member's Public folder.

You can also use the server address

```
http://idisk.me.com/username-Public?
```

to connect to an iDisk from computers running Windows and Linux. Check the Help for your operating system to determine how to connect to a WebDAV server (usually called a *Web folder* in the Windows world). When prompted for your access username and password, use your MobileMe account name and password. If you're using Windows XP, Windows Vista, or Windows 7, Apple has provided an even easier way to manage your iDisk: Use MobileMe Control Panel for Windows, which you can download from www.me.com.

Chapter 10

Hooking Up with Handy Helpers

In This Chapter

▶ Adding a printer or a scanner to your system

▶ Using Photo Booth and Front Row

▶ Watching cable or satellite TV on your iMac

This chapter is all about getting interesting things into — and out of — your iMac. Some are more common (almost mundane these days) and pretty easy to take care of, such as scanners and printers. Then I might surprise you with something new to you, like your iMac's built-in video camera.

I also show you how to turn your iMac into a photo booth. Heck, I'll even describe how you can pull that fancy satellite or cable TV signal into your iMac.

It's perfectly okay to tell everyone else that you're watching the financial channel. But watching a little football never hurt anyone. . . .

Connecting Printers

All hail the USB port! It's the primary connection point for all sorts of goodies. In this section, I concentrate on adding a local USB printer and the basics of adding a network printer to your system. (Find more on connecting a wireless Bluetooth printer in the Bonus Chapter at www.mlcbooks.com.)

USB printers

Connecting a USB printer to your iMac is duck soup. Don't you want all things in life were this easy? You might very well be able to skip most of the steps in this section entirely, depending on whether your printer came with an installation disc. (Virtually all do, of course, but you might have bought yours used, say from eBay.)

Your printer needs to be fully supported within Mac OS X:

✔ If the software is designed for earlier versions of Mac OS X (say, v. 10.4 or v. 10.5), it probably works with Snow Leopard.

✔ I always recommend visiting the manufacturer's Web site to download the latest printer driver and support software *before* you install your printer. That way, you know that you're up to date. (Don't forget to check the Read Me file that accompanies your new software to make sure there are no new system requirements!)

Save and close open files and applications before installing your printer. You might have to restart your iMac to complete the installation.

The physical connections for your printer are pretty simple:

✔ Make sure that your printer's USB cable is plugged in to both your iMac and the printer itself. (Naturally, you'll use one of the iMac's USB ports on the back of the computer.)

✔ After the USB connection is made, plug the printer in to an AC wall socket and turn it on.

Don't forget to add the paper and check the ink cartridge(s)!

Additional printer installation steps depend on whether you have a manufacturer's installation disc for your printer.

Sure, I've got the install disc

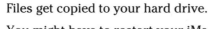

If your printer comes with its manufacturer's installation disc, follow these steps when everything is connected and powered on:

1. **Insert the installation disc in the iMac.**

   The disc contents usually appear in a Finder window. If they don't, double-click the installation disc icon on the Desktop to open the window.

2. **Double-click the installation application to start the ball rolling.**

3. **Follow the onscreen instructions.**

   Files get copied to your hard drive.

   You might have to restart your iMac.

You're ready to print!

Don't forget to visit your printer manufacturer's Web site to check whether any driver updates are available for your particular model.

Whoops, I've got diddly-squat (Software-wise)

Didn't get an installation CD? Try installing the printer without software, or download the software from the manufacturer's Web site.

Installing without software

If you didn't get an installation CD with your printer, you might be lucky enough that your printer's driver was included in your installation of Mac OS X. First, press ⌘+P within an application to display the Print dialog, where you can check see whether the printer you connected is already recognized.

If it's not displayed, here's how to check for that pesky driver after you connect the printer and switch it on:

1. **Open the System Preferences window.**

2. **Click the Print & Fax icon.**

3. **Click the Add button (which sports a plus sign).**

4. **Check the Printer list in the Printer Setup Utility window to see whether your printer has already been added automatically within Snow Leopard.**

   If your printer appears here, dance a celebratory jig. You can close System Preferences and choose that printer from the Print dialog in your applications. (You can even set it as the default from the System Preferences Print & Fax pane. Just click the Default Printer pop-up menu to select your new printer.)

Downloading software

If you don't have installation software and your iMac doesn't automatically match your USB printer with a driver, it's time to check the Internet to locate a Snow Leopard-compatible driver for your printer.

Check the manufacturer's Web site for your printer's software. Look for

- ✔ **Special software drivers that the printer might need**

  Install any drivers you find *before* you run an installation application. Otherwise, the installation app might not be able to recognize or configure the printer if the driver hasn't been installed first.

- ✔ **Installation application**

  If the manufacturer offers an installation application for your printer, download the application and run it.

Network printers

Your wired or wireless Ethernet network provides a quick-and-easy way to share any printer that's connected to your iMac. Follow these steps to share your printers across the network with others:

1. **Click the System Preferences icon on the Dock.**

2. **Click the Sharing icon.**

3. **Select the On check box next to the Printer Sharing service entry.**

4. **Click Close to exit System Preferences.**

In most cases, a printer that you share automatically appears in the Print dialog on other computers connected to your network. Therefore, if you want to access a printer being shared by another Mac across your network, open the Print dialog within your application and click the Printer pop-up menu to select it.

If the remote printer isn't listed automatically, you can dig a little further. To add a printer that another Mac on your network is sharing to your list of printers, follow these steps:

1. **Click System Preferences on the Dock.**

2. **Click the Print & Fax icon.**

3. **Click the Add button (which carries a plus sign).**

4. **Click the Default button on the toolbar.**

   Snow Leopard displays all the available local shared printers. Click the desired printer and then click Add. (Depending on the built-in support within Snow Leopard for the printer you're accessing or sharing, you may have to install the driver on your Mac or the other Macs on your network as well.)

Connecting Scanners

USB and FireWire scanners practically install themselves. As long as the model is listed as Mac OS X-compatible and it supports the TWAIN device standard (just about all scanners do), things really *are* plug-and-play. (Not sure if a scanner is Mac OS X-compatible? Check the system requirements on the scanner's box or on the manufacturer's Web site.)

If you have the scanner manufacturer's installation disc, go ahead and use it. However, most scanners don't require specialized drivers, so even that orphan model that you picked up from Uncle Milton last year should work (if it's recognized by Mac OS X). It doesn't hurt to check the manufacturer's Web site to see whether any of the software has been updated since the disc was produced.

If Mac OS X doesn't support your older scanner, a third-party application might be able to help. Get thee hence to Hamrick Software at `www.hamrick.com` and download a copy of the latest version of VueScan. This great scanning application supports over 750 scanner models, including a number that don't work with Snow Leopard otherwise. At $40, it's a world-class bargain, to boot.

Ready to go? Make sure that your scanner is powered on and connected to your iMac (and that you load a page or photograph to scan). If your scanner's installation disc provided you with a proprietary scanning application, I recommend that you use that application to test your scanner. In fact, it's Mark's Maxim time!

If your printer or scanner includes bundled applications, *use them!*

Sure, Mac OS X has the Print & Fax pane within System Preferences for printers and the Image Capture application for scanners and digital cameras, but these are bare-bones tools compared with the print manager and image acquisition software that comes bundled with your hardware. I turn to Snow Leopard's built-in hardware handling stuff only when I don't have anything better.

Hey, I'm not saying that anything's wrong with Image Capture, which is in your Applications folder, if you need to use it. However, don't expect Image Capture to support any specialized features offered by your scanner (like one-button e-mail or Web publishing). You have to use the application especially designed for your manufacturer and model to take advantage of any extras that it offers — alternately, many image-editing applications (like Photoshop or Photoshop Elements) might offer more scanning features than Image Capture.

Using Photo Booth and Front Row

Many Apple switchers and first-time owners quickly notice the tiny square lens and LED light at the top of the iMac's svelte frame. What gives?

Mystery solved, good reader: That's the lens of your iMac's built-in iSight camera, which allows you to capture video or snap a quick fun series of photos via Snow Leopard's Photo Booth application.

But there's more: If you invest in an Apple Remote (sold separately), you can control your iMac from the comfort of your lounge chair or breakfast nook via Snow Leopard's Front Row software.

Capturing the moment with Photo Booth

What's that you say? You've never used a computer video camera? Well then, good reader, you've come to the right place!

The iSight camera's indicator light glows green whenever you're taking a snapshot or recording video . . . which, when you think about it, is A Good Thing (especially if you prefer chatting at home in Leisure Mode).

If you need a quick picture of yourself for use on your Web page, or perhaps your iChat icon needs an update to show off your new haircut, use Photo Booth to capture images at 640 x 480 resolution and 32-bit color. Although today's digital cameras can produce a much higher-quality photo, you can't beat the built-in convenience of Photo Booth for that quick snapshot!

To snap an image in Photo Booth, follow these steps:

1. **Launch Photo Booth from the Dock or from the Applications folder.**

   Check out that glowing LED!

2. **(Optional) Click the Effects button to choose an effect you'd like to apply to your image.**

   Photo Booth displays four screens of thumbnail preview images so that you can see how each effect changes the photo (see Figure 10-1). To move through the thumbnail screens, click the Previous and Next arrow buttons that appear around the Effects button.

   You can produce some of the simple effects you might be familiar with from Photoshop, such as a black-and-white image or a fancy, colored pencil filter . . . but it can also deliver some mind-blowing distortion effects, and even an Andy Warhol–style pop-art image!

   Of course, you can always launch your favorite image editor afterward to use a filter or effect on a photo — for example, the effects available in iPhoto — but Photo Booth can apply these effects automatically as soon as you take the picture.

3. **(Optional) Click a thumbnail to select the desired effect.**

   To return the display to normal, click the Normal thumbnail, which appears in the center. (Um, that would be Paul Lynde's spot, for those of you old enough to remember *Hollywood Squares.*)

4. **Click the Camera button.**

Figure 10-1:
Photo Booth
does one
thing
particularly
well —
candid
photography.

The image appears in the film strip at the bottom of the window. Photo Booth keeps a copy of all the images you take in the film strip so that you can use them later. After you click a photo in the filmstrip, a series of buttons appear, inviting you take any one of a series of actions, including

🖊 Sending the photo in an e-mail message

🖊 Saving the photo directly to iPhoto

🖊 Using the image as your Snow Leopard user account icon

🖊 Using the image as your iChat Buddy icon

To delete an image from the Photo Booth filmstrip, click the offending photo and then click the X button that appears underneath.

If you're itching to connect a USB digital camera for use with iPhoto, let me redirect you to Chapter 12, where I cover the iPhoto experience in depth.

To capture a video clip, click the Movie Clip button (which bears frames from an old-fashioned movie reel) at the lower left of the Photo Booth window. Click the Big Red Movie Button to start recording, and click again to end the clip.

Controlling your iMac remotely with Front Row

Okay, you've seen some neat stuff so far, but things get *really* cool about now! With Apple's Front Row software, you can turn your iMac into a multimedia presentation center that can show off all your digital media to your adoring public (and friends and family to boot). In fact, if you buy an Apple Remote ($19 from the Apple Store), you don't even have to leave the comfort of the couch to start the show.

The Front Row application performs four different functions:

- **Watching DVD movies with DVD Player:** If you already loaded a DVD into your optical drive, you can watch it. (Sorry, your iMac doesn't load the DVD for you. I guess *some* things have to remain manually driven for a few years yet.)

- **Viewing photos and slideshows:** Front Row calls upon iPhoto so that you can see your albums, film rolls, and slideshows.

- **Displaying videos in QuickTime Player:** You can choose any video you download from the iTunes Music Store or save (in a format recognized by QuickTime) to your Movies folder.

- **Coaxing your favorite music, podcasts, and TV shows from your iTunes library:** Find your media and playlists available from Front Row.

All this is accomplished by using the awesome, infrared Apple Remote. If your last computer — the beige box — didn't *have* a remote control, don't panic. The remote's as simple to use as an iPod Shuffle!

To launch the application, press the Menu button on the remote. As long as your iMac is on, Front Row runs automatically. To put your iMac to sleep after a night of fun, press and hold the Select/Play/Pause button.

Table 10-1 includes the important functions of the Apple Remote in Front Row.

Table 10-1	Using the Apple Remote in Front Row
Action	*Purpose*
Menu	Press to launch Front Row or to return to the previous menu.
Volume/Menu Down	Press to navigate down through menu options or to lower the volume while media is playing.
Volume/Menu Up	Press to navigate up through menu options or to raise the volume while media is playing.
Select/Play/Pause	Press to select a menu item, or play or pause media from within iTunes, DVD Player, QuickTime, or iPhoto.
Next/Fast Forward	Press to skip to the next song or DVD chapter, or hold down to fast-forward through a song.
Previous/Rewind	Press to skip to the previous song or DVD chapter, or hold down to rewind a song.

You can also go the mundane route and use keyboard shortcuts to control Front Row (but it's nowhere near as cool). Table 10-2 explains the keyboard shortcuts.

Table 10-2	Using the Keyboard in Front Row
Action	*Keyboard Equivalent*
Menu	⌘+Esc to enter the menu; Esc to exit it
Volume/Menu Down	Down arrow (↓)
Volume/Menu Up	Up arrow (↑)
Select/Play/Pause	Spacebar or Return
Next/Fast Forward	Right arrow (→)
Previous/Rewind	Left arrow (←)

Note that Front Row has no complex configuration. Front Row is what designers call a *front-end application;* that is, it launches the Snow Leopard applications necessary to display or play the media you select. (There is a simple Settings menu in Front Row, offering you the chance to toggle your screen saver and menu sound effects off or on. Both options are turned on by default.)

Your Apple Remote isn't designed to work with any other third-party applications at the time of this writing. For example, you can't use it as a presentation aide in PowerPoint. However, some Apple applications do recognize the Apple Remote (like Keynote).

Turning Your iMac into a TV — And More

Your iMac's beautiful LCD screen would seem to be the perfect artist's canvas for watching cable or satellite TV broadcasts, but there's no co-ax input on the back of your computer. Therefore, unless you invest in some additional hardware, you're restricted to watching DVD movies.

Such an obvious need is going to be filled quickly, and a number of different hardware manufacturers have produced external devices that can merge your iMac and your TV signal. Most are USB or FireWire peripherals, and many have all the features of today's TiVo and digital video recorders.

My favorite example is the EyeTV Hybrid Plus, from Elgato (www.elgato.com), which uses a USB connection. Check out what this superstar includes for your investment of $150:

- Built-in NTSC (analog) and ATSC (digital TV) tuners, cable-ready with a coaxial connector
- The ability to pause, fast-forward, record, or even edit the video you stored on your iMac's hard drive
- Capability to schedule recordings with an onscreen program guide
- Full-screen TV display or in a window anywhere on your Desktop
- No external power supply required

I really love the ability to fast-forward through commercials, and I can take anything that I record on my iMac and use it in iDVD and iMovie. The addition of TV under your control sorta finalizes the whole digital hub thing, now doesn't it?

Part IV
Living the iLife

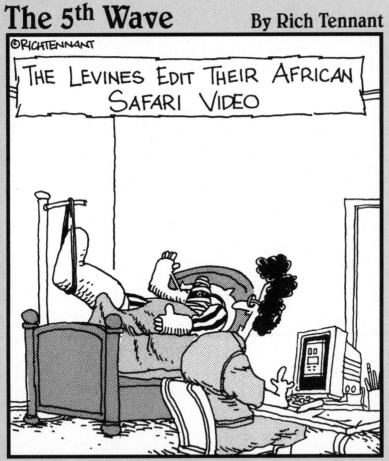

"Do you think the 'Hidden Rhino' clip should come before or after the 'Waving Hello' video clip?"

In this part . . .

Here they are, the applications that everyone craves: This part covers iTunes, iPhoto, iMovie, iDVD, iWeb and GarageBand like your Grandma's best quilt. You find out how to share your images, music, and video clips between the major iLife '09 applications on your iMac, and how to create everything from your own DVDs to a truly awesome hardcover photo album!

Chapter 11

The Multimedia Joy of iTunes

Sometimes, words just aren't enough. iTunes is that kind of perfection.

To envision how iTunes changes your iMac, you have to paint the picture with *music* — music that's easy to play, easy to search, and easy to transfer from device to device. Whether it be classical, alternative, jazz, rock, hip-hop, or folk, I can guarantee you that you won't find a better application than iTunes to fill your life with your music. And podcasts. And video. And TV shows. And Internet radio. (See how hard it is to pin down this wonderful application? Along with your iMac, iTunes really does form the hub of your digital lifestyle.)

In this chapter, I lead you through all the features of my absolute favorite member of the iLife suite . . . and it's going to be pretty doggone obvious how much I appreciate this one piece of software.

What Can I Play on iTunes?

Simply put, iTunes is a media player; it plays audio and video files. These files can be in any of many different formats. Some of the more common audio formats that iTunes supports are

✔ **MP3:** The small size of MP3 files has made them popular for file trading on the Internet. A typical CD-quality, three-minute pop song in MP3 format has a size of 3–5MB.

✔ **AAC:** *AAC* (short for Advanced Audio Coding) is an audio format that's very similar to MP3; in fact, AAC files offer better recording quality at the same file sizes. However, this format originally supported a built-in copy protection scheme that prevented AAC music purchased from iTunes from being widely distributed on Macs. (Luckily, this copy protection is no longer applied to iTunes tracks, and you can still burn protected AAC tracks to an audio CD, just as you can MP3 tracks.) The tracks that you download from the iTunes Store are in AAC format.

The iTunes Store's *iTunes Plus* tracks are also in AAC format, but these tracks are not copy-protected, and they're encoded at a higher-quality 256 Kbps rate.

✔ **Apple Lossless:** Another format direct from Apple, *Apple Lossless* format provides the best compromise between file size and sound quality: These tracks are encoded without loss of quality. However, Apple Lossless tracks are somewhat larger than AAC, so it's generally the favorite of the most discerning audiophile for his or her entire music library.

✔ **AIFF:** The standard Macintosh audio format produces sound of the absolute highest quality. This high quality, however, also means that the files are pretty doggone huge. A typical pop song in AIFF format has a size of 30–50MB (about 10MB per minute of audio).

✔ **WAV:** Not to be outdone, Microsoft created its own audio file format (WAV) that works much like AIFF. It can reproduce sound at higher quality than MP3, but the file sizes are very large, virtually identical in size to AIFF files.

✔ **CD audio:** iTunes can play audio CDs. Because you don't usually store CD audio anywhere but on an audio CD, file size is no big whoop.

✔ **Movies and video:** You can buy and download full-length movies, TV shows, music videos, and movie trailers from the iTunes Store . . . and, with an Apple TV unit connected to your home theater system, you can watch those movies and videos from the comfort of your sofa on the other side of your house.

✔ **Podcasts:** These audio downloads are like radio programs for your iPod — but iTunes can play and organize them, too. Some podcasts also include video and photos to boot.

✔ **Ringtones:** iPhone owners, rejoice! iTunes automatically offers to create ringtones for your iPhone from the tracks you've bought on the iTunes Store. (You can also create ringtones with GarageBand, using songs you've added to your iTunes library.)

✔ **Audiobooks:** No longer do you need cassettes or audio CDs to enjoy your spoken books — iTunes can play them for you, or you can send them to your iPod for listening on the go.

✔ **Streaming Internet radio:** You can listen to a continuous broadcast of songs from one of tens of thousands of Internet radio stations, with quality levels ranging from what you'd expect from FM radio to the full quality of an audio CD. You can't save the music in iTunes, but it's still great fun. (In fact, I run my own station . . . more on MLC Radio later in the chapter.)

Playing an Audio CD

To play an audio CD in iTunes, insert the CD in your iMac's disc slot, start iTunes by clicking its icon in the Dock, and click the Play button. (Note that your Mac might be set to automatically launch iTunes when you insert an audio CD.) The iTunes interface resembles that of a traditional cassette or CD player. The main playback controls of the iTunes are Play, Previous Song, Next Song, and the volume slider, as shown in Figure 11-1.

Play/Pause

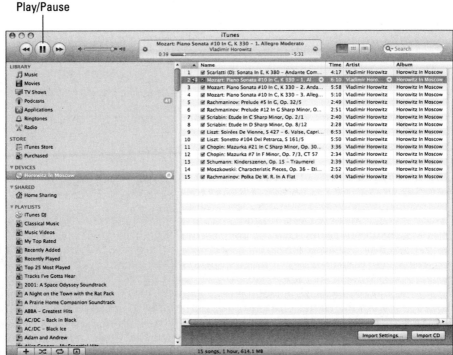

Figure 11-1:
The main
playback
controls:Play,
Previous,
and Next.

Click the Play button to begin listening to a song. While a song is playing, the Play button toggles to a Pause button. Clicking that button again pauses the music.

Click the Next Song button to advance to the next song on the CD. The Previous Song button works like the Next Song button but with a slight twist: If a song is currently playing and you click the Previous Song button, iTunes first returns to the beginning of the current song (just like a CD player). To advance to the previous song, double-click the Previous Song button. To change the volume of your music, click and drag the volume slider.

As with other Macintosh applications, you can control much of iTunes with the keyboard. Table 11-1 lists some of the more common iTunes keyboard shortcuts.

Table 11-1	Common iTunes Keyboard Shortcuts
Press This Key Combination	*To Do This*
Spacebar	Play the currently selected song if iTunes is idle.
Spacebar	Pause the music if a song is playing.
Right-arrow key	Advance to the next song.
Left-arrow key	Go back to the beginning of a song. Press a second time to return to the previous song.
⌘+Up-arrow key	Increase the volume of the music.
⌘+Down-arrow key	Decrease the volume of the music.
⌘+Option+down-arrow key	Mute the audio if any is playing. Press again to play the audio.

Playing Digital Audio and Video

In addition to playing audio CDs, iTunes can play the digital audio files that you download from the Internet or obtain from other sources in the WAV, AAC, Apple Lossless, AIFF, and MP3 file formats. Enjoying a digital audio file is just slightly more complicated than playing a CD. After downloading or saving your audio files to your iMac, open the Finder and navigate to the stored files. Then simply drag the music files (or an entire folder of music) from the Finder into the Music entry in the iTunes Source list. The added files appear in the Music section of your iTunes Library. Think of the Library as a master list of your digital media. To view the Music Library, select the Music entry in the left-hand column of the iTunes player, as shown in Figure 11-2. Heck, you can also drag a song file from a Finder window and drop it on the iTunes icon in the Dock, which adds it to your Music Library as well.

If you drop the file on top of a playlist name in the Source list, iTunes adds it to that particular *playlist* as well as the main Library. (More about playlists in a bit.) If you drop a folder of songs on top of the Playlists header, iTunes creates a new playlist using the name of the folder and adds all the songs in the folder to the new playlist.

Figure 11-2:
The Music Library keeps track of all your audio files.

To play a song, just double-click it in the Music list. Alternatively, you can use the playback controls (Play, Previous Song, and Next Song) that I discuss earlier in this chapter (refer to Figure 11-1).

The Source list of iTunes can list up to five possible sources for music:

- ✔ **Library:** This section includes Music, Movies, TV Shows, Podcasts, Audiobooks, iPod Games, and Radio. (Think *Internet radio,* which I discuss further in the section "iTunes Radio.")

- ✔ **Devices:** If an iPod is connected, it appears in the list. (And yes, Virginia, other models of MP3 players from other companies will also appear in the list if they support iTunes.) If you load an audio CD, it appears in the Devices heading . . . anything from the Bee Gees to Fall Out Boy.

✔ **Store:** I discuss the iTunes Store in the section "Buying Digital Media the Apple Way."

✔ **Shared:** If another Mac or PC on your local network is running iTunes and is set to share part or all of its library, you can connect to the other computer for your music. (Shared music on another Mac appears as a separate named folder in the Source list.)

✔ **Playlists:** Think of playlists as folders you use to organize your music. (More on playlists later in this chapter.)

If you've invested in an Apple TV, it will appear in the list as well, allowing iTunes to share media with your Apple TV, which in turn sends it to your ED- or HD-TV.

Notice also that the Library lists information for each song that you add to it, such as

✔ **Song Name:** The title of the song

✔ **Time:** The length of the song

✔ **Artist:** The artist who performs the song

✔ **Album:** The album on which the song appears

If some of the songs that you're adding don't display anything for the title, album, or artist information, don't panic; most MP3 files have embedded data that iTunes can read. If a song doesn't include any data, you can always add the information to these fields manually. I show you how later, in the section "Setting or changing the song information manually."

Clicking any of the column headings in the Library causes iTunes to reorder the Library according to that category. For example, clicking the Song Name column heading alphabetizes your Library by song title. I click the Time heading often to sort my Library according to the length of the songs. Oh, and you can drag column titles to reorder them any way you like (as long as the Name column remains at the far left of the named columns).

iTunes can display your Music Library in three ways: By default, the application uses the *list view* you see in Figure 11-1, where each song is one entry. Click the second View button (at the top of the iTunes window) to group tracks together by album artwork in *grid view*. Click the third View button, and you're browsing by album cover in *cover flow view*, complete with reflective surface!

Browsing the Library

After you add a few dozen songs to iTunes, viewing the Library can become a task. Although a master list is nice for some purposes, it becomes as cumbersome as an elephant in a subway tunnel if the list is very long. To help out, iTunes can display your Library in another format, too: namely, browsing mode. To view the Library in browsing mode, click the View menu and click the Show Browser item, or press the ⌘+B keyboard shortcut.

The Browse mode of iTunes displays your library in a compact fashion, organizing your tunes into four sections:

- ✔ **Genre**
- ✔ **Artist**
- ✔ **Album**
- ✔ **Song Name**

Selecting an artist from the Artist list causes iTunes to display that artist's albums in the Album list. Select an album from the Album list, and iTunes displays that album's songs in the bottom section of the Browse window. (Those Apple software designers . . . always thinking of you and me.)

Finding songs in your Music Library

After your collection of audio files grows large, you might have trouble locating that Swedish remix version of "I'm Your Boogie Man." To help you out, iTunes has a built-in Search function. To find a song, type some text into the search field of the main iTunes window. While you type, iTunes tries to find a selection that matches your search text. The search is quite thorough, showing any matching text from the artist, album, song title, and genre fields in the results. For example, if you type **electronic** into the field, iTunes might return results for the band named *Electronic* or other tunes that you classified as *electronic* in the Genre field. (The section "Know Your Songs," later in this chapter, tells you how to classify your songs by genre, among other options.) Click the magnifying glass at the left side of the Search field to restrict the search by Artists, Albums, Composers, and Songs.

Removing old music from the Library

After you spend some time playing songs with iTunes, you might decide that you didn't *really* want to add 40 different versions of "Louie Louie" to your Library. (Personally, I prefer either the original or the cast from the movie *Animal House*.) To remove a song from the Library, click the song to select it and then press the Delete key on your keyboard.

Will I trash my Count Basie?

Novice iTunes users, take note: iTunes watches your back when you trash tracks.

To illustrate: Suppose you delete a song from the Library that's located only in the iTunes music folder (which you didn't copy into iTunes from another location on your hard drive). That means you're about to delete the song entirely, and there'll be no copy remaining on your iMac at all. Rest assured, though, that iTunes prompts you to make sure that you really want to move the file to the Trash. (I get fearful e-mail messages all the time from readers who are loath to delete anything from iTunes because they're afraid they'll trash their digital music files completely.)

Remember: If you delete a song from the Library that *also* exists elsewhere on your hard drive (outside the reach of the iTunes music folder), it isn't deleted from your hard drive. In fact, if you mistakenly remove a song that you meant to keep, just drag it back into iTunes from the Finder, or even from the Trash. 'Nuff said.

You can also remove a song from the Library by dragging it to the Trash in your Dock.

Watching video

Watching video in iTunes is similar to listening to music. To view your video collection, click one of these entries in the Source list:

- ✔ **Movies**
- ✔ **TV Shows**

If you select Movies or TV Shows, iTunes displays your videos as thumbnails or in cover flow view. Music videos appear as a smart playlist.

From your collection, you can

- ✔ **Double-click a video thumbnail or an entry in the list.**
- ✔ **Drag a QuickTime video clip from the Finder window to the iTunes window.** Video files that can be viewed using QuickTime typically have file extensions ending in .mov or .mp4.

iTunes plays video in the box below the Source list, within the iTunes window, in a separate window, or in full-screen mode, depending on the settings you've chosen on the General pane in the iTunes Preferences window. In full-screen mode, move your pointer to display a control strip at the bottom of the screen. The control strip sports a slider bar that you can drag to move through the video, a volume control, Play/Pause, and Fast Forward/Reverse buttons.

Keeping Slim Whitman and Slim Shady Apart: Organizing with Playlists

Your iTunes Music Library can contain thousands upon thousands of songs: If your Library grows anywhere near that large, finding all the songs in your lifelong collection of Paul Simon albums is *not* a fun task. Furthermore, with the Library, you're stuck playing songs in the order that iTunes lists them.

To help you organize your music into groups, use the iTunes playlist feature. A *playlist* is a collection of some of your favorite songs from the Library. You can create as many playlists as you want, and each playlist can contain any number of songs. Whereas the Library lists all available songs, a playlist displays only the songs that you add to it. Further, any changes that you make to a playlist affect only that playlist, leaving the Library intact.

To create a playlist, you can do any of the following:

- **Choose File⇨New Playlist.**

- **Press ⌘+N.**

- **Choose File⇨New Playlist from Selection.** This creates a new playlist and automatically adds any tracks that are currently selected.

- **Click a song to select it; then click the Genius button at the lower-right corner of the window.** (The Genius button bears a striking "atom" symbol.) iTunes builds a playlist of songs that are similar in some way (typically by matching the genre of the selection or the beats per minute, but also based on recommendations from other iTunes members). Your iMac needs an Internet connection to create a Genius playlist, and the larger your music library the longer it will take iTunes to build the playlist.

- **Click the iTunes DJ entry in the Playlist section on the left side of the window.** iTunes delivers a random selection of songs taken from your iTunes Music Library — perfect for your next spontaneous party! You can change the order of the songs in the iTunes DJ playlist (known as Party Shuffle in older versions of iTunes), add songs from your Library, or delete songs that don't fit the scintillating ambience of your gathering. Enjoy!

- **Click the New Playlist button in the iTunes window** (the plus sign button in the lower-left corner). You get a newly created empty playlist (the toe-tappin' *untitled playlist*).

Some playlists are smarter than others

Click the File menu and you'll see the New Smart Playlist menu command. The contents of a *smart* playlist are automatically created from a specific condition or set of conditions that you set via the Smart Playlist dialog: You can limit the track selection by mundane things, such as album, genre, or artist; or you can get funky and specify songs that were played last, or by the date you added tracks, or even by the sampling rate or total length of the song. For example, iTunes can create a playlist packed with songs that are shorter than three minutes, so you can fill your iPod Shuffle with more stuff! Ah, but wait, you're not limited to a single criterion. If you want to add another criterion, click the plus sign at the right side of the dialog and you get another condition field to refine your selection even further.

You can choose the maximum songs to add to the smart playlist, or limit the size of the playlist by the minutes or hours of play or the number of megabytes or gigabytes the playlist will occupy. (Again, great for automatically gathering as much from your KISS collection as will fit into a specific amount of space on a CD or your iPod.) Mark the Live Updating check box for the ultimate in convenience. iTunes automatically maintains the contents of the smart playlist to keep it current with your conditions at all times in the future. (If you remove tracks manually from a smart playlist, iTunes adds other tracks that match your conditions.)

Now think about what all these settings mean when combined . . . *whoa*. Here's an example yanked directly from my own iTunes library. I created a smart playlist that selects only those songs in the Rock genre. It's limited to 25 songs, selected by least often played, and live updating is turned on. The playlist is named Tracks I've Gotta Hear because it finds the 25 rock songs (from my collection of 1,654 songs) that I've heard least often! After I listen to a song from this smart playlist, iTunes automatically "freshens" it with another song, allowing me to catch up on the tracks I've been ignoring. Completely, unbelievably *sweet*— and another reason that iTunes is the best music player on Planet Earth!

All playlists appear in the Source list. To help organize your playlists, it's a good idea to . . . well, *name* them. (Aren't you glad now that you have this book?) For example, suppose that you want to plan a party for your polka-loving friends. Instead of running to your computer after each song to change the music, you could create a polka-only playlist. Select and start the playlist at the beginning of the party, and you won't have to worry about changing the music the whole night. (You can concentrate on the accordion.) To load a playlist, select it in the Source list; iTunes displays the songs for that playlist.

The same song can appear in any number of playlists because the songs in a playlist are simply pointers to songs in your Music Library — not the songs themselves. Add and remove them at will to or from any playlist, secure in the knowledge that the songs remain safe in the Library. Removing a playlist is simple: Select the playlist in the Source list and then press Delete.

Removing a playlist doesn't actually delete any songs from your Library.

Know Your Songs

Besides organizing your music into Elvis and non-Elvis playlists, iTunes gives you the option to track your music at the song level. Each song that you add to the Music Library has a complete set of information associated with it. iTunes displays this information in the Info dialog, including

- **Name:** The name of the song
- **Artist:** The name of the artist who performed the song
- **Composer:** The name of the astute individual who actually *wrote* the song
- **Album Artist:** The name of the artist responsible for a compilation or tribute album
- **Album:** The album where the song appears
- **Grouping:** A group type that you assign
- **Year:** The year the artist recorded the song
- **BPM:** The beats per minute (which indicates the song's tempo)
- **Track Number:** The position of the song on the original album
- **Disc Number:** The original disc number in a multi-CD set
- **Comments:** A text field that can contain any comments on the song
- **Genre:** The classification of the song (such as rock, jazz, or pop)

You can display this information by clicking a song name and pressing ⌘+I — the fields appear on the Info tab.

Setting the song information automatically

Each song that you add to the iTunes Music Library might have song information included with it. If you add music from a commercial audio CD, iTunes connects to a server on the Internet and attempts to find the information for each song on the CD. If you download a song from the Internet, it often comes with some information embedded in the file already; the amount of included information depends on what the creator supplied. (And believe me, it's often misspelled as well — think *Leenard Skeenard.*) If you don't have an Internet connection, iTunes can't access the information and displays generic titles instead.

Setting or changing the song information manually

If iTunes can't find your CD in the online database or someone gives you an MP3 with incomplete or inaccurate information, you can change the information yourself — believe me, you want at least the artist and song name, as well as the genre! To view and change the information for a song, perform the following steps:

1. **Select the song in either the Music Library list or a Playlist.**

2. **Press ⌘+I or choose File⇨Get Info.**

3. **Edit the song's information under the Info tab, as shown in Figure 11-3.**

Keep in mind that the more work you put into setting the information of the songs in your Music Library, the easier it is to browse and use iTunes. Incomplete song information can make it more difficult to find your songs in a hurry. If you prefer, you don't have to change all information about a song (it just makes life easier later if you do). Normally, you can get away with setting only a song's title, artist, and genre. The more information you put in, however, the faster you can locate songs and the easier they are to arrange. iTunes tries to help by automatically retrieving known song information, but sometimes you have to roll up your sleeves and do a little work. (Sorry, but the Data Elves are out to lunch.)

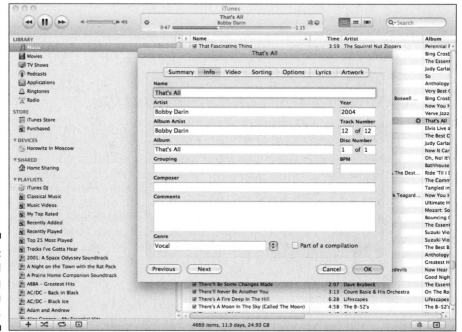

Figure 11-3:
View and edit song information here.

"What about cover art, Mark?" Well, I'm overjoyed that you asked! iTunes can try to locate artwork automatically for the tracks you select. (Note that adding large images can significantly increase the size of the song file.) Follow these steps:

1. **Select the desired songs from the track list.**

2. **Click Advanced⇨Get Album Artwork.**

You can set iTunes to automatically attempt the addition of album artwork every time you rip tracks from an audio CD, or when you add songs without artwork to your Music Library. Click iTunes and choose Preferences; then click the Store button and click the Automatically Download Missing Album Artwork check box to enable it.

Want to manually add album covers to your song info? Select one (or all) of the songs from a single album in the track list, display the Info dialog, and click the Artwork tab. Now launch Safari, visit Amazon.com, and do a search on the same album. Drag the cover image from the Web page right into the Info dialog, and drop it on top of the "sunken square" image well. When you click OK, the image appears in the Summary pane, and you can display it while your music is playing by pressing ⌘+G, or by pressing the Show or Hide Song Artwork button at the lower left of the iTunes window! (Note that adding large images can significantly increase the size of the song file.)

By the way, if you buy tracks or an album from the iTunes Store, Apple always includes album covers automatically. Thanks, Steve!

Ripping Audio Files

You don't have to rely on Internet downloads to get audio files: You can create your own MP3, AAC, Apple Lossless, AIFF, and WAV files from your audio CDs with iTunes. The process of converting audio files to different formats is called *ripping.* (Audiophiles with technical teeth also call this process *digital extraction,* but they're usually ignored at parties by the popular crowd.) Depending on what hardware or software you use, each has its own unique format preferences. For example, most iPod owners prefer MP3 or AAC files, but your audio CDs aren't in that format. Being able to convert files from one format to another is like having a personal translator in the digital world. You don't need to worry if you have the wrong format: You can simply convert it to the format that you need.

The most common type of ripping is to convert CD audio to AAC or MP3 format. To rip MP3s from an audio CD, follow these simple steps:

1. **Launch iTunes by clicking its icon in the Dock.**

   Alternatively, you can locate it in your Applications folder.

2. **Load an audio CD into your iMac.**

   The CD title shows up in the iTunes Source list (under the Devices heading), which is on the left side of the iTunes window. The CD track listing appears on the right side of the window.

   If iTunes asks you whether you want to import the contents of the CD into your Music Library, you can click Yes and skip the rest of the steps; however, if you've disabled this prompt, just continue with the remaining two steps.

3. **Click the CD entry under the Devices listing.**

4. **Click the Import Settings button.**

5. **Choose MP3 Encoder from the Import Using pop-up menu.**

6. **Choose High Quality (160 Kbps) from the Setting pop-up menu and then click OK.**

   This bit rate setting provides the best compromise between quality and file size (tracks you rip will be significantly smaller than "audiophile" bit rates such as 192 Kbps or higher).

7. **Clear the check box of any song that you don't want to import from the CD.**

   All songs on the CD have a check box next to their title by default. Unmarked songs aren't imported.

8. **After you select the songs that you want added to the Library, click the Import CD button.**

Tweaking the Audio for Your Ears

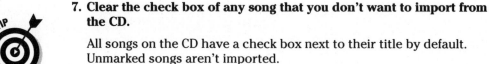

Besides the standard volume controls that I mention earlier in this chapter, iTunes offers a full equalizer. An *equalizer* permits you to alter the volume of various frequencies in your music, allowing you to boost low sounds, lower high sounds, or anything in between. Now you can customize the way your music sounds and adjust it to your liking.

To open the Equalizer (as shown in Figure 11-4), do one of the following:

✔ **Choose Window⇨Equalizer.**

✔ **Press ⌘+Option+2.**

The Equalizer window has an impressive array of 11 sliders. Use the left-most slider (Preamp) to set the overall level of the Equalizer. The remaining sliders represent various frequencies that the human ear can perceive. Setting a slider to a position in the middle of its travel causes that frequency to play back with no change. Move the slider above the midpoint to boost that frequency; conversely, move the slider below the midpoint to reduce the volume of that frequency.

Continue adjusting the equalizer sliders until your music sounds the way you like it. When you close the Equalizer window, iTunes remembers your settings until you change them again. In case you prefer to leave frequencies to the experts, the iTunes Equalizer has several predefined settings to match most musical styles. Click the pop-up menu at the top of the Equalizer window to select a genre.

After you adjust the sound to your satisfaction, close the Equalizer window to return to the iTunes interface and relax with those funky custom notes from James Brown.

Figure 11-4: Use the Equalizer sliders to tweak the sound of your music.

A New Kind of Radio Station

Besides playing back your favorite audio files, iTunes can also tune in Internet radio stations from around the globe. You can listen to any of a large number of preset stations, seek out lesser-known stations not recognized by iTunes, or even add your favorite stations to your playlists. This section shows you how to do it all.

iTunes Radio

Although it's not a radio tuner in the strictest sense, iTunes Radio can locate virtual radio stations all over the world that send audio over the Internet — a process usually dubbed *streaming* amongst the "in" Internet crowd. iTunes can track down hundreds of Internet radio stations in a variety of styles with only a few clicks.

To begin listening to Internet radio with iTunes, click the Radio icon located beneath the Library icon in the Source list. The result is a list of more than 20 types of radio stations, organized by genre.

When you expand a Radio category by clicking its triangle, iTunes queries a tuning server and locates the name and address of dozens of radio stations for that category. Whether you like Elvis or not-Elvis (those passing fads, like new wave, classical, or alternative), something's here for everyone. The Radio also offers news, sports, and talk radio.

After iTunes fetches the names and descriptions of radio stations, double-click one that you want to hear. iTunes immediately jumps into action, loads the station, and begins to play it.

Tuning in your own stations

Although iTunes offers you a large list of popular radio stations on the Web, it's by no means comprehensive. Eventually, you might run across a radio station that you'd like to hear, but it's not listed in iTunes. Luckily, iTunes permits you to listen to other stations, too. To listen to a radio station that iTunes doesn't list, you need the station's Web address.

In iTunes, choose Advanced➪Open Audio Stream (or press ⌘+U). In the Open Stream dialog that appears (as shown in Figure 11-5), enter the URL of your desired radio station and then click OK. Within seconds, iTunes tunes in your station.

What's with the numbers next to the station names?

When choosing an Internet radio station, keep your Internet connection speed in mind. If you're using a broadband DSL or cable connection — or if you're listening at work over your company's high-speed network — you can listen to stations broadcasting at 128 Kbps (or even higher). The higher the bit rate, the better the music sounds. At 128 Kbps, for example, you're listening to sound that's almost as good as an audio CD.

However, if you're listening over a dial-up modem connection, iTunes can't keep up with audio streaming at higher bit rates, so you're limited to stations broadcasting at 56 Kbps or lower.

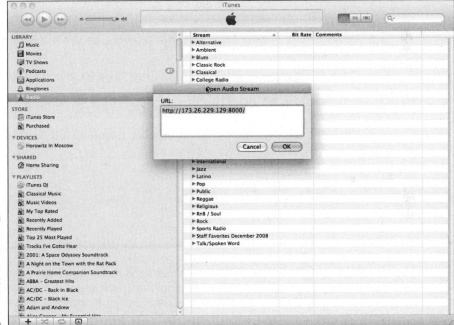

Figure 11-5:
Tuning into MLC Radio, my Internet radio station.

Radio stations in your playlists

If you find yourself visiting an online radio station more than once, you'll be glad to know that iTunes supports radio stations in its playlists. To add a radio station to a playlist from the Radio list, do the following:

1. **Open the category that contains the station you want to add to your playlist.**

2. **Locate the station that you want to add to your playlist and drag it from the Radio list to the desired playlist on the left.**

   If you haven't created any playlists yet, see the section "Keeping Slim Whitman and Slim Shady Apart: Organizing with Playlists" earlier in this chapter to find out how.

Adding a radio station that doesn't appear in the Radio list is a bit trickier but possible nonetheless. Even though iTunes allows you to load a radio station URL manually by using the Open Stream command in the Advanced menu, it doesn't give you an easy way to add it to the playlist. Follow these steps to add a specific radio station to a playlist:

1. **Add any radio station from the Radio list to your desired playlist.**

   Any station in the list will do, as you'll immediately change both the station's URL and name to create your new station entry in the Playlist.

2. **Press ⌘+I or choose File⇨Get Info to bring up the information dialog for that station.**

3. **Click the Summary section and change the URL by clicking the Edit URL button.**

4. **Enter the desired URL and click OK.**

5. **Click the Info tab, type the new station name, and then click OK.**

iSending iStuff to iPod

If you're lucky enough (like me) to own an iPod, you'll be happy to know that iTunes has features for your personal audio and video jukebox as well. *iPods,* Apple's multimedia players, comprise an entire family of portable devices (ranging from $59 to about $399) that can hold anywhere from about 300 songs to literally thousands of songs, as well as podcasts, photos, and video. This great gadget and those like it have become known worldwide as *the* preferred portable digital media player. (Heck, even the iPhone can act as an iPod!)

You connect your iPod to any Macintosh or Windows PC with USB 2.0 ports with the included cable. After the iPod's connected, you can synchronize the iPod with iTunes. By default, this process is automatic: The iPod and the iTunes software communicate with each other and figure out what items are in your iTunes Library (as compared with the iPod Library). If they discover songs, podcasts, and video in your iTunes Library that are missing from your iPod, the items automatically transfer to the iPod. Conversely, if the iPod contains stuff that's no longer in iTunes, the iPod automatically removes those files from its drive.

"I have an itch to hear 'Kung Fu Fighting'!"

This particular technology author has a preference for a certain hot Net jam spot: *MLC Radio,* the Internet radio station I've been running for several years now. I call my station a '70s Time Machine because it includes hundreds of classic hits from 1970–1979, inclusive. You hear everything from "Rock and Roll Hoochie Koo" by Rick Derringer to "Moonlight Feels Right" by Starbuck. (Hey, I'm summing up a decade here, so be prepared for both Rush and the Captain and Tennille, too.) The station broadcasts at 128 Kbps (near audio CD quality), so you need a broadband connection to listen. For the radio's Internet address or help connecting to MLC Radio, visit my Web site at www.mlcbooks.com — and then follow the steps in the next section to add MLC Radio to your playlists!

Go back and reread that last sentence above about the iPod **automatically removing** files from its drive. (I'll wait here.) Apple added this feature in an effort to be attentive to copyright concerns. The reasoning is that if you connect your iPod to your friend's computer, you can't transfer songs from the iPod to that computer. Of course, you could always look at it from the marketing perspective as a feature that makes sure your iMac and iPod are always in total sync. Whatever the case, pay close attention and read all warning dialogs when connecting to a computer other than your own, or you might wipe out your iPod's library.

You can change your settings so that iTunes auto-syncs only selected playlists. Or if you're really nervous, you can manually sync your iPod with iTunes.

This chapter — even as long as it is — just can't explain all the ins and outs of the iTunes/iPod relationship! For a complete look at both iTunes and the iPod, I can heartily recommend a fellow *For Dummies* book, *iPod & iTunes For Dummies,* 7th Edition, by Tony Bove (Wiley Publishing).

Sharing Media across a Network

Ready to share music, podcasts, and video — *legally,* mind you — with other folks on your local network? You can offer your digital media to other iTunes users across your home or office. Follow these steps:

1. **Choose iTunes⇨Preferences to open the Preferences dialog.**
2. **Click Sharing.**
3. **Select the Share My Library on My Local Network check box.**

4. **Specify whether you want to share your entire library or only selected playlists and files.**

Sharing selected playlists is a good idea for those Meatmen and Sex Pistols fans who work at a cubicle farm in a big corporation.

5. **If you want to restrict access to just a few people, select the Require Password check box; then type a password in the text box.**

6. **Click OK.**

Your shared folder appears within the Source list for all iTunes users who enabled the Look for Shared Libraries check box on the same pane of their iTunes Preferences dialog. Note that the music you share with others can't be imported or copied, so everything stays legal.

Want to change that frumpy default name for your shared media library to something more exotic, like "Dan's Techno Beat Palace"? No problem — display the Preferences dialog again, but this time click the General button and click in the Library Name text box. Edit your network entertainment persona to your heart's content.

Burning Music to Shiny Plastic Circles

Besides being a great audio player, iTunes is adept at creating CDs, too. iTunes makes the process of recording songs to a CD as simple as a few clicks. Making the modern version of a compilation (or *mix*) tape is easier than getting a kid to eat ice cream. iTunes lets you burn CDs in one of three formats:

- **Audio CD:** This is the typical kind of commercial music CD that you buy at a store. Most typical music audio CDs store 700MB of data, which translates into about 80 minutes of music.

- **Data CD or DVD:** A standard CD-ROM or DVD-ROM is recorded with the audio files. This disc can't be played in any standard audio CD player (even if it supports MP3 CDs, which I discuss next). Therefore, you can listen to these songs only by using iTunes (or another media player) on an iMac or a PC.

- **MP3 CD:** As does the ordinary computer CD-ROM that I describe, an MP3 CD holds MP3 files in data format. However, the files are arranged in such a way that they can be recognized by audio CD players that support the MP3 CD format (especially boom boxes, DVD players, personal CD players, and car stereos). Because MP3 files are so much smaller than the digital audio tracks found on traditional audio CDs, you can fit as many as 160 typical 4-minute songs on one disc. These discs can also be played on your iMac via iTunes.

Sending music elsewhere with AirTunes

If you're using an AirPort Express portable wireless Base Station, you can ship your songs right to your Base Station from within iTunes, and from there to your home stereo or boom box!

After your AirPort Express Base Station is plugged in and you connect your home stereo (or a boom box, or a pair of powered stereo speakers) to the stereo minijack on the Base Station, you see a Speakers pop-up list button appear at the bottom of the iTunes window.

(If the Speakers button doesn't appear, choose iTunes➪Preferences to open the Preferences dialog and click the Devices button on the toolbar. Make sure that the Look for Remote Speakers Connected with AirTunes check box is enabled.)

Click the Speakers button, and you can choose to broadcast the music you're playing in iTunes across your wireless network. Ain't technology truly *grand?*

Keep in mind that MP3 CDs aren't the same as the standard audio CDs that you buy at the store, and you can't play them in older audio CD players that don't support the MP3 CD format. Rather, this is the kind of archival disc that you burn at home for your own collection.

To begin the process, build a playlist (or select an existing playlist that you want to record). If necessary, create a new Playlist and add to it whatever songs you would like to have on the CD. (See the earlier section, "Keeping Slim Whitman and Slim Shady Apart: Organizing with Playlists," if you need a refresher.) With the songs in the correct order, select the playlist. Click the Burn Disc button at the bottom of the iTunes window to commence the disc burning process. Click the desired recording format (again, usually Audio CD) in the Burn Settings dialog that appears.

To save yourself from sonic shock, I always recommend that you enable the Sound Check check box before you burn. iTunes will adjust the volume on all the songs on your audio CD so that they'll play at the same volume level.

Ready to go? Click OK, and iTunes lets you know when the recording is complete.

Feasting on iTunes Visuals

By now, you know that iTunes is a feast for the ears, but did you know that it can provide you with eye candy as well? With just a click or two, you can view mind-bending graphics that stretch, move, and pulse with your music, as shown in Figure 11-6.

Figure 11-6:
iTunes
can dis-
play some
awesome
patterns!

To begin viewing iTunes visuals, choose View⇨Show Visualizer (or press ⌘+T). Immediately, most of your iTunes interface disappears and begins displaying groovy lava lamp-style animations (like, *sassy,* man). To stop the visuals, choose View⇨Hide Visualizer (or press ⌘+T again). The usual sunny aluminum face of iTunes returns.

Backing up within iTunes

iTunes offers a built-in backup feature for your media library — I told you this was the best media player ever designed!

Choose File⇨Library⇨Back Up to Disc to start the process. You can choose to back up your entire iTunes library and all your playlists (which I recommend) or just the content you've purchased from the iTunes Store. Personally, if I lost everything in my collection except for what I've bought from the iTunes Store, I'd be just as crushed. Back it all up, and you won't be sorry.

Click Back Up, and iTunes will prompt you for blank CDs or DVDs. If you need to restore from your completed backup, just launch iTunes and load the first backup disc into your drive.

How often is often enough when it comes to backing up your content? That depends completely on how often your media library changes. The idea is to back up often enough so that you always have a recent copy of your media files close by.

You can also change the viewing size of the iTunes visuals in the View menu. From the View menu item, choose Full Screen (or press ⌘+F). To escape from the Full Screen mode, move the mouse or press Esc.

You can still control iTunes with the keyboard while the visuals are zooming around your screen. See Table 11-1 earlier in this chapter for a rundown on common keyboard shortcuts.

The iTunes Visualizer has many hidden features. While viewing the Visualizer, press **?** to see a list of hidden Visualizer settings.

But wait, more Easter eggs are to be found! Again, while viewing the Visualizer, press one of following keys:

- **M:** Changes the Visualizer pattern
- **P:** Changes the Visualizer color scheme

Press either of these keys repeatedly to cycle through the various patterns and color schemes lurking deep within the Visualizer. (Personally, I'm a random Visualizer guy . . . there are so many patterns and schemes, I just let my iMac do all the work.)

Additionally, you'll find third-party Visualizer plug-ins available for downloading on Apple's Web site and other Mac-related download sites — heck, some even display lyrics, karaoke-style! Choose a different Visualizer plug-in from the View⇨Visualizer menu item. (Call me old-fashioned, but I like the default, iTunes Visualizer.)

Buying Digital Media the Apple Way

Before we wave goodbye to the happy residents of iTunes iSland, I won't forget to mention the hottest spot on the Internet for buying music and video: the iTunes Store, which you can reach from the cozy confines of iTunes. (That is, as long as you have an Internet connection. If you don't, it's time to turn the page to a different chapter.) If you're not in iTunes, go to www. apple.com/itunes/store.

Click the iTunes Store item in the Source list, and after a few moments you're presented with the latest offerings. Click a link in the store list to browse according to media type, or click the Power Search link to search by song title, artist, album, or composer. The Back/Forward buttons at the top of the iTunes Store window operate much the same as those in Safari, moving you backward or forward in sequence through pages you've already seen. Clicking the Home button (which, through no great coincidence, looks like a miniature house) takes you back to the Store's main page.

To display the details on a specific album, track, video, podcast, or audio-book (whew), just click it. If you're interested in buying just certain tracks (for that perfect road warrior mix), you get to listen to 30 seconds of any track — for free, no less, and at full sound quality. To add an item to your iTunes Store shopping cart, click the Add Song/Movie/Album/Video/Podcast/Audiobook button (sheesh!). When you're ready to buy, click the Shopping Cart item in the Source list and then click the Buy Now button. (At the time of this writing, tracks are usually 99 cents a pop, and an entire album is typically $9.99 . . . what a bargain!

The iTunes Store creates an account for you based on your e-mail address, and it keeps secure track of your credit card information for future purchases. After you use the iTunes Store once, you never have to log in or retype your credit card information again (as long as you're logged in using your account).

The tracks and files that you download are saved to a separate playlist called Purchased. After the download is finished, you can play them, move them to other playlists, burn them to CD or DVD, share 'em over your network, or ship them to your iPod, just as you can any other item in your iTunes Library.

You can also put the Genius button to work for you, in league with the iTunes store. Click the Show Genius Sidebar button at the lower-right corner of the iTunes window — it looks like an arrow inside a square — and iTunes displays the Genius Sidebar, where iTunes recommends music that you can buy on the iTunes Store that's similar to the albums in your Music Library. Click the button again to banish the sidebar.

Remember all those skeptics who claimed that buying digital audio and video could never work over the Internet because of piracy issues and high costs? Well, bunkie, hats off to Apple: Once again, our favorite technology leader has done something the *right* way!

Chapter 12

The Masterpiece That Is iPhoto

*V*irtually every iMac owner is likely to have a digital camera or a scanner. Digital video (DV) camcorders have certainly grown more plentiful over the past three or four years, and the iPod is the hottest piece of music hardware on the planet at the time of this writing. The digital camera, however, has reached what those funny (strange) marketing people refer to as *saturation,* and iPhoto was written to address the needs of every person with a digital camera and an iMac!

With iPhoto, you organize, edit, and even publish your photographs. (It sports more features than a handful of Swiss Army knives.) After you shoot your photos with a digital camera, you can import them into iPhoto, edit them, and publish them. You're not limited to photos that you take yourself, either; you can edit, publish, and organize all kinds of digital image files. You can even create a photo album and use the iPhoto interface to order a handsome hard-bound copy shipped to you.

To sum it all up, I'm willing to bet that iPhoto is either the first or the second iLife '09 application that you fall in love with (running neck and neck with iTunes). In this chapter, I show you how you can work digital image magic with true Apple panache!

Delving into iPhoto

In Figure 12-1, you can see most of the major controls offered in iPhoto '09. (Other controls automatically appear when you enter different modes; I cover them in upcoming sections of this chapter.)

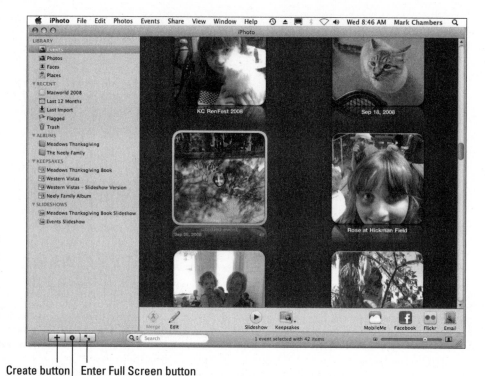

Figure 12-1:
iPhoto
greets you
with an
attractive
window.

Create button | Enter Full Screen button

Get Info button

Although these controls and sections of the window are covered in more detail in the following sections, here's a quick rundown of what you're looking at:

✔ **Source list:** This list of image locations determines which photos iPhoto displays.

- You can choose to display either your entire image library or just the last "roll" of digital images that you downloaded from your camera.

- You can create new *albums* of your own that appear in the source list; albums make it much easier to organize your photos.

- Photos can be grouped by *Event* (when they were taken), *Faces* (who appears in the photos), *Places* (where photos were taken) and *Albums* (the traditional method you may be familiar with from older versions of iPhoto).

- You can create books, calendars, cards, and slideshows.

✔ **Viewer:** This pane displays the images from the currently selected photo source.

You can drag or click to select photos in the Viewer for further tricks, such as assigning keywords and image editing.

✔ **Create button:** Click this button to add a new blank album, smart album, MobileMe gallery, book, calendar, card, or slideshow to your source list.

✔ **Get Info button:** Click this button to display information on the currently selected photos.

✔ **Enter Full Screen button:** Click this button to switch to a full-screen display of your photos. In full-screen mode, the images in the selected album appear in a filmstrip across the top of the screen, and you can click one to view that image using your Mac's entire screen real estate. You can also use the same controls that I discuss later in this chapter for editing and adjusting images; just move the cursor to the top edge of the full-screen display to show the menu or to the bottom edge to show the editing toolbar.

✔ **Play Slideshow:** Select an event, album, book or slideshow in the Source list (or multiple images you've selected in the Viewer) and click this button to start a full-screen slideshow using those images.

✔ **Search box:** Click the button next to the Search text box to locate photos by specific criteria, or just click in the box and start typing to search by description and title.

✔ **Toolbar buttons:** This group of buttons selects an operation you want to perform on the images you've selected in the Viewer. (Note that the toolbar buttons you see may depend on your screen resolution. If you resize the iPhoto window so that it is sufficiently small, some toolbar buttons will "collapse" into a Keepsakes button with a drop-down menu attached.)

✔ **Thumbnail Resize slider:** Drag this slider to the left to reduce the size of the thumbnails in the Viewer. This allows you to see more thumbnails at one time, which is a great boon for quick visual searches. Drag the slider to the right to expand the size of the thumbnails, which makes it easier to differentiate details between similar photos in the Viewer.

Working with Images in iPhoto

Even a superbly designed image display and editing application, such as iPhoto '09, would look overwhelming if everything were jammed into one window. Thus, Apple's developers provide different operation modes (such as editing and book creation) that you can use in the one iPhoto window. Each mode allows you to perform different tasks, and you can switch modes at just about any time by clicking the corresponding toolbar button.

In this section, I discuss three of these modes — import, organize, and edit — and what you can do when you're in them. Then I conclude the chapter with sections on publishing and sharing your images.

Import Images 101

In *import* mode, you're ready to download images directly from your digital camera — as long as your specific camera model is supported in iPhoto. The Apple iPhoto support page at www.apple.com/macosx/upgrade/cameras.html lists many of the cameras that are supported in iPhoto.

Follow these steps to import images:

1. **Connect your digital camera to your iMac.**

   Plug one end of a USB cable into your camera and the other end into your iMac's USB port, and prepare your camera to download images.

2. **Launch iPhoto.**

   Your iMac will probably launch iPhoto automatically when your camera is detected, but you can always launch iPhoto manually by clicking its icon in the Dock (or double-clicking it in your Applications folder).

3. **Type an event name for the imported photos, such as** Birthday Party **or** Godzilla Ravages Tokyo (depending on your birthday parties, this could be the same event).

4. **Type a description for the Event.**

5. **To allow iPhoto to automatically separate images into separate events based on the date they were taken, click to select the Autosplit Events after Importing check box.**

6. **Click the Import All button to import your photographs from the camera.**

   The images are added to your Photo Library, where you can organize them as you want.

   To select specific images to import, hold down the ⌘ key and click each desired photo; then click Import Selected instead of Import All.

7. **Specify whether the images you're importing should be deleted from the camera afterward.**

   If you don't expect to download these images again to another computer or another device, you can choose to delete the photos from your camera automatically. This saves you a step, frees space for new photos, and helps eliminate the guilt that can crop up when you nix your pix. (Sorry, I couldn't resist.)

Importing images from your hard drive

If you have a folder of images that you've collected already on your hard drive, a CD, a DVD, an external drive, or a USB Flash drive, adding them to your library is easy. Just drag the folder from a Finder window and drop it into the Albums header (within the source list in the iPhoto window). iPhoto automatically creates a new album using the folder name, and you can sit back while the images are imported into that new album. iPhoto recognizes images in several formats: JPEG, GIF, RAW, PNG, PICT, PSD, PDF, and TIFF.

If you have individual images, you can drag them as well. Select the images in a Finder window and drag them into the desired album in the source list. To add them to the album currently displayed in the Viewer, drag the selected photos and drop them in the Viewer instead.

If you'd rather import images by using a standard Mac Open dialog, choose File⇨Import to Library. Simplicity strikes again!

"What's that about an Event, Mark?" After you download the contents of your digital camera, those contents count as a virtual *Event* in iPhoto — based on either the date that you imported them or the date they were taken. For example, you can always display the last images you imported by clicking Last Import. If you want to see photos from your son's graduation, they appear as a separate Event. (Both of these organizational tools will appear in the source list.) Think about that . . . it's pretty tough to arrange old-fashioned film prints by the moment in time that they document, but iPhoto makes it easy for you to see just which photos are part of the same group! I explain more about Events in the next section.

Organize mode: Organizing and sorting your images

In the days of film prints, you could always stuff another shoebox with your latest photos or buy another sticky album to expand your library. Your digital camera, though, stores images as files instead, and many folks don't print their digital photographs. Instead, you can keep your entire collection of digital photographs and scanned images well ordered and easily retrieved by using iPhoto's *organize* mode. Then you can display them in a slideshow, e-mail them, print them, use them as Desktop backgrounds, or burn them to an archive disc.

A new kind of photo album

The most familiar method of organizing images in iPhoto is the *album*. Each album can represent any designation you like, be it a year, a vacation, your daughter, or your daughter's ex-boyfriends. Follow these steps:

1. **Create a new album.**

   You can either choose File⇨New Album or click the plus (+) button at the bottom of the source list. Click the Album button at the top of the sheet to display the settings you see in Figure 12-2.

2. **Type the name for your new photo album.**

   If you want to create an empty album (without automatically including any images that might be selected), make sure you click the Use Selected Items in New Album check box to deselect it.

3. **Click OK.**

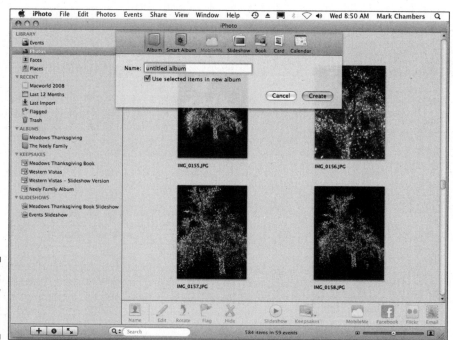

Figure 12-2:
Add a new album in iPhoto.

iPhoto also offers a special type of album called a *Smart Album,* which you can create from the File menu. (For even faster action, hold down the Option key while you click the Add button.) A Smart Album contains only photos that match certain criteria that you choose, using the keywords and rating that you assign your images. Other criteria text in the photo filenames, dates the images were added to iPhoto, and any comments you might have added. Now here's the really nifty angle: iPhoto *automatically* builds and maintains Smart Albums for you, adding new photos that match the criteria (and deleting those that you remove from your Photo Library)! Smart Albums carry a gear icon in the source list.

You can display information about the currently selected item in the information pane under the source list. Just click the Show Information button at the bottom of the iPhoto window, which sports the familiar "*i*-in-a-circle" logo. You can also type a short note or description in the Description box that appears in the Information pane. For more in-depth information, select the desired item and then press ⌘+I.

You can also change information on an image by selecting it in the Viewer and clicking the Show Information button. Click any of the headings in the pane (Title, Date, Time, and so on) to display a text edit box, and you can simply click in either box to type a new name or alter the photo's date stamp.

You can drag images from the Viewer into any album you choose. For example, you can copy an image to another album by dragging it from the Viewer to the desired album in the Source list.

To remove a photo that has fallen out of favor, follow these steps:

1. **In the source list, select the desired album.**

2. **In the Viewer, select the photo (click it) that you want to remove.**

3. **Press Delete.**

When you remove a photo from an album, you *don't* remove the photo from your collection (which is represented by the Photos entry under the Library heading in the source list). That's because an album is just a group of links to the images in your collection. If you want to completely remove an offending photo from iPhoto, click the Photos entry under the Library heading to display your entire collection of images and delete the picture there. The photo disappears from all albums with which it is associated.

To remove an entire album from the source list, just click it in the source list to select it — in the Viewer, you can see the images that it contains — and then press Delete. (Alternatively, right-click or Control-click the offending album and choose Delete Album.)

To rename an album, click the entry under the Albums heading in the Source list to select it and then click again to display a text box. Type the new album name and press Return.

Change your mind? iPhoto comes complete with a handy-dandy Undo feature. Just press ⌘+Z, and it's as though your last action never happened. (A great trick for those moments when you realize you just deleted your only image of your first car from your Library.)

Arranging stuff by Events

As I mention earlier, an Event is a group of images that you shot or down-loaded at the same time — iPhoto figures that those images belong together (which is usually a pretty safe assumption). Figure 12-3 illustrates some of the Events I've created in my iPhoto collection.

As can an album, an Event can be renamed — you just use a different proce-dure. Click the Events entry under the Library heading in the Source list to display your Events in the Viewer; then click the existing Event name in the caption underneath the thumbnail. A text box appears in which you can type a new name; click Return to update the Event.

Try moving your cursor over an Event thumbnail in the Viewer and you'll see that iPhoto displays the date range when the images were taken, as well as the total number of images in the Event. Ah, but things get *really* cool when you move your cursor back and forth over an Event with many images: The thumbnail animates and displays all the images in the Event, without your using old-fashioned scroll bars or silly arrows! (Why can't I think of this stuff? This is the future, dear readers.)

Notice that "i-in-a-circle" that appears when you hover your cursor over an Event thumbnail? Click it to display the location where the shot was taken, using the Places feature I describe in a page or two.

To display the contents of an Event in the Viewer, just double-click the Event thumbnail. To return to the Events thumbnails, click the All Events button at the top of the Viewer.

Decided to merge those Prom Event pictures with your daughter's Graduation Event? No problem! You could drag one Event thumbnail on top of another, but that's the easy way. Alternatively, click the Events entry under the Library heading in the Source list to display your Events and then hold down ⌘ while you click the Events that you want to merge. Click the Merge button in the toolbar at the bottom of the window, or click Events⇨Merge Events. (Forgot about that menu bar, didn't you?) Click Merge in the confirmation dialog that appears.

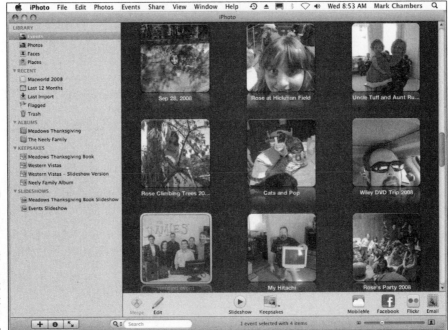

Figure 12-3:
Events help
you orga-
nize by what
happened,
not just
when it
happened!

Whilst organizing, you can create a brand-new empty Event by clicking Events⇨Create Event. Feel free to drag photos from albums, other Events, or your Photo library into your new Event.

Working with Faces and Places

iPhoto '09 includes two new organizational tools called Faces and Places. These two categories now appear in the Library section of the Source list.

First, let's tackle Faces. This feature is a sophisticated recognition system that automatically recognizes human faces within the photos that you add to your Library. (I don't know whether it works well with pets — but you can try, anyway.) Naturally, you have to identify faces first before iPhoto can recognize them, which it does through a process called *tagging*.

To tag a face, follow these steps:

1. **In the Source list, click the Photos item to display your image library.**

2. **In the Viewer, click the photo with a person you want to tag.**

   The photo is selected, as indicated by the yellow border.

3. Click the Name button in the iPhoto toolbar at the bottom of the window.

iPhoto displays the tagging pane you see in Figure 12-4. Note that iPhoto has indicated each person's face in the photo with a label.

4. If the face is unrecognized (labeled as unnamed), click the label to open a text box and type the person's name.

If iPhoto recognizes the face correctly and the name matches the person, click the check mark to confirm the tag. If the face is incorrectly identified, click the X and you can enter a new name.

If the name appears on an Address Book contact card, you can click the matching entry that appears to confirm the identity. Wowzers!

If iPhoto doesn't recognize a face at all in the photo (which can happen if the person's face is turned at an angle to the camera, or is in a darker area of the photo), click the Add Missing Face button, and iPhoto places a box in the center of the image. Drag the box over the person's face. If necessary, you can resize the box using the four handles at the corners of the box. Now you can click the label and type the person's name.

Figure 12-4:
Adding another mug to my collection of Faces.

5. **Press Return to save the face.**

   Notice the expansion button that appears next to the person's name? Click it, and iPhoto displays other photos that likely contain this person's face, allowing you to tag them there as well.

6. **Click Done after you've identified all the faces in the photo.**

After you've tagged an image, it appears in your Faces collection, which you can view by clicking the Faces entry in the Source list. You can click a portrait in your Faces collection to see all the images that contain that person. As you might expect, the more tags you add for a specific person, the better iPhoto gets at recognizing that person!

Places makes it easy to track the location where photos were taken, but it requires a digital camera that includes GPS tracking information in the image metadata. (This is a relatively new feature for digital cameras, so older models aren't likely to support GPS tracking.) Places also requires an Internet connection, because it uses Google Maps.

Click the Places entry in the Source list to display a global map, with push-pins indicating where your photos were taken. You can switch the Places map between terrain and satellite modes, or choose a hybrid display. If you're familiar with Google Maps, these settings are old friends of yours.

Alternatively, click the List View button to display a character-based browser, where you can click on country, state, and city names.

No matter which view mode you choose, clicking a pushpin or location displays the images taken in that area.

Organizing with keywords

"Okay, Mark, albums, Events, Faces, and Places are great ideas, but there has to be a way to search my collection by category!" Never fear, good iMac owner. You can also assign descriptive *keywords* to images to help you organize your collection and locate certain pictures fast. iPhoto comes with a number of standard keywords, and you can create your own as well.

To illustrate, suppose you'd like to identify your images according to special events in your family. Birthday photos should have their own keyword, and anniversaries deserve another. By assigning keywords, you can search for Elsie's sixth birthday or your silver wedding anniversary (no matter what Event or album they're in), and all related photos with those keywords appear like magic! (Well, *almost* like magic. You need to choose View⇨Keywords, which toggles the Keyword display on and off in the Viewer.)

iPhoto includes a number of keywords that are already available:

- ✔ **Favorite**
- ✔ **Family**
- ✔ **Kids**
- ✔ **Vacation**
- ✔ **Birthday**
- ✔ **Movie**
- ✔ **Checkmark**

What's the Checkmark all about, you ask? It's a special case: Adding this keyword displays a tiny check mark icon in the bottom-right corner of the image. The checkmark keyword comes in handy for temporarily identifying specific images because you can search for just your checkmarked photos.

To assign keywords to images (or remove keywords that have already been assigned), select one or more photos in the Viewer. Choose Window➪Show Keywords or press ⌘+K to display the Keywords window, as shown in Figure 12-5.

Click the keyword buttons that you want to attach to the selected images to mark them. Or click the highlighted keyword buttons that you want to remove from the selected images to disable them.

You're gonna need your own keywords

I'll bet you take photos of things other than just kids and vacations — and that's why iPhoto allows you to create your own keywords. Display the iPhoto Keywords window by pressing ⌘+K, clicking the Edit Keywords button, and then clicking Add (the button with the plus sign). iPhoto adds a new unnamed keyword to the list as an edit box, ready for you to type its name.

You can rename an existing keyword from this same window, too. Click a keyword to select it

and then click Rename. Remember, however, that renaming a keyword affects *all the images that were tagged with that keyword.* That might be confusing when, for example, photos originally tagged as Family suddenly appear with the keyword Foodstuffs. To remove an existing keyword from the list, click the keyword to select it and then click the Delete button, which bears a minus sign.

Figure 12-5:
Time to add
keywords
to these
selected
images.

Digging through your library with keywords

Behold the power of keywords! To sift through your entire collection of images by using keywords, click the magnifying glass button next to the Search box at the bottom of the iPhoto window and then choose Keyword from the pop-up menu. iPhoto displays a pop-up Keywords panel, and you can click one or more keyword buttons to display just the photos that carry those keywords.

The images that remain in the Viewer after a search must have *all* the keywords that you specified. If an image is identified, for example, by only three of four keywords you chose, it isn't a match and it doesn't appear in the Viewer. (You can create a Smart Album with specific keywords to get around this limitation.)

To search for a photo by words in its description, just click in the Search box and start typing. You can also click that same magnifying glass by the Search box to search through your images by date and rating as well.

Speaking of ratings . . .

Playing favorites by assigning ratings

Be your own critic! iPhoto allows you to assign any photo a rating of anywhere from zero to five stars. I use this system to help me keep track of the images that I feel are the best in my library. Select one (or more) image and then assign a rating using one of the following methods:

✔ Choose Photos➪My Rating and then choose the desired rating from the pop-up submenu.

✔ Use the ⌘+0 through ⌘+5 shortcuts.

Sorting your images just so

The View menu provides an easy way to arrange your images in the Viewer by a number of different criteria. Choose View➪Sort Photos and then click the desired sort criteria from the pop-up submenu. You can arrange the display by date, keyword, title, or rating. If you select an album in the source list, you can also choose to arrange photos manually, which means that you can drag and drop thumbnails in the Viewer to place them in the precise order you want them.

Naturally, iPhoto allows you to print selected images, but you can also send photos directly to iWeb for use on your MobileMe Web site. Click Share➪Send to iWeb and then choose either Photo Page or Blog from the submenu. iPhoto automatically sends the selected images or album to iWeb and launches the application! You can also use iPhoto's Web Gallery feature to get your photos on the Web. (More on the Web Gallery at the end of this chapter.)

Edit mode: Removing and fixing stuff the right way

Not every digital image is perfect — just look at my collection if you need proof. For those shots that need a pixel massage, iPhoto includes a number of editing tools that you can use to correct common problems.

The first step in any editing job is to select the image you want to fix in the Viewer. Then click the Edit button on the iPhoto toolbar to switch to the Edit mode controls, as shown in Figure 12-6. Now you're ready to fix problems, using the tools that I discuss in the rest of this section. (If you're editing a photo that's part of an Event, album, Faces, or Places, note the spiffy scrolling photo strip at the top, which allows you to switch to another image to edit from the same grouping.)

When you're done with Edit mode, click the . . . (wait for it) . . . Done button!

Figure 12-6:
iPhoto is now in edit mode — watch out, image problems!

Rotating tipped-over shots

If an image is in the wrong orientation and needs to be turned to display correctly, click the Rotate button to turn it once in a counterclockwise direction. Hold down the Option key while you click the Rotate button to rotate in a clockwise direction.

Crop 'til you drop

Does that photo have an intruder hovering around the edges of the subject? You can remove some of the border by *cropping* an image, just as folks once did with film prints and a pair of scissors. (We've come a long way.) With iPhoto, you can remove unwanted portions of an image; it's a great way to get Uncle Milton's stray head (complete with toupee) out of an otherwise perfect holiday snapshot.

Follow these steps to crop an image:

1. **Click the Crop button in the Edit toolbar.**
2. **Select the portion of the image that you want to keep.**

In the Viewer, click and drag the handles on the rectangle to outline the part of the image that you want. Remember, whatever's outside this rectangle disappears after the crop is completed.

TIP

When you drag a corner or edge of the outline, a semi-opaque grid (familiar to amateur and professional photographers as the nine squares from the Rule of Three) appears to help you visualize what you're claiming. (Check it out in Figure 12-7.)

3. **(Optional) Choose a preset aspect ratio.**

   If you want to force your cropped selection to a specific aspect ratio — such as 4 x 3 or 16 x 9 for an iDVD project — click the Constrain check box and select that ratio from the Constrain pop-up menu.

4. **Click the Apply button.**

   Oh, and don't forget that you can use iPhoto's Undo feature if you mess up and need to try again. Just press ⌘+Z.

REMEMBER

iPhoto features multiple Undo levels, so you can press ⌘+Z several times to travel back through your last several changes.

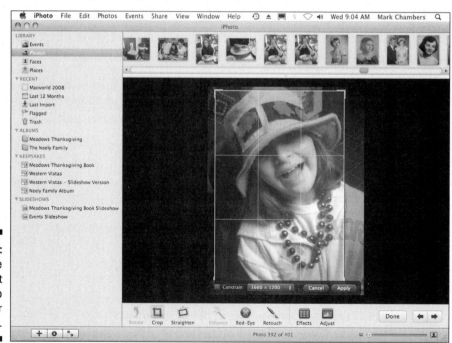

Figure 12-7:
Select the stuff that you want to keep in your photo.

Straightening what's crooked

Was your camera slightly tilted when you took the perfect shot? Never fear! Click the Straighten button and then drag the slider to tilt the image in the desired direction. Click the Close button to return to Edit mode.

Enhancing images to add pizzazz

If a photo looks washed out, click the Enhance button to increase (or decrease) the color saturation and improve the contrast. Enhance is automatic, so you don't have to set anything.

Removing rampant red-eye

Unfortunately, today's digital cameras can still produce the same "zombies with red eyeballs" as traditional film cameras. *Red-eye* is caused by a camera's flash reflecting off the retinas of a subject's eyes, and it can occur with both humans and animals. (I'm told pets get *green-eye*, but iPhoto can handle them, too!)

iPhoto can remove that red- and green-eye and turn frightening zombies back into your family and friends! Click the Red-Eye button and then select a demonized eyeball by clicking in the center of it. (If the new eyeball is too small or too large, drag the Size slider to adjust the dimensions.) To complete the process, click the X in the button that appears in the image.

Retouching like the stars

The iPhoto Retouch feature is perfect for removing minor flecks or lines in an image (especially those you've scanned from prints). Click Retouch and you'll notice that the cursor turns into a crosshair; just drag the cursor across the imperfection.

Switching to black-and-white or sepia

Ever wonder whether a particular photo in your library would look better as a black-and-white (or *grayscale*) print? Or perhaps an old-fashioned *sepia* tone in shades of copper and brown? Just click the Effects button to display the Effects window, which offers eight different effects you can apply to the photo.

Adjusting photo properties manually

Click Adjust to perform manual adjustments to brightness and contrast (the light levels in your image), as well as the sharpness, shadow, and highlight levels. To adjust a value, make sure that nothing's selected in the image and then drag the corresponding slider until the image looks the way you want. Click the Close button to return to Edit mode.

While you're editing, you can use the Next and Previous buttons at the lower-right corner of the iPhoto window to move to the next image in the current group (or back to the previous image).

Producing Your Own Coffee-Table Masterpiece

Book mode unleashes what I think is probably the coolest feature of iPhoto: the chance to design and print a high-quality bound photo book! After you complete an album — all the images have been edited just the way you want, and the album contains all the photos you want to include in your book — iPhoto can send your images as data over the Internet to a company that prints and binds your finished book for you. (No, they don't publish *For Dummies* titles, but then again, I don't get high-resolution color plates in most of my books, either.)

At the time of this writing, you can order many different sizes and bindings, including an 8.5-by-11-inch soft-cover book with 20 double-sided pages for about $20 and a hardbound 8.5-by-11-inch keepsake album with 10 double-sided pages for about $30 (shipping included for both). Extra pages can be added for about $0.70 and $1.00 a pop, respectively.

iPhoto '09 can also produce and automatically order calendars and greeting cards, using a process similar to the one I describe in this section for producing a book. Who needs that stationery store in the mall anymore?

 If you're going to create a photo book, make sure that the images have the highest quality and highest resolution. The higher the resolution, the better the photos look in the finished book. I personally always try to use images of over 1,000 pixels in both the vertical and horizontal dimensions.

To create a photo book, follow these steps:

1. **Click the desired album in the source list to select it.**

2. **Click the Keepsakes toolbar button and click Book from the pop-up menu.**

   Depending on your screen resolution, iPhoto may have room to display the Book button by itself — no big deal, because things work the same.

3. **Select the size of the book and a theme.**

   Your choices determine the number of pages and layout scheme, as well as the background graphics for each page.

4. **Click Choose.**

   You'll see the controls shown in Figure 12-8.

   In Book mode, the Viewer changes in subtle ways. It displays the current page at the bottom of the display and adds a scrolling row of thumbnail images above it. This row of images represents the remaining images from the selected album that you can add to your book. You can drag any image thumbnail into one of the photo placeholders to add it to the page. You can also click the Page button at the left of the thumbnail strip — it looks like a page with a turned-down corner — to display thumbnails of each page in your book. (To return to the album image strip, click the Photos button under the Page button.)

5. **Rearrange the page order to suit you by dragging the thumbnail of any page from one location to another in the strip.**

6. **In the Book toolbar below the page view, you can adjust a variety of settings for the final book, including the book's theme, background, page numbers, and text fonts.**

   At this point, you can also add captions and short descriptions to the pages of your photo album. Click any one of the text boxes in the page display and begin typing to add text to that page.

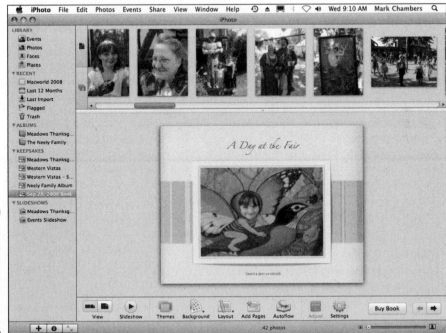

Figure 12-8: Preparing to publish my own coffee-table master-piece.

7. **When you're ready to publish your book, click the Buy Book button.**

8. **In a series of dialogs that appears, iPhoto guides you through the final steps to order a bound book.**

Note that you're asked for credit card information, so have that plastic ready.

I wouldn't attempt to order a book using a dial-up modem connection. The images are likely far too large to be sent successfully. If possible, use a broadband or network connection to the Internet while you're ordering. If your only connection to the Internet is through a dial-up modem, I recommend saving your book in PDF format and having it printed at a copy shop or printing service instead. (Choose File⇨Print and then click the Save as PDF button.)

I really need a slideshow

You can use iPhoto to create slideshows! Click the album or Event you want to display and click the Add button; then choose Slideshow from the toolbar and click Create. Notice that iPhoto adds a Slideshow item in the source list. The same scrolling thumbnail strip appears at the top of the Viewer — this time displaying the images in the album or Event. Click and drag the thumbnails so that they appear in the desired order.

To choose background music for your slideshow, click the Music button in the Slideshow toolbar to display Apple's theme music, as well as the tracks from your iTunes library. To choose a standard theme, click the Source pop-up menu and choose Theme Music; then select that perfect song and click Apply. To choose an iTunes song or playlist, click the Source pop-up menu and choose either the Music item (for your entire library) or a playlist. You can also create a custom playlist by selecting the Custom Playlist for Slideshow check box. Then, drag the individual songs you want to the song list at the bottom of the sheet. (You can drag them to rearrange their order in the list as well.) Click Apply to accept your song list.

To configure your slideshow, click the Settings button in the Slideshow toolbar and click the All Slides tab. In the dialog that appears, you can specify the amount of time that each slide

remains on the screen, as well as an optional title and rating displays. You can choose the transition that occurs between photos, too, or specify a random transition each time. iMac owners appreciate the Aspect Ratio pop-up menu, which allows you to choose a 16:9 widescreen display for your slideshow.

Click the This Slide tab to modify the settings for a specific slide (useful for keeping a slide on-screen for a longer period of time or for setting a different transition than the default transition you choose from the Slideshow toolbar). I can recommend the Automatic Ken Burns effect — yep, the same one in iMovie — which lends an animated movement to the selected image. You can also set the selected photo to display in black and white, sepia, or antique coloring.

To display a preview of a single slide and its transitions, click the desired slide and then click Preview; this is a handy way of determining whether your delay and transition settings are really what you want for a particular slide. When you're ready to play your slideshow, click the Play button, and iPhoto switches to full-screen mode. You can share your completed slideshow by clicking Share in the iPhoto menu, where you can send the slideshow to iDVD (for later burning onto a DVD) or send it through e-mail.

You'll Love MobileMe Gallery!

iPhoto '09 includes a feature called MobileMe Gallery that does for images what podcasting does for audio: You can share your photos with friends, family, business clients, and anyone else with an Internet connection! (Your adoring public doesn't even require a Mac; it can use That Other Kind of Computer.) iPhoto automatically uploads the selected images and leads you through the process of creating a new Web page to proudly display your photos. However, you *must* be a MobileMe subscriber to use the MobileMe Gallery feature. If you haven't heard the news on Apple's MobileMe service yet, see Chapter 9 for the details.

To create a MobileMe Gallery, you designate one or more photos in the Viewer (or even select entire albums or Events in the Source list) and then click the Add button. Click the MobileMe toolbar button in the sheet that appears to display the Web Gallery settings.

Type a name for your new Web Gallery. You can elect to show the title of each photo, allow your visitors to download your images or upload their own, and even allow photos to be uploaded by other computer owners using an e-mail or a Web browser!

By default, any visitor to your MobileMe Web site can see your gallery. But what if you prefer a little security for those images? In that case, click the Album Viewable By pop-up menu, where you can limit your viewing audience (you can even require that your visitors enter a login name and password before they can receive your photos).

Click Publish, and you'll see that iPhoto indicates that your images are being uploaded with a cool twirling progress icon to the right of the album in the source list. When the process is complete, iPhoto indicates that the photos appear in a MobileMe Gallery with a new heading in the Source list. You're on the air!

Now for the other side of the coin: By selecting your MobileMe Gallery in the Source list and clicking Tell a Friend in the iPhoto toolbar, iPhoto automatically prepares an e-mail message in Apple Mail that announces your new Gallery! Just add the recipient names and click Send. This spiffy message includes instructions for

> ✔ **Folks using iPhoto '09 on a Mac:** As you can imagine, this is the easiest receive option to configure. After these folks are subscribed, they get an automatically updated album of the same name that appears in their source list, and they can use those images in their own iPhoto projects! From within iPhoto, your visitors can subscribe to your MobileMe Gallery by clicking File➪Subscribe to Photo Feed and entering the subscription URL.

✔ **Folks using Windows or an older version of iPhoto:** These subscribers can use any Web browser with RSS support (such as the Safari browser that comes with Snow Leopard and is available from Apple for Windows) or any RSS reader. (In effect, your MobileMe Gallery becomes an RSS feed for those without iPhoto '09.)

By default, any changes you make to the contents of your MobileMe Gallery are updated automatically on your MobileMe account, and, in turn, are updated automatically to everyone who receives your images. You can turn this feature off, however, if you have a large number of images and you update often (which can result in your sister's computer downloading a lot of data). To display the Check for New Photos setting for MobileMe Gallery, click iPhoto➪Preferences and click the Web button on the Preferences window toolbar. (You can also change the title for your Gallery and monitor your iDisk usage from this pane.)

Mailing Photos to Aunt Mildred

iPhoto can help you send your images through e-mail by automating the process. The application can prepare your image and embed it automatically in a new message.

To send an image through e-mail, select it and then click the Email button in the toolbar. The dialog, as shown in Figure 12-9, appears, allowing you to choose the size of the images and whether you want to include their titles, descriptions, and Places location information as well.

Keep in mind that most ISP (Internet service provider) e-mail servers don't accept an e-mail message that's more than 3MB or 4MB, so watch that Size display. If you're trying to send a number of images and the size goes over 2MB, you might have to click the Size pop-up menu and choose a smaller size (reducing the image resolution) to get them all embedded in a single message.

When you're satisfied with the total file size and you're ready to create your message, click the Compose button. iPhoto automatically launches Apple Mail (or whatever e-mail application you specify) and creates a new message containing the images, ready for you to click Send!

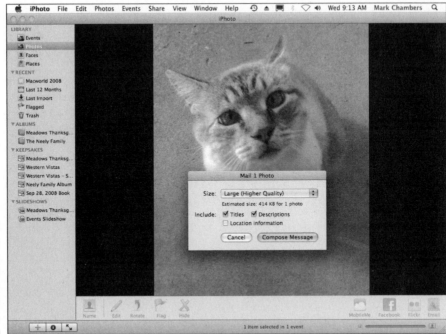

Figure 12-9:
Preparing
to send
an image
through
Apple Mail.

Is that Facebook and Flickr I spy?

Indeed it is! iPhoto '09 introduces a direct connection to both your Facebook social networking account (at www.facebook.com) and your Flickr online gallery account (at www.flickr.com), allowing you to simply select one or more photos and send them automatically to either service! These two buttons appear on the toolbar when you're organizing your photos.

The first time you select photos in the Viewer (or an album or Event in the Source list) and

click either button, iPhoto prompts you for permission to set up your connection. (Of course, this will require you to enter your Facebook and Flickr account information — hence the confirmation request.) Click Set Up and provide the data that each site requires.

After you've set up your accounts, simply select your photos, albums, or Events and click the toolbar button for the desired service. Apple, you absolutely *rock*!

Chapter 13

Making Film History with iMovie

Remember those home movies that you used to make in high school? They were entertaining and fun to create, and your friends were impressed. In fact, some kids are so downright inspired that you're not surprised when you discover at your high school reunion that they turned out to be graphic artists, or got involved in video or TV production.

iMovie, part of the iLife '09 suite, makes moviemaking as easy as those home-made movies. Apple simplified all the technical stuff, such as importing video and adding audio, leaving you free to concentrate on your creative ideas. In fact, you won't find techy terms such as *codecs* or *keyframes* in this chapter at all. I guarantee that you'll understand what's going on at all times. (How often do you get a promise like that with video-editing software?)

With iMovie, your digital video (DV) camcorder, and the other parts of the iLife suite, you can soon produce and share professional-looking movies, with some of the same creative transitions and titles used by Those Hollywood Types every single day. All on your iMac, all by yourself.

If you turn out to be a world-famous Hollywood Type Director in a decade or so, don't forget the little people along the way!

Shaking Hands with the iMovie Window

If you've ever tried a professional-level video-editing application, you probably felt as though you were suddenly dropped in the cockpit of a jumbo jet. In iMovie, though, all the controls you need are easy to use and logically placed.

Video-editing software takes up quite a bit of desktop space. In fact, you can't run iMovie at resolutions of less than 1024 x 768, and even the minimum is far too constrained for most iMovie users.

To launch iMovie, click the iMovie icon in the Dock. (It looks like a star from the Hollywood Walk of Fame.) You can also click the Application folder in any Finder window sidebar and then double-click the iMovie icon.

To follow the examples I show you here, follow these strenuous steps and create a new movie project:

1. **Click the File menu and choose New Project (or press ⌘+N).**

   iMovie displays the sheet you see in Figure 13-1.

2. **Type a name for your project.**

3. **Select the aspect ratio (or screen dimensions) for your movie.**

   You can select a widescreen display (16:9), a standard display (4:3), or a display especially suited for an iPhone (3:2). If compatibility with the familiar SDTV format is important, I always recommend that you choose standard (4:3) ratio; choosing 16:9 for an SDTV set will result in those familiar black "letterbox" bars at the top and bottom of the screen. On the flip side, choosing 4:3 results in *pillarboxing* (black bars on the left and right) when shown on an HD set.

Figure 13-1:
Creating a
new movie
project
within
iMovie.

4. Click a thumbnail to select a theme to apply to your finished movie.

If you choose a theme, iMovie automatically adds the transitions and titles that correspond to that theme. (Normally, this is what you want to do. However, if you want to add transitions and titles manually, click the Automatically Add Transitions and Titles check box to deselect it.)

If you decide not to use a theme (by selecting the None thumbnail), iMovie can still add an automatic effect between clips. Click the Automatically Add check box and click the pop-up menu to choose the desired effect.

5. Click Create.

You're on your way! Check out Figure 13-2: This is the whole enchilada, in one window.

The controls and displays that you'll use most often follow:

- ✔ **Monitor:** Think of this as being just like your TV or computer monitor. Your video clips, still images, and finished movie play here. You'll also crop and rotate your video within the monitor.

- ✔ **Browser toolbar:** This row of buttons allows you to switch between your media clips (video clips, photos, and audio) and the various tools that you use to make your film. The selected items fill the right side of the browser pane below the monitor.

- ✔ **Event pane:** All the video clips that you use to create your movie are stored in the Event pane. I show you what each of the panes in the iMovie workspace looks like when you tackle different tasks in this chapter.

- ✔ **Project pane:** iMovie displays the elements that you've added to your movie project in this pane.

- ✔ **Playhead:** The red vertical line that you see in the Event and Project panes is the *playhead,* which indicates the current editing point while you're creating your movie. When you're playing your movie, the playhead moves to follow your progress through the movie.

- ✔ **Editing toolbar:** This strip of buttons allows you to control editing functions such as cropping, audio, and video adjustments, voiceovers, and selecting items.

- ✔ **Camera Import window:** Click this switch to import DV clips from your DV camcorder or iSight camera.

Those are the major highlights of the iMovie window. A director's chair and megaphone are optional, of course, but they do add to the mood.

Playhead   Editing toolbar   Project pane   Monitor

Figure 13-2:
iMovie
is a lean,
mean video
producing
machine.

Camera Import   Event pane   Browser toolbar

A Bird's-Eye View of Moviemaking

I don't want to box in your creative skills here — after all, you can attack the moviemaking process from a number of angles. (Pun, unfortunately, intended.) However, I've found that my movies turn out the best when I follow a linear process, so before I dive into specifics, allow me to provide you with an overview of moviemaking with iMovie.

Here's my take on the process, reduced to seven steps:

1. **Import your video clips either directly from your DV camcorder, iSight camera, or your hard drive.**

2. **Drag your new selection of clips from the Event pane to the Project pane and arrange them in the desired order.**

3. **Import or record audio clips (from iTunes, GarageBand, or external sources, such as audio CDs or audio files that you've recorded yourself) and add them to your movie.**

4. **Import your photos (directly from iPhoto or from your hard drive) and place them where needed in your movie.**

5. **Add professional niceties, such as voiceovers, transitions, effects, and text to the project.**

6. **Preview your film and edit it further if necessary.**

7. **Share your finished film with others through the Web, e-mail, or a DVD that you create and burn with iDVD.**

As you might imagine, this chapter simply can't hold a full description of every setting and every procedure within iMovie '09 — but luckily, my good friend Dennis Cohen has done exactly that in his new book *iMovie '09 & iDVD '09 For Dummies* (Wiley Publishing). Dennis will take you from basics to all the in-depth features of these two iLife applications!

Importing the Building Blocks

Sure, you need video clips to create a movie of your own, but don't panic if you have but a short supply. You can certainly turn to the other iLife applications for additional raw material. (See, I told you that integration thing would come in handy.)

Along with video clips you import from your DV camcorder, built-in iSight camera, and hard drive, you can also call on iPhoto for still images (think credits) and iTunes for background audio and effects. In this section, I show you how.

Pulling in video clips

Your iMac is equipped already with the two extras that come in handy for video editing — namely, a large hard drive and a FireWire port. Because most mini-DV camcorders today use a FireWire connection to transfer clips, you're all set. (And even if your snazzy new DV camcorder uses a USB 2.0 connection, you're still in the zone, although you will need to modify the steps I provide in this section for your particular device.) Oh, and since your iMac has an iSight camera on board, you're a self-contained movie studio!

Here's the drill if your clips are on your FireWire-equipped mini-DV camcorder:

1. **Plug the proper cable into your iMac.**

2. **Set the DV camcorder to VTR (or VCR) mode.**

   Some camcorders call this Play mode.

3. **Click the Camera Import button (labeled in Figure 13-2).**

iMovie opens a new window.

4. **Click the Camera pop-up menu (at the bottom of the Import window) and select your DV camcorder or iSight camera.**

   Playback controls appear under the Camera Import window, mirroring the controls on your FireWire DV camcorder. This allows you to control the unit from iMovie. *Keen!*

   To capture video from your iSight camera, click the Video Size pop-up menu to choose the dimensions of the clip; then click Capture. On the sheet that appears, choose the location where the video will be saved, and choose whether to add this video to an existing event or create a new event. Click Capture to start recording, and click Stop when your video is complete. (You can skip the rest of the steps in this section, which deal only with DV camcorders.)

5. **Click the Import button.**

6. **Click the Save To pop-up menu and choose the drive that should store your clips.**

   You can choose to add the new clips to an existing Event or create a new Event. Heck, if the event spanned more than one day, you can create a new Event for each day. (How do they think up these things?)

7. **Click OK and admire your handiwork.**

   iMovie begins transferring the footage to your iMac and automatically adds the imported clips to your Event Library.

If your clips are already on your hard drive, rest assured that iMovie can import them, including those in *high-definition video* (HDV) format. iMovie also recognizes a number of other video formats, as shown in Table 13-1.

Table 13-1	Video Formats Supported by iMovie
File Type	*Description*
DV	Standard 4:3 digital video
DV Widescreen	Widescreen 16:9 digital video
MOV	QuickTime movies
HDV & AVCHD	High-definition (popularly called widescreen) digital video, in 720p and 1080i
MPEG-2	Digital video format used for DVD movies
MPEG-4	A popular format for streaming Internet and wireless digital video

To import a movie file, follow this bouncing ball:

1. **Choose File⇨Import and choose Movies from the submenu.**

2. **If you're importing 1080i video clips, choose the quality setting.**

   The Large setting will save you a significant amount of hard drive space, but the Full setting preserves the original resolution and detail. (If you're not importing 1080i video, use the default Large setting and click OK. The Full setting demands all the CPU and RAM resources your iMac can offer, so don't expect to do much multitasking while importing.)

3. **Click the drive that should store your clips in the sidebar and then navigate to the desired location.**

4. **Specify whether you want to add the imported video to an existing Event or create a new Event.**

   If you choose to add the video to an existing Event, click the pop-up menu and select an Event.

5. **Specify whether you want to copy the video (leaving the original movie intact) or have the movie deleted after a successful import.**

6. **Click Import.**

   Alternatively, you can also drag a video clip from a Finder window and drop it in the Project pane.

Making use of still images

Still images come in handy as impressive-looking titles or as ending credits to your movie. (Make sure you list a gaffer and a best boy to be truly professional.) However, you can use still images also to introduce scenes or to separate clips according to your whim. For example, I use stills when delineating the days of a vacation within a movie or different Christmas celebrations over time.

Here are two methods of adding stills to your movie:

- ✔ **Adding images from iPhoto:** Click the Photo Browser button in the Browser toolbar (or press ⌘+2) and you'll experience the thrill that is your iPhoto Library, right from iMovie (as shown in Figure 13-3). You can elect to display your entire iPhoto Library or more selective picks such as specific albums or Events. When you find the image you want to add, just drag it to the right spot in the Project pane.

- ✔ **Importing images from your hard drive:** If you're a member of the International Drag-and-Drop Society, you can drag TIFF, JPEG, GIF, PICT, PNG, and PSD images directly from a Finder window and drop them into the Project pane as well.

Figure 13-3:
Pulling still images from iPhoto is child's play.

Importing and adding audio from all sorts of places

You can pull in everything from Wagner to Weezer as both background music and sound effects for your movie. In this section, I focus on how to get those notes into iMovie and then how to add them to your movie by dragging them to the Project pane.

You can add audio from a number of sources:

✔ **Adding songs from iTunes:** Click the Show Music and Sound Effects button in the Browser toolbar (or press ⌘+1) to display the contents of your iTunes Library. Click the desired playlist in the scrolling list box, such as the Dinah Washington playlist I selected in Figure 13-4. (If you've exported any original music you've composed in GarageBand to your iTunes Library, you can use those songs in your own movie!) You can add a track to your movie by dragging the song entry from the Music and Sound Effects list to the desired spot in the Project pane.

Figure 13-4: Calling on my iTunes Library to add Dinah Washington to my iMovie.

✔ **Adding sound effects:** Yep, if you need the sound of a horse galloping for your Rocky Mountain vacation clips, click either iMovie Sound Effects or iLife Sound Effects in the scrolling list box. iMovie includes a number of top-shelf audio effects that you can use in the second audio track on the timeline viewer. This way, you can add sound effects even when you've already added a background song. Again, to add a sound effect, drag it to the perfect spot in the Project pane.

If you have several gigabytes of music in your iTunes Library, it might be more of a challenge to locate "Me and Bobby McGee" by Janis Joplin, especially if she's included in a compilation. Let your iMac do the digging for you! Click in the Search box below the track list and begin typing a song name. iMovie narrows down the song titles displayed to those that match the characters you type. To reset the search box and display all your songs in the Library or selected playlist, click the X icon that appears to the right of the box.

✔ **Ripping songs from an audio CD:** Load an audio CD and then choose Audio CD from the scrolling list box. iMovie displays the tracks from the CD, and you can add them at the current playhead position the same way as iTunes songs.

✔ **Recording directly from a microphone:** Yep, if you're thinking voiceover narration, you've hit the nail on the head. Check out the sidebar, "Narration the easy way," for the scoop.

Narration the easy way

Ready to create that award-winning nature documentary? You can add voiceover narration to your iMovie project that would make Jacques Cousteau proud. In fact, you can record your voice while you watch your movie playing, allowing perfect synchronization with the action! To add narration, follow these steps:

1. **Click the Voiceover button in the Editing toolbar — it sports a microphone icon — to open the Voiceover window.**

2. **Click the Record From pop-up menu and select the input device.**

   iMacs sport a decent internal microphone, but you can always add a USB or digital TOSlink microphone to your system.

3. **Drag the input volume slider to a comfortable level.**

   You can monitor the volume level of your voice with the left and right input meters — try to keep the meters at 50 percent or so for the proper volume level.

4. **To block out ambient noise levels, drag the Noise Reduction slider to the right if necessary.**

If you'd like iMovie to enhance your voice electronically for a more professional sound, click the Voice Enhancement check box to select it. If you need to hear the audio from your movie project while you speak, click the Play Project Audio While Recording check box to select it — note, however, that you'll need to listen to the audio while using a set of headphones (plugged in to your Mac's headphone jack) to avoid feedback problems.

5. **Click in the desired spot within a clip in the Project pane where the narration should begin.**

6. **Begin speaking when prompted by iMovie.**

7. **Watch the video while you narrate so that you can coordinate your narration track with the action.**

8. **Click anywhere in the iMovie window to stop recording (or wait until the clip ends).**

   iMovie adds an icon to the Project pane underneath the video with the voiceover.

9. **Click the Close button in the Voiceover window.**

You can fine-tune both the audio within a video clip or the audio clips that you add to your project. With the desired clip selected, click the Inspector button in the Editing toolbar (it bears a proud letter *i*) and click the Audio tab. The Audio Adjustments window that appears includes an array of audio controls that allow you to change the volume of the selected clip, or to give that audio priority over other audio playing simultaneously (such as a sound effect that needs to be clearly heard over background music and the video clip). If your clips dramatically vary in volume, click the Normalize Clip Volume button and then select each clip that you want to set to the same volume; click Normalize Clip Volume again for each clip. You can also set an automatic or manual Fade-in/Fade-out for the audio. When you're done tweaking, click Done. (Oh, and don't forget that you can always return the clip to its original volume; just open this window again and click Revert to Original.)

Building the Cinematic Basics

Time to dive in and add the building blocks to create your movie. Along with video clips, audio tracks, and still images, you can add Hollywood-quality transitions, optical effects, and animated text titles. In this section, I demonstrate how to elevate your collection of video clips into a real-life furshlugginer *movie*.

Adding clips to your movie

You can add clips to your movie by using the Project pane and the Event pane. The Dynamic Duo works like this:

- **Project pane:** This displays the media you've added to your project so far, allowing you to rearrange the clips, titles, transitions and still images in your movie.

- **Event pane:** This displays your video clips arranged by Event (the date they were shot or the date they were imported), acting as the source repository for all your clips. Movies pulled into iMovie, imported into iPhoto, or added manually from the Finder appear here.

To add a clip to your movie, follow these steps:

1. **Move your cursor across clips in the Event pane to watch a preview of the video.**

2. **When you've decided what to add to your project, you can either add the entire clip or a selection.**

   - To select an entire clip, right-click the clip's thumbnail and choose Select Entire Clip from the menu that appears.

   - To select a portion of a clip, drag your cursor across the thumbnail. A yellow frame appears around your selection. To change the length of the selected video, drag the handles that appear on either side. If you make a mistake while selecting video, just click any empty space within the Event pane to remove the selection frame and try again.

3. **Drag the selection from the Event pane to the spot where it belongs in the Project pane.**

   Alternatively, you can press the E key or click the Add to Project button (the first button in the Editing toolbar).

Preview your work — and do it often.

iMovie offers two Play Full screen buttons: one under the Event Library and one under the Project Library. Select the project or Event you want to play and then click the corresponding button (or press ⌘+G). You can also choose View⇨Play Full Screen to watch the selection. Press the spacebar to pause, and press Esc to return to iMovie. You can also move your cursor to display a filmstrip that you can click to skip forward or backward in the project or Event.

To play a selection from the beginning, press \ (the slash that leans to the left). (If you've ever watched directors at work on today's movie sets, you may have noticed that they're constantly watching a monitor to see what things will look like for the audience. You have the same option in iMovie!)

While you're watching video in the Event pane, you may decide that a certain clip has a favorite scene or that another clip has material you don't want, such as Uncle Ed's shadow puppets. (Shudder.) iMovie '09 features *Favorite* and *Rejected* frames, allowing you to view and use your best camera work (and ignore the worst stuff). To mark video, select a range of frames or an entire clip and then click the Mark as Favorite button in the Editing toolbar. Click the Reject button to hide the selected video or frames from view. (You can always unmark a Favorite or Rejected scene using the Unmark button in the Editing toolbar.)

Removing clips from your movie

Don't like a clip? Bah. To banish a clip from your movie, follow these steps

1. **Click the offending clip in the Project pane to select it.**

2. **Press Delete.**

   Alternatively, you can right-click the clip (or a selection you've made by dragging) and choose either Delete Entire Clip or Delete Selection from the menu that appears.

If you remove the wrong clip, don't panic. Instead, use iMovie's Undo feature (press ⌘+Z) to restore it.

Reordering clips in your movie

If Day One of your vacation appears after Day Two, you can easily reorder your clips and stills by dragging them to the proper space in the Project pane. When you take your finger off the mouse, iMovie automatically moves the rest of your movie aside with a minimum of fuss and bother.

Editing clips in iMovie

If a clip has extra seconds of footage at the beginning or end, you don't want that superfluous stuff in your masterpiece. Our favorite video editor gives you the following functions:

✔ **Crop:** Removes unwanted material from a video clip or still image

✔ **Rotate:** Rotates a clip or image on its center axis

✔ **Trim:** Trims frames from a video clip

Before you can edit, however, you have to select a section of a clip:

1. **Click a clip or image in either the Project pane (where changes you make are specific to this project) or the Event pane (where edits you make are reflected in any project using that footage).**

   iMovie displays the clip or image in the monitor.

2. **To select the entire clip or image, simply click it.**

3. **Drag your cursor across the thumbnail to select the section of the media you want to edit. (Note that some editing functions, such as Crop and Rotate, will automatically apply to the entire clip.)**

   The selected region is surrounded by a yellow frame. You're ready to edit that selected part of the clip.

Note the handles that appear at the beginning or ending of the selection. You can make fine changes to the selected section by dragging them.

✔ **To crop:** Click the Crop button in the Edit toolbar to display the frame in the Monitor pane and then click Crop at the top of the Monitor pane. Drag the edges of the frame and the handles to select the section you want to keep. To preview your selection, click the Play button at the top of the monitor. When you're ready, click Done, and everything but the selected region is removed.

✔ **To rotate:** Click the Crop button in the Edit toolbar and then click one of the two rotation buttons (which carry a curved arrow icon). Each click rotates the media 90 degrees in that direction. Click Done when the clip or image is properly oriented.

✔ **To trim:** Choose Edit⇨Trim to Selection. iMovie removes the frames from around the selected video.

Edits that you make to one clip or still image can actually be copied to multiple items! Select the edited clip and click Edit➪Copy from the iMovie menu. Now you can select one or more clips and choose Edit➪Paste Adjustments to apply Video, Audio, or Crop edits. (To apply all three types of edits, just choose All.)

Transitions for the masses

Many iMovie owners approach transitions as *visual bookends:* They merely act as placeholders that appear between video clips. Nothing could be farther from the truth, because judicious use of transitions can make or break a scene. For example, which would you prefer after a wedding ceremony — an abrupt, jarring cut to the reception or a gradual fadeout to the reception?

Today's audiences are sensitive to transitions between scenes. Try not to overuse the same transition. Also weigh the visual impact of a transition carefully.

iMovie includes a surprising array of transitions, including old favorites (such as Fade In and Dissolve) and some nifty stuff you might not be familiar with (such as Cube and Page Curl). To display your transition collection (Figure 13-5), click the Show Transitions button on the Browser toolbar (or press ⌘+4).

To see what a particular transition looks like, move your cursor over the thumbnail to display the transition in miniature.

Adding a transition couldn't be easier: Drag the transition from the list in the Transitions Browser pane and drop it between clips or between a clip and a still image in the Project pane. In iMovie '09, transitions are applied in real time.

Even Gone with the Wind had titles

The last stop on our iMovie Hollywood Features Tour is the Titles Browser, shown in Figure 13-6. You'll find it by clicking the Title button on the Browser toolbar (which bears a big capital T), or by pressing ⌘+3. You can add a title with a still image, but iMovie also includes everything you need to add basic animated text to your movie.

Chapter 13: Making Film History with iMovie

Figure 13-5:
Add transitions for flow between clips in iMovie.

Figure 13-6:
Add titles for your next silent film.

Most of the controls you can adjust are the same for each animation style. You can change the font, the size of the text, and the color of the text. To add a title manually, follow these steps:

1. **Select an animation thumbnail from the Title Browser pane and drag it to the desired spot in the Project pane.**

2. **Click a background thumbnail to select a background for your title.**

3. **Click the Show Fonts button in the monitor window to make any changes to the fonts or text attributes.**

4. **Click in a text box to type your own line of text.**

5. **Click the Play button to preview your title.**

   iMovie displays a preview of the effect in the monitor with the settings that you choose.

6. **Click Done.**

   The title appears in the Project pane.

Sharing Your Finished Classic with Others

Your movie is complete, you've saved it to your hard drive, and now you're wondering where to go from here. Click Share on the application menu bar, and you'll see that iMovie can unleash your movie upon your unsuspecting family and friends (and even the entire world) in a number of ways:

- ✔ **iTunes:** Send your movie to your iTunes Library as a movie.

- ✔ **Media Browser:** Make your iMovie project available within other iLife '09 applications, in five different sizes suited to different display devices. Note that the Media Browser is also available for other Apple applications, like Final Cut Studio, and to third-party applications like Toast Titanium.

- ✔ **YouTube:** Yep, you read right, you can send your iMovie directly to the YouTube Web site! Can it get more convenient than that? (I think not.)

- ✔ **MobileMe Gallery:** Share your movie with the world at large by posting it within a Gallery on your MobileMe Web site. (I provide more MobileMe details to chew on in Chapter 9.)

- ✔ **Export Movie:** Create a copy of your movie on your hard drive in one of five different sizes.

✔ **Export using QuickTime:** Create a QuickTime movie with your project using the QuickTime encoding engine (allowing greater control over the export process and the attributes of the finished movie file).

If you use this option, any computer with an installed copy of QuickTime can display your movies, and you can use QuickTime movies in Keynote presentations as well.

✔ **Export to Final Cut XML:** If you'd like to transfer your iMovie '09 project to Final Cut Pro, use this option to create a compatible XML file.

When you choose a sharing option, iMovie displays the video quality for the option and makes automatic changes to the movie attributes. (For example, choosing Tiny reduces the finished movie as far as possible in file size, and the audio is reduced to mono instead of stereo.)

If you're worried about permanently reducing the quality of your project by sharing it in a smaller size, fear not! When you choose a sharing option to export your movie, your original project remains on your hard drive, unchanged, so you can share a better-quality version at any time in the future!

Chapter 14

iDVD — Your DVD Movie Factory

*H*ow does the old adage go? Oh, yes, it's like this:

> Any DVD movie must be a pain to create. You'll need a ton of money for software, too. And you'll have to take hours of training that will cause your brain to explode.

Funny thing is, *DVD authoring* — designing and creating a DVD movie — really was like that for many years. Only video professionals could afford the software and tackle the training needed to master all the intricacies of DVD Menu design.

Take one guess as to the company that changed all that. (No, it wasn't Coca-Cola.) Apple's introduction of iDVD was (quite literally) a revolution in DVD authoring. Suddenly you, your kids, and Aunt Harriet could all design and burn DVD movies and picture slideshows. Dear reader, this iDVD thing is *huge*.

Plus, you'll quickly find out that iDVD is tightly connected to all the other slices of your digital hub. In plain English, you can pull content from iTunes, iPhoto, and iMovie as easily as a politician makes promises. And that, friends and neighbors, is the quintessential definition of *cool*.

In this chapter, I show you how your iMac can take on Hollywood as well as how you can produce a DVD movie with content that's as good as any you'd rent at the video store!

Hey, Where's the Complex Window?

Figure 14-1 shows iDVD in all its glory. You have to supply your own digital video clips, background audio, and digital photographs, of course.

Menu display

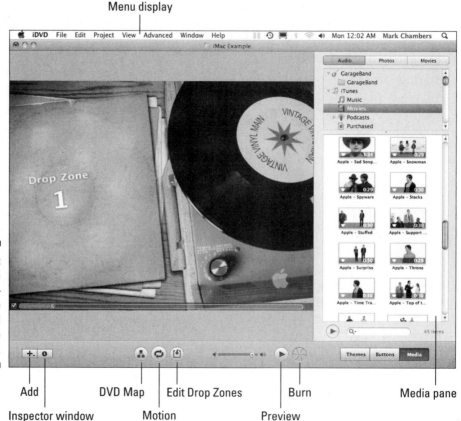

Figure 14-1:
iDVD is a
jewel —
easy to
use and
powerful, to
boot.

Add   DVD Map Edit Drop Zones   Burn   Media pane

Inspector window   Motion   Preview

Take a moment to appreciate iDVD — no secondary windows to fiddle with or silly palettes strung out everywhere. (Can you tell that I've had my fill of old-style DVD authoring applications?) Allow me to list the highlights of the iDVD window:

 ✔ **Menu display:** This section takes up the largest part of the iDVD window, with good reason. You create your project here. In this case, *Menu* refers to your DVD Menu, not the menu at the top of your iMac's display.

✔ **Media pane:** You add video, still images, and audio to your project from here, as well as tweak and fine-tune things. The Media pane actually comprises three separate panes. To choose a new pane, click one of these buttons at the bottom of the screen:

  • *Themes:* You apply themes (such as Travel Cards, Wedding White, and Baby Mobile) to your DVD Menu to give it a certain look and feel.

  • *Buttons:* These options apply to the item currently selected, such as drop shadows on your text titles or the appearance of your Menu buttons.

  • *Media:* From here, you can add media items, such as video clips and photos, to your Menu.

✔ **Add button:** From this pop-up menu (which sports a dapper plus sign), you can choose one of three types of buttons to add to a project. The choices are

  • *Add Submenu:* Choose this item to add a new submenu button to your DVD Menu. The person using your DVD Menu can click a button to display a new submenu that can include additional movies or slideshows. (If that sounds like ancient Greek, hang on. All becomes clearer later in the chapter, in the section "Adding movies.")

  A Menu can hold only a maximum of 12 buttons (depending on the theme you choose), so submenus let you pack more content on your DVD. (Older versions of the application allowed only six buttons, so don't feel too cheated.) Anyway, each submenu you create can hold another 12 buttons.

  • *Add Movie:* Yep, this is the most popular button in the whole shooting match. Click this menu item to add a new movie clip to your Menu.

  • *Add Slideshow:* If you want to add a slideshow to your DVD — say, using photos from your hard drive or pictures from your iPhoto library — click this menu item.

✔ **Inspector button:** Click this button to display the Inspector window for the current Menu or a highlighted object. From this window, you can change the look of an individual submenu button or an entire Menu.

✔ **DVD Map:** Click the Map button to display the organizational chart for your DVD Menu. Each button and submenu that you add to your top-level DVD Menu is displayed here, and you can jump directly to a particular item by double-clicking it. Use this road map to help design the layout of your DVD Menu system or to get to a particular item quickly. To return to the Menu display, click the Map button again.

✔ **Motion:** Click this button to start or stop the animation cycle used with the current iDVD theme. The animation repeats (just as it will on your finished DVD) until you click the Motion button again.

Need a visual indicator of the length of your Menu's animation cycle? Click View➪Show Motion Playhead to display the animation *playhead*, which moves below the Menu display to indicate where you are in the animation cycle. As you can with other playheads in the iLife suite, you can click and drag the diamond-shaped playhead button to move anywhere in the animation cycle.

✔ **Edit Drop Zones:** This button allows you to edit the look and contents of a drop zone on your Menu. (Don't worry, I explain more about drop zones in the sidebar titled, "Taking advantage of drop zones," later in this chapter.)

✔ **Preview:** To see how your DVD Menu project looks when burned to a DVD, click Preview. You get a truly nifty on-screen remote control that you can use to navigate your DVD Menu, just as if you were watching your DVD on a standard DVD player. To exit Preview mode, click the Stop button on the remote control.

✔ **Burn:** Oh, yeah, you know what this one is for — recording your completed DVD movie to a blank disc.

That's the lot! Time to get down to the step-by-step business of making movies.

Starting a New DVD Project

When you launch iDVD for the first time (or if you close all iDVD windows), you get the sporty dialog box shown in Figure 14-2. Take a moment to discover more about these four choices.

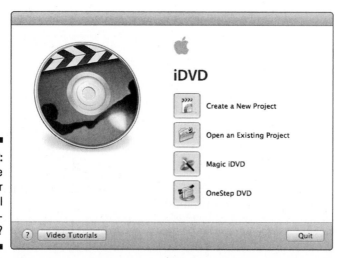

Figure 14-2: Will that be create or edit, manual or automatic?

Creating a new project

If you choose Create a New Project, iDVD prompts you to type a name for your new DVD project and to set a location where the project files should be saved. By default, the very reasonable choice is your Documents folder. You also get to choose whether your project will display in a Standard (full-screen) aspect ratio of 4:3 or a Widescreen aspect ratio of 16:9. If you've been watching DVD movies for some time, you probably recognize these two terms.

You'll probably crave Widescreen format if you have a widescreen TV — go figure — but both formats will display on both types of televisions, complete with those black bars we all know and love at the top and bottom (or left and right sides) of the screen.

Click Create, and the iDVD window appears in all its glory.

Opening an existing project

If you've used iDVD and had a DVD project open the last time you quit the application, iDVD automatically loads the DVD project you were working on. However, you can open any DVD you've created by clicking Open an Existing Project. (To choose a different existing project from the iDVD window, press ⌘+O or choose File➪Open Recent.)

Automating the whole darn process

If you're a fan of click-it-and-forget-it (or you're in a hurry), you can throw caution to the wind and allow iDVD to create your latest epic for you! iDVD offers two automated methods of creating a DVD movie disc.

Using OneStep DVD

With OneStep, iDVD does almost all the work automatically, by using the media clips and photos that you specify. To allow iDVD to help you create a movie, click the OneStep DVD button on the top-level menu (refer to Figure 14-2). If you've already opened a project, choose File➪OneStep DVD from the application's menu bar (to import clips directly from your FireWire mini-DV camera) or OneStep DVD from Movie (to select a clip to import from your hard drive). OneStep DVD does not work with camcorders that use a USB connection to your iMac. I tell you more about the OneStep DVD feature later, in the section "A Word about Automation."

Using Magic iDVD

Magic iDVD is the newcomer on the block, and it falls neatly between total automation (with OneStep DVD) and total manual control. Click the Magic iDVD button on the top-level menu (refer to Figure 14-2). If you've already opened a project, you can choose File➪Magic iDVD from the menu bar to choose a theme, drop specific movies and specific photos into filmstrips, and choose an audio track.

In contrast to OneStep DVD, you get to preview the finished product. If it's to your liking, you can choose to either burn the disc directly or create a full-blown iDVD project with the results. *Sweet.*

You find out more about the new Magic iDVD feature later, in the section "A Word about Automation."

Creating a DVD from Scratch

Doing things the old-fashioned, creative, and manual way (following the examples in this section) involves four basic steps:

1. **Design the DVD Menu.**

   Choose a theme and any necessary buttons or links.

2. **Add media.**

   You can drag movie files from iMovie, still images from iPhoto, and music from iTunes.

3. **Tweak.**

   Adjust and fine-tune your DVD Menu settings.

4. **Finish things up.**

   Preview and burn your DVD or save it to your hard drive.

Choosing just the right theme

The first step to take when manually designing a new DVD Menu system is to add a theme. In the iDVD world, a *theme* is a preset package that helps determine the appearance and visual appeal of your DVD Menu, including a background image, Menu animation, an audio track, and a group of settings for text fonts and button styles.

Taking advantage of drop zones

Most of Apple's animated themes include special bordered areas marked as drop zones. These locations have nothing to do with skydiving; rather, a *drop zone* is a placeholder in the Menu that can hold a single video clip or photograph. When you drag a video clip or an image to a drop zone, that clip or picture is added to the animation in Apple's theme! Think about that for a moment; I know I did. You can actually personalize a Hollywood-quality animated DVD Menu with *your own photos and video!*

Most of the themes included with iDVD include at least one drop zone, and some are practically jam-packed with drop zones. For example, the amazing Forever theme has a whopping six drop zones! If you think a Menu looks just fine without anything in a drop zone, however, you don't have to put anything there. The words *Drop Zone* disappear when you preview or burn your DVD. (Empty frames do tend to look a bit silly in some themes, though.)

To add a video clip or image to a drop zone, simply drag the clip or photo from a Finder window and drop it on the desired drop zone. You can also drag clips or photos from other sources, including the Movies and Photos panes in iDVD's Media pane, the iMovie window, or the iPhoto window (Apple is anything but strict on these matters).Remember, drop zones don't act as links or buttons to other content; the stuff you add to a Menu's drop zones appears only as part of the theme's animation cycle. You can even drag an iPhoto event or album to a drop zone, and it will continuously cycle through the images. *Wowzers!*

To see all the drop zones at one time (without cycling through the animation), click the Edit Drop Zones button at the bottom center of the iDVD window; when you do, you see a thumbnail display of each zone. You can drag items to these thumbnails or jump right to one in the animation by clicking the thumbnail. To delete the contents of a drop zone, click the thumbnail in the editor and press Delete.

If you're adding something to a dynamic drop zone (which disappears and reappears during the menu animation cycle), click the Motion button to activate the animation and then click it again to stop the animation cycle. Now click and drag the scrubber bar until the desired drop zone is in view. To delete the contents of a drop zone, Control-click (or right-click) the drop zone and choose Clear.

iDVD helps those of us who are graphically challenged by including a wide range of professionally designed themes for all sorts of occasions, ranging from old standbys such as weddings, birthdays, and vacations to more generic themes with the accent on action, friendship, and technology. To view the included themes, click the Themes button in the lower-right corner of the iDVD window (see Figure 14-3).

To choose a theme for your project — or to see what a theme looks like on your Menu — click any thumbnail and watch iDVD update the Menu display.

Figure 14-3:
Select a
new theme
from the
Themes
pane.

If you decide while creating your DVD Menu that you need a different theme, you can change themes at any time. iDVD won't lose a single button or video clip that you add to your DVD Menu. You'll be amazed at how the look and sound of your DVD Menu completely change with just the click of a theme thumbnail.

Adding movies

Drop zones and themes are cool, but most folks want to add video to their DVDs. To accomplish this, iDVD uses *buttons* as links to your video clips. In fact, some iDVD Movie buttons display a preview of the video they'll display! To play the video on a DVD player, select the Movie button with the remote control, just as you do for a commercial DVD.

To add a Movie button, drag a QuickTime movie file from the Finder and drop it onto your DVD Menu display. (Only MPEG-4 QuickTime movies and DV streams are supported — MPEG-1 and MPEG-2 movie clips may be rejected or automatically converted, or they may even be added without audio.) Alternatively, click the Add button and choose Add Movie from the pop-up menu.

iDVD and iMovie are soul mates, so you can also display the iDVD Media pane and then click Movies from the pop-up menu. Now you can drag clips from your Movies folder.

No matter the source of the clip, when you drop it onto your DVD Menu, iDVD adds a Movie button, as you can see in Figure 14-4. Note that some buttons appear as text links rather than actual buttons. The appearance of a Movie button in your DVD Menu is determined by the theme you choose.

A Movie button doesn't have to stay where iDVD places it! By default, iDVD aligns buttons and text objects using an invisible grid, but if you don't want such order imposed on your creativity, just drag the object where you'd like it to be to turn on Free Positioning. (You can also right-click the object and select the Free Positioning item from the menu that appears.) iDVD provides cool new automatic guides that help you align objects when you're using Free Positioning! You'll see them as yellow lines that appear when objects are aligned along a vertical or horizontal plane.

You can have up to 12 buttons on your iDVD Menu (the theme you choose determines the maximum number of buttons you can add). To add more content than 12 buttons allow, add a submenu by clicking the Add button and choosing Add Submenu from the pop-up menu. Now you can click the submenu button to jump to that screen and drag up to another 12 movie files into it.

Figure 14-4:
A new Movie button appears on your pristine DVD Menu.

A word on image dimensions

For best playback results on a standard TV, make sure that your background image has the same dimensions as standard digital video — 640 x 480 pixels. If the dimensions of your image don't match the dimensions of digital video, iDVD will stretch or shrink the image to fit, which is likely to have undesirable effects. When your image is stretched and skewed to fit the DVD Menu, Aunt Harriet might end up looking like Shrek.

You can use QuickTime player or iPhoto to change the dimensions of your background image for import into iDVD. For example, you can use the iPhoto crop feature to alter the overall shape of the image and then resize it within iPhoto. Use the Size setting when you export the image from iPhoto and then save the

file in the Pictures folder located in your Home folder so that you can find it easily later. (For more on working in iPhoto, see Chapter 12.)

If you enjoy a cutting-edge widescreen (16:9) or HD (high-definition) TV display, you won't have the standard TV dimension restriction of 640 x 480 pixels. And because iDVD supports HD video and 16:9 video with a number of widescreen themes, be prepared to kiss the phrases *pan-and-scan* and *full-screen* goodbye and forget about the Show TV Safe Area feature. If your completed DVD projects are purely for your own enjoyment, that's a great idea. However, don't forget that if you distribute your discs to others with old-fashioned TVs dating back to the archaic '80s and '90s, they might not be pleased with what they see!

Keep your target audience in mind while you create your DVD. Standard TV sets have a different *aspect ratio* (height to width) and *resolution* (number of scan lines on the screen) than a digital video clip, and a standard TV isn't as precise in focusing that image on the tube. If you selected the Standard aspect ratio when you created the project, you can make sure that your DVD content looks great on a standard TV screen by following these steps:

1. **Click View on the old-fashioned iDVD menu (the one at the top of the screen).**

2. **Choose the Show TV Safe Area command.**

   You can also press the convenient ⌘+T shortcut. iDVD adds a smaller rectangle within the iDVD window to mark the screen dimensions of a standard TV.

If you take care that your Menu buttons and (most of) your background image fit within this smaller rectangle, you're assured that folks with a standard television can enjoy your work. To turn off the TV Safe Area rectangle, press ⌘+T again.

If your entire family is blessed with a fleet of HD TVs (or you chose the Widescreen aspect ratio for this project), leave the Show TV Safe Area option off. Today's widescreen displays can handle just about any orientation.

Great, now my audience demands a slideshow

Many Mac owners don't realize that you don't have to use iDVD just for video clips. In fact, you can use the Slideshow buttons to add a group of digital photos to your DVD Menu . The Slideshow buttons allow the viewer to play back a series of digital photographs — set to music if you like. iDVD handles everything for you, so there's no tricky timing to figure out or weird scripts to write. Just click the Add button at the bottom of the iDVD window and choose Add Slideshow. iDVD places a Slideshow button on your DVD Menu.

After the Slideshow button is on tap, add the content — in this case, by choosing the images that iDVD adds to your DVD Menu. Follow these steps to select your slideshow images:

1. **Double-click the Slideshow Menu button — the one you just added to the Menu — to open the Slideshow display (see Figure 14-5).**

2. **Click the Media button (bottom right of the screen).**

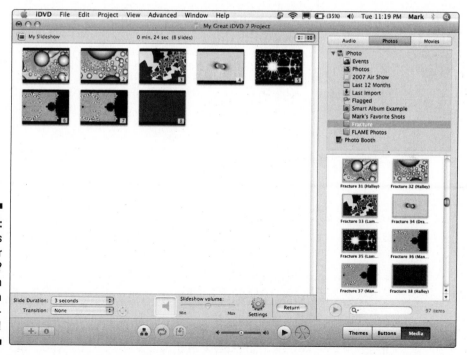

Figure 14-5: Who needs a projector anymore? iDVD can create a great slideshow!

3. **Click the Photos tab (top right of the screen) to display your iPhoto library and photo albums.**

4. **Drag your favorite image thumbnails from the Photos list and drop them into the My Slideshow window.**

   You can also drag images straight from a Finder window or the iPhoto window itself. (Those Apple folks are sooooo predictable.)

5. **Drag around the photos in the My Slideshow window to set their order of appearance in your slideshow.**

   Note that you can click on the Slide Duration pop-up menu to change the length of time that images are displayed.

6. **To add audio to these pictures, drag your favorite audio file from the Finder and drop it in the Audio well in the My Slideshow window.**

   The *Audio well* is the box bearing the speaker icon, next to the volume control below the My Slideshow window.

   Alternatively, click the Audio tab to select an audio track from your iTunes library, iTunes playlists, or GarageBand creations.

7. **Click the Return button to return to your DVD Menu.**

If you're using a Menu with animated buttons that display an image (rather than text buttons), you can choose which image you want to appear on the Slideshow button. Click the Slideshow button that you added and see the slider that appears above the Slideshow button. Drag this slider to scroll through the images you added. When you find the image that you want to use for the Slideshow button in the DVD Menu, click the Slideshow button again to save your changes.

Now for the music . . .

Most of the Apple-supplied themes already have their own background music, so you might not even need to add music to your DVD Menu. However, if you want to change the existing background music (or if your DVD Menu currently doesn't have any music), adding your own audio to the current Menu is child's play!

1. **Click the Media button.**

2. **Click the Audio tab to reveal the musical Shangri-La, as shown in Figure 14-6.**

3. **Drag an audio file from the iTunes playlist or GarageBand folder display and drop it on the Menu background.**

   iDVD accepts every sound format that you can use for importing and encoding in iTunes: AIFF, MP3, AAC, Apple Lossless, and WAV audio files.

4. **Click the Motion button (labeled in Figure 14-1) to watch your DVD Menu animation cycle set to the new background audio.**

5. **Click the Motion button again to stop the animation and return to serious work.**

Figure 14-6:
You do a lot of fine-tuning from the Audio pane.

Giving Your DVD the Personal Touch

You can easily make changes to the default settings provided with the theme you chose. iDVD offers all sorts of controls that allow you to change the appearance and behavior of buttons, text, and the presentation of your content. In this section, I show you how to cast out iDVD's (perfectly good) defaults and then tweak things to perfection.

Using Uncle Morty for your DVD Menu background

Hey, Uncle Morty might not be a supermodel, but he has birthdays and anniversaries, and iDVD is more than happy to accommodate you in documenting those milestones! Follow these steps to change the background of your DVD Menu:

1. **Click the Inspector button.**

2. **Get an image using one of the following methods:**

   • *Drag an image from the Finder* and drop it into the Background well.

   • *Drag the image directly into the Menu display.*

   • *To use an image from your iPhoto library,* click the Media button and click the Photos tab, and then drag the desired image into the Menu display.

   iDVD updates the DVD Menu to reflect your new background choice.

Adding your own titles

The one tweak you'll probably have to perform in every iDVD project is changing titles. Unfortunately, the default labels provided by iDVD are pretty lame, and they appear in two important places:

✔ **Menu title:** Your large main title usually appears at the top of the DVD Menu.

✔ **Button captions:** Each Submenu, Movie, and Slideshow button that you add to your Menu has its own title.

To change the text in your Menu title or the titles below your buttons, follow these steps:

1. **Select the text by clicking it.**

2. **Click it again to edit it.**

   A rectangle with a cursor appears to indicate that you can now edit the text.

3. **Type the new text and press Return to save the change.**

Changing buttons like a highly paid professional

Customizing Movie buttons? You can do it with aplomb! Follow these steps:

1. **Click Buttons.**

2. **Click any Movie button from the DVD Menu to select it.**

   A slider appears above the button, which you can drag to set the thumbnail picture for that button in your DVD Menu. (Naturally, this is only for animated buttons, not text buttons.)

   Enable the Movie check box to animate the button.

3. **To create a Movie button with a still image, drag a picture from a Finder window or the Media pane and drop it on top of the button.**

4. **To adjust the properties for the button, click the Inspector button.**

Table 14-1 describes the button properties — note that some properties won't appear for text buttons.

Table 14-1	Button Settings You Can Customize
Movie Button Property	*What It Does*
Label Font	Changes the label font, text size, color, and attributes.
Label Attributes	Specifies the position of the label and whether it has a shadow.
Custom Thumbnail	Drag an image to the Custom Thumbnail well. For Slideshow buttons, drag the Thumbnail slider to select the image that will appear on the button.
Transition	Determines the transition that occurs when the button is clicked (before the action occurs).
Size	Adjusts the size of the button. Move the slider to the right to increase the button size.

Giving motion to your creation

Earlier in this chapter, you find out how to use a different image for your background (in the section titled, "Using Uncle Morty for your DVD Menu background"), but what about using an animated background? You can use any QuickTime movie from your iMovie library (including those you've taken with your iMac's iSight camera) to animate your DVD Menu background! Didn't I tell you that this iDVD thing was *huge*?

Keep in mind that your background movie should be a short clip; 20–30 seconds is optimal. A clip with a fade-in at the beginning and a fade-out at the end is the best choice because iDVD loops your background clip continuously, and your animated background flows seamlessly behind your Menu.

I'm not talking drop zones here. (See the sidebar "Taking advantage of drop zones," earlier in this chapter, for an explanation of drop zones.) You can add a movie to a drop zone, of course, but by using a movie clip as a background, you're replacing the entire animation sequence rather than just a single area of the background. Drop zones also don't provide audio, whereas a clip background does include the clip audio.

Follow these steps to add a new animated background:

1. **Click your old friend, the Inspector button.**

   Make sure that no individual objects are highlighted so that the Inspector window displays the Menu properties instead.

2. **Drag a movie from the Finder and drop it into the Background well.**

   You can click the Movies tab in the Media pane to instantly display your iMovie collection.

3. **Click the Motion button in the iDVD window to try out your new background.**

4. **Click the Motion button again to stop the animation cycle.**

Previewing Your Masterpiece

Figure 14-7 captures the elusive Preview remote control — truly an awesome sight. When you click Preview, the Media pane disappears, and your DVD Menu appears exactly as it will on the finished DVD.

Ah, but appearances aren't everything: You can also use your DVD Menu! Click the buttons on the remote control to simulate the remote on your DVD player or think outside the box and click a Menu button directly with your mouse pointer. iDVD presents the video clip, runs the slideshow, or jumps to a submenu, just as it will with the completed disc.

This is a great time to test-drive a project before you burn it to disc. To make sure you don't waste a blank DVD, make certain that everything you expect to happen actually happens. Nothing worse than discovering that

Aunt Edna's slideshow from her Hong Kong trip actually displays your family's summer trip to the zoo (whoops). If you made a mistake or something needs tweaking, click the Preview button again, and you're back to the iDVD window proper, where you can edit or fine-tune your project.

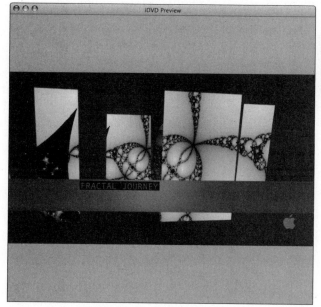

Figure 14-7:
Preview
mode — an
incredible
simulation,
indeed.

 iDVD allows you to save your project as a standard Mac OS X *disc image* rather than as a simple project file (or a physical DVD) — you can use Apple's Disk Utility to open and mount the disc image as if it were a burned disc. If you move the disc image to another Mac with a SuperDrive, you can use Disk Utility to burn it to disc using that machine. To save an iDVD project as a disc image, choose File⇨Save as Disc Image (or press ⌘+Shift+R). To save your project as a standard VIDEO_TS folder (suitable for burning with another video-editing or DVD recording application), choose File⇨Save as VIDEO_TS Folder.

 Interested in tweaking settings across your entire project? Perhaps you'd like to reduce the time it takes to create and edit your DVD or switch video modes from NTSC to PAL for a DVD that's to be sent overseas. If you'd like to view or change the overall settings for your entire DVD, click Project⇨Project Info to display the Project Info dialog. Heck, you can even switch aspect ratios or change the project name. Thanks, Apple!

A Word about Automation

At the beginning of the chapter, I mention the easy way to produce an iDVD disc or project, using either OneStep DVD (for complete automation) or Magic iDVD (for partial automation). In this section, I provide you with the details.

One-click paradise with OneStep DVD

If you're in a hurry to create a DVD from clips on your DV camcorder and you don't mind losing your creative input, OneStep DVD is just the ticket. In short, iDVD allows you to plug in your FireWire-equipped mini-DV camcorder, answer a question or two, and then sit back while the application does *all* the work. iDVD imports the DV clips, creates a basic Menu design, and burns the disc automatically! (Again, note that OneStep DVD doesn't support USB camcorders.)

Using OneStep DVD will appeal to any iMac owner. Why not produce a DVD right after a wedding or birthday that you can give as a gift? Photographers who cover those same special events might consider selling a DVD made with OneStep DVD. If you happen to capture something incredibly unique — such as a UFO landing or an honest politician — you can use OneStep DVD to create an instant backup of the clips on your DV camcorder. You could even keep your friends and family up-to-date with the progress of your vacation by sending them a daily DVD of your exploits! (You gotta admit, even Grandma would consider that eminently *sassy!*)

Follow these steps to start the OneStep DVD process:

1. **Click the OneStep DVD button on the iDVD top-level menu (refer to Figure 14-2).**

   Alternatively, choose File⇨OneStep DVD.

   iDVD displays the dialog shown in Figure 14-8.

Figure 14-8:
Connect
your DV
camcorder,
and
OneStep
DVD does
the rest.

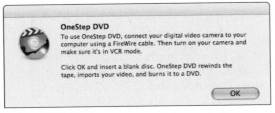

OneStep DVD
To use OneStep DVD, connect your digital video camera to your computer using a FireWire cable. Then turn on your camera and make sure it's in VCR mode.

Click OK and insert a blank disc. OneStep DVD rewinds the tape, imports your video, and burns it to a DVD.

OK

If you want to use OneStep DVD with an existing movie on your iMac's hard drive, choose File⇨OneStep DVD from Movie instead. iDVD prompts you for the video file to use.

2. **Following the prompts, connect the FireWire cable from your DV camcorder; then turn on the camcorder and set it to VCR mode.**

3. **Click OK.**

4. **Load a blank DVD.**

Exercising control with Magic iDVD

Got a little extra time? For those who prefer to make just a few choices and let iDVD do the rest, the new Magic iDVD feature just plain rocks! However, you can't import clips directly from your mini-DV camcorder as you can with OneStep DVD; instead, you select one of the following:

✔ **An iDVD theme**

✔ **Video clips** you've already created with iMovie or dragged from the Finder (perfect for use with a USB 2.0 DV camcorder)

✔ **Photos** from your iPhoto library or dragged from the Finder

✔ **Audio** from your iTunes playlist or dragged from the Finder

Follow these steps to start the OneStep DVD process:

1. **Click the Magic iDVD button on the iDVD top-level dialog (refer to Figure 14-2).**

   iDVD displays the window you see in Figure 14-9.

2. **Click in the DVD Title box and type a name for your disc (or project).**

3. **Click to select a theme from the Theme strip.**

4. **Click the Movies tab and drag the desired clips into the Drop Movies Here strip.**

5. **To add a slideshow, click the Photos tab and drag the desired photos into the Drop Photos Here strip.**

6. **To add audio for your slideshow, click the Audio tab and drag the desired song into the Drop Photos Here strip (a speaker icon appears in the first cell of the strip to indicate that you've added a soundtrack).**

7. **Click Preview to see a preview of the finished project, complete with remote control. To exit Preview mode, click Exit.**

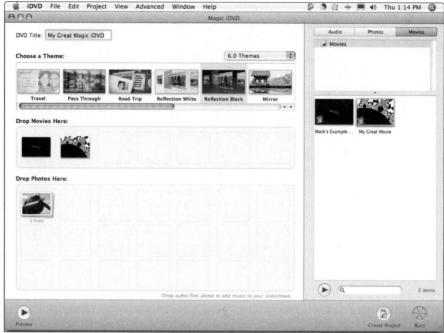

Figure 14-9:
With Magic
iDVD,
you make
some basic
choices,
and iDVD
does the
work.

8. **To open the project in its current form in the main iDVD window, click Create Project.**

9. **To record your completed project directly to DVD, load a blank DVD and click Burn.**

To return to the iDVD main window at any time, just click the Close button on the Magic iDVD window.

Recording a Finished Project to a Shiny Disc

When you're ready to record your next Oscar-winning documentary on family behaviors during vacation, just follow these simple words:

1. **Click the Burn button at the bottom of the iDVD window.**

   I have to admit, the Burn button that appears has to be my favorite single control in all my 20+ years of computing! It looks powerful, it looks sexy . . . it wants to *burn*. (Sorry about that.)

2. **After iDVD asks you to insert a blank DVD-R into the SuperDrive, load a single or dual-layer blank DVD-R, DVD-RW, DVD+R, or DVD+RW (depending on the media your Mac can handle).**

Your SuperDrive might be able to burn and read a DVD+R, DVD-RW, or DVD+RW, but what about your DVD player? Keep in mind that only DVD-Rs are likely to work in older DVD players. The latest generation of DVD players is likely DVD+R compatible as well, but I've seen only a handful of DVD players that can handle rewriteable media at the time of this writing. Therefore, remember the destination for the discs you burn and choose your media accordingly.

After a short pause, iDVD begins burning the DVD. The application keeps you updated with a progress bar.

When the disc is finished, you're ready to load it into your favorite local DVD player or back into your iMac and enjoy your work using Apple's DVD Player.

Either way, it's all good!

Chapter 15

Recording Your Hits with GarageBand

Do you dream of making music? I've always wanted to join a band, but I never devoted the time nor learned to play the guitar. You know the drill: Those rock stars struggled for years to gain the upper hand over an instrument, practicing for untold hours, memorizing chords, and. . . . Wait a second. I almost forgot. You don't need to do *any* of that now!

Apple's GarageBand '09 lets a musical wanna-be (like yours truly) make music with an iMac — complete with a driving bass line, funky horns, and perfect drums that never miss a beat. In fact, the thousands of prerecorded loops on tap in this awesome application allow you to design your music to match that melody running through your head, from techno to jazz to alternative rock.

Oh, and did I mention that you can also use GarageBand '09 to produce podcasts? That's right! You can record your voice and easily create your own show, and then share it with others from your iWeb site! Heck, add photos if you like. You'll be the talk of your family and friends and maybe even your Mac user group.

This chapter explains everything you need to know to create your first song. I also show you how to import your hit record into iTunes so you can listen to it on your iPod with a big silly grin on your face (like I do) or add it to your next iMovie or iDVD project.

Don't be too smug when you think of all that practicing and hard work you missed out on. What a shame!

Shaking Hands with Your Band

As you can see in Figure 15-1, the GarageBand window isn't complex at all, and that's good design. In this section, I list the most important controls so that you know your Play button from your Loop Browser button.

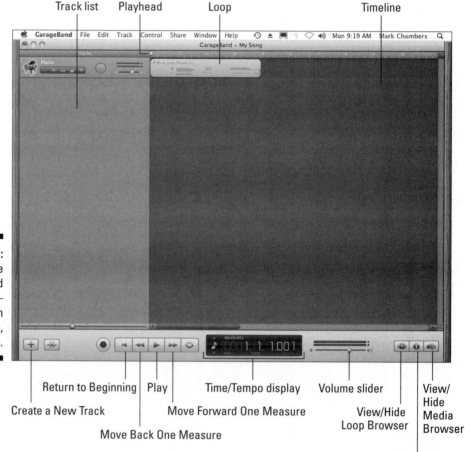

Figure 15-1: The GarageBand window — edged in wood grain, no less.

Your music-making machine includes

✔ **Track list:** In GarageBand, a *track* is a discrete instrument that you set up to play one part of your song. For example, a track in a classical piece for string quartet would have four tracks — one each for violin, viola, cello, and bass. The track list contains all the tracks in your song arranged so that you can easily see and modify them, like the rows in a spreadsheet. A track begins in the list, stretching out to the right all the way to the end of the song. As you can see in the upper left of Figure 15-1, I already have one track defined — a Grand Piano.

If you're creating a podcast, a *Podcast artwork track* can also appear. Video podcasts can include a movie track as well.

✔ **Timeline:** This scrolling area holds the loops (see the following bullet) that you add or record, allowing you to move and edit them easily. When a song plays, the Timeline scrolls to give you a visual look at your music. (Bear with me; you'll understand that cryptic statement in a page or two.)

✔ **Loop:** This is a prerecorded clip of an instrument being played in a specific style and tempo. Loops are the building blocks of your song. You can drag loops from the Loop Browser to a track and literally build a bass line or a guitar solo. (It's a little like adding video clips in iMovie to build a film.)

✔ **Playhead:** This vertical line is a moving indicator that shows you the current position in your song while it scrolls by in the Timeline. You can drag the playhead to a new location at any time. The playhead also acts like the insertion cursor in a word processing application: If you insert a section of a song or a loop from the Clipboard, it appears at the current location of the playhead. (More on copying and inserting loops later, so don't panic.)

✔ **Create a New Track button:** Click this button to add a new track to your song.

✔ **Track Info button:** If you need to display the instrument used in a track, click the track to select it and then click this button. You can also control settings, such as Echo and Reverb, from the Edit pane of the Track Info display.

✔ **View/Hide Loop Browser button:** Click the button with the striking eye icon to display the Loop Browser at the bottom of the window; click it again to close it. You can see more of your tracks at a time without scrolling by closing the Loop Browser.

✔ **View/Hide Media Browser button:** Click this button (which bears icons of a filmstrip, slide, and musical note) to display the media browser at the right side of the window; click it again to close it. By closing the media browser, you'll see more of your tracks. If you're already familiar with iDVD, iWeb, or iMovie, you recognize this pane in the GarageBand window; it allows you to add media (in this case, digital song files, still images or video clips) to your GarageBand project for use in a podcast or as iPhone ringtones.

✔ **Return to Beginning button:** Clicking this button immediately moves the playhead back to the beginning of the Timeline.

✔ **Move Back/Forward One Measure buttons:** To move quickly through your song by jumping to the previous or next measure, click the corresponding button.

✔ **Play button:** Hey, old friend! At last, a control that you've probably used countless times before — and it works just like the same control on your audio CD player. Click Play, and GarageBand begins playing your entire song. Notice that the Play button turns blue. To pause the music, click Play again; the button loses that sexy blue sheen and the playhead stops immediately.

✔ **Time/Tempo display:** This cool-looking LCD display shows you the current playhead position in seconds.

You can click the icon at the left of the display to choose other modes, such as

- **Measures** (to display the current measure and mark the beat)

- **Chord** (to display note and chord names)

- **Project** (to show or change the key, tempo, and signature for the song).

✔ **Volume slider:** Here's another familiar face. Just drag the slider to raise or lower the volume.

Of course, more controls are scattered around the GarageBand window, but these are the main controls used to compose a song . . . which is the next stop!

Composing and Podcasting Made Easy

In this section, I cover the basics of composition in GarageBand, working from the very beginning. Follow along with this running example:

1. **Close all existing GarageBand windows.**

   GarageBand displays the top-level New Project dialog.

2. **Click New Project on the list at the left.**

3. **Click the Piano icon and click Choose.**

   GarageBand displays the New Project dialog, as shown in Figure 15-2.

   By choosing the Piano, my new GarageBand project will have one track already in place — a grand piano. If you choose Electric Guitar or Voice, you'll have a project automatically created with an electric guitar track or male and female voice tracks. To create a completely empty project, choose Loops.

Figure 15-2: Start creating your new song here.

4. **Type a name for your new song and then drag the Tempo slider to select the beats per minute (bpm).**

   A GarageBand song can have only one *tempo* (or speed) throughout, expressed as beats per minute.

5. **If you want to adjust the settings for your song, you can select the**

   - *Time signature (the Time box)*

   - *Key (the Key box)*

   If you're new to music *theory* (the rules and syntax by which music is created and written), just use the defaults. Most of the toe-tappin' tunes that you and I are familiar with fit right in with these settings.

6. **Click the Create button.**

   You see the window shown in Figure 15-1. (The Blues Jazz Piano 01 loop in Figure 15-1 — which I show you how to add in the next section — is an example of a typical loop.)

Adding tracks

Although I'm not a musician, I am a music lover, and I know that many classical composers approached a new work in the same way you approach a new song in GarageBand: by envisioning the instruments that they wanted to hear. (I imagine Mozart and Beethoven would've been thrilled to use GarageBand, but I think they did a decent job with pen and paper, too.)

In fact, GarageBand '09 introduces a *Songwriting* project (also available from the top-level New Project dialog). When you choose the Songwriting project, GarageBand presents you with a full set of four instrument tracks, plus a real instrument track for your voice. (More on software versus real instrument tracks in a page or two.) You're instantly ready to start adding loops and recording your own voice!

If you've followed along to this point, you've noticed two problems with your GarageBand window:

✔ **There's no keyboard.** You can record the contents of a software instrument track by "playing" the keyboard, clicking the keys with your mouse. (As you might imagine, this isn't the best solution.) If you're a musician, the best method of recording your own notes is with a MIDI instrument, which I discuss later in the chapter. For now, you can display the keyboard window by pressing ⌘+K. If the keyboard window is on the screen and you don't need it, banish the window by clicking the Close button.

Even if you're not interested in the "point-and-click" keyboard, GarageBand offers a musical typing keyboard, where you press the keys on your keyboard to simulate the keys on a musical keyboard. (Hey, if you don't have a MIDI instrument, at least it's better than nothing.) To display the musical typing keyboard window, press Shift+⌘+K.

✔ **The example song has only one track.** If you want to write the next classical masterpiece for Grand Piano, that's fine. Otherwise, on the GarageBand menu bar, choose Track➪Delete Track to start with a clean slate. (I know, I could have started with a Loops project, but this way you get to see how to delete a track.)

These are the five kinds of tracks you can use in GarageBand '09:

✔ **Software instrument tracks:** These tracks aren't audio recordings. Rather, they're mathematically precise algorithms that your Mac *renders* (or builds) to fit your needs. If you have a MIDI instrument connected to your Mac, you can create your own software instrument tracks. (More on MIDI instruments later in this chapter.)

In this chapter, I focus on software instrument tracks, which are the easiest for a nonmusician to use.

✔ **Real instrument tracks:** A real instrument track is an actual audio recording, such as your voice or a physical instrument without a MIDI connection. (Think microphone.)

✔ **Electric Guitar tracks:** GarageBand includes a real instrument track especially made for an electric guitar, which allows you to use one of five different amplifiers and a number of stompboxes (those effect pedals that guitarists are always poking with their foot to change the sound of their instruments).

✔ **Podcast artwork track:** You get only one of these; it holds photos that will appear on a video iPod (or a window on your iWeb site) when your podcast is playing.

✔ **Movie tracks:** The video sound track appears if you're *scoring* (adding music) to an iMovie movie. Along with the video sound track, you get a cool companion video track that shows the clips in your movie. (More on this in the "Look, I'm John Williams!" sidebar, later in this chapter.)

Time to add a software instrument track of your very own. Follow these steps:

1. **Click the Create a New Track button (which carries a plus sign), labeled in Figure 15-1.**

   GarageBand displays the New Track dialog.

2. **Click the Software Instrument radio button and then click Create.**

   See all those great instruments in the Track Info pane on the right?

3. **Choose the general instrument category by clicking it.**

   I chose Drum Kits.

4. **From the right column, choose your specific style of weapon, such as Rock Kit for an arena sound.**

   Figure 15-3 illustrates the new track that appears in your list when you follow these steps.

Figure 15-3:
The new
track
appears,
ready
to rock.

If you're creating a podcast and you want to add a series of still images that will appear on a video iPod's screen (or on your iWeb page), follow these steps:

1. **Click the View Media Browser button (labeled in Figure 15-1).**

2. **Click the Photos button.**

   GarageBand displays all the photos in your iPhoto library and Events.

3. **Drag an image from your iPhoto library in the media browser to the Track list.**

   The Podcast track appears at the top of the Track list, and you can add and move images in the list at any time, just like the loops that you add to your instrument tracks. (More on adding and rearranging the contents of a track later in this section.)

Choosing loops

When you have a new, empty track, you can add loops to build your song. You do that by adding loops to your track from the Loop Browser — Apple provides you with thousands of loops to choose from — and photos from your media browser. Click the Loop Browser button (which bears the all-seeing eye) to display your collection, as shown in Figure 15-4.

If your Loop Browser looks different from what you see in Figure 15-4, that's because of the view mode you're using, just like the different view modes available for a Finder window. The three-icon button in the upper-left corner of the Loop Browser toggles the browser display between column, musical button, and podcast sounds view. Click the middle of the three buttons to switch to button mode.

Figure 15-4:
The Loop Browser, shown in button view.

Search box

Looking for just the right loop

The track in this running example uses a Rock drum kit, but you haven't added a loop yet. (Refer to Figure 15-3.) Follow these steps to search through your loop library for just the right rhythm:

1. **Click the button that corresponds to the instrument you're using.**

   I chose the Kits button in the Loop Browser. Click it, and a list of different beats appears in the pane at the bottom of the Loop Browser window. (Check out Figure 15-4 for a sneak peek.)

2. Click one of the loops with a green musical-note icon.

Go ahead; this is where things get fun! GarageBand begins playing the loop nonstop, allowing you to get a feel for how that particular loop sounds.

The examples I chose for this chapter are software instruments, which are identified by a green musical-note icon (If you've got a band at home, have at it with live instruments).

3. Click another entry in the list, and the application switches immediately to that loop.

Now you're beginning to understand why GarageBand is so cool for both musicians and the note-impaired. It's like having your own band, with members who never get tired and play whatever you want while you're composing. (Mozart would've *loved* this.)

If you want to search for a particular instrument, click in the Search box (labeled in Figure 15-4) and type the text you want to match. GarageBand returns the search results in the list.

4. Scroll down the list and continue to sample the different loops until you find one that fits like a glove.

For this reporter, it's Southern Rock Drums 01.

5. Drag the entry to your Rock Kit track and drop it at the very beginning of the Timeline (as indicated by the playhead).

Your window will look like Figure 15-5.

If you want that same beat throughout the song, you don't need to add any more loops to that track. (More on extending that beat in the next section.) However, if you want the drum's beat to change later in the song, you add a second loop after the first one in the *same* track. For now, leave this track as is.

Whoops! Did you do something that you regret? Don't forget that you can undo most actions in GarageBand by pressing the old standby ⌘+Z immediately afterward.

Second verse, same as the first

When you compose, you can add tracks for each instrument that you want in your song:

✔ Each track can have more than one loop.

✔ Loops *don't* have to start at the beginning; you can drop a loop anywhere in the Timeline.

For example, in Figure 15-6, you can see that my drum kit kicks in first, but my bass line doesn't begin until some time later (for a funkier opening).

Figure 15-5:
A track with a loop added.

Look, I'm John Williams!

You, too, can be a famous composer of soundtracks . . . well, perhaps not quite as famous as Mr. Williams, but even he had to start somewhere. To add a GarageBand score to an iMovie, click the Track menu in Garage Band and then click Show Movie Track to display the Movie track. Choose a movie to score from the familiar confines of the Media Browser, and drag it to the Movie Track.

At this point, you add and modify instrument tracks and loops just as you would any other GarageBand project. The existing sound for the iMovie project appears in the Movie Sound track. A Video Preview pane appears on top of the Track Info pane on the right side of the GarageBand window. When you click the Play button, the video is shown as well so that you can check your work and tweak settings (as described later in the chapter).

After you've finished composing, you can click Share on the menu bar and choose to export your work to iDVD, as a QuickTime movie directly to your hard drive, or to iTunes as a movie. Note that you can't return to iMovie with your project, so scoring should be a final step in the production of your movie.

You put loops on separate tracks so that they can play simultaneously on different instruments. If all your loops in a song are added on the same track, you hear only one loop at any one time, and all the loops use the same software instrument. By creating multiple tracks, you give yourself the elbow room to bring in the entire band at the same time. It's über-convenient to compose your song when you can see each instrument's loops and where they fall in the song.

Click the Reset button in the Loop Browser to choose another instrument or genre category.

Figure 15-6: My Timeline with a synth and an electric bass onboard. Let's rock!

Resizing, repeating, and moving loops

If you haven't already tried listening to your entire song, try it now. You can click Play at any time without wreaking havoc on your carefully created tracks. Sounds pretty good, doesn't it?

But wait: I bet the song stopped after about five seconds, right? (You can watch the passing seconds using either the Time/Tempo display or the second rule that appears at the very top of the Timeline.) I'm sure that you want your song to last more than five seconds! After the playhead moves past the end of the last loop, your song is over. Click Play again to pause the playback; then click the Return to Beginning button (labeled in Figure 15-1) to move the playhead back to the beginning of the song.

The music stops so soon because your loops are only so long. Most are five seconds in length, and others are even shorter. To keep the groove going, you have to do one of three things:

✔ **Resize the loop.** Hover your cursor over either the left or right edge of most loops, and an interesting thing happens: Your cursor changes to a vertical line with an arrow pointing away from the loop. That's your cue to click and drag — and as you drag, most loops expand to fill the space you're making, repeating the beats in perfect time. By resizing a loop, you can literally drag the loop's edge as long as you like.

✔ **Repeat the loop.** Depending on the loop that you chose, you might find that resizing it doesn't repeat the measure. Instead, the new part of the loop is simply dead air. In fact, the length of many loops is limited to anywhere from one to five seconds. However, if you move your cursor over the side of a loop that you want to extend, it turns into a vertical line with a circular arrow, which tells you that you can click and *repeat* the loop. GarageBand actually adds multiple copies of the same loop automatically, for as far as you drag the loop. In Figure 15-7, I've repeated the bass loop that you see in Figure 15-6.

✔ **Add a new loop.** You can switch to a different loop to change the flow of the music. Naturally, the instrument stays the same, but there's no reason you can't use a horn-riff loop in your violin track (as long as it sounds good played by a violin)! To GarageBand, a software instrument track is compatible with *any* software instrument loop that you add from the Loop Browser as long as that loop is marked with our old friend the green musical note.

You can also use the familiar cut (⌘+X), copy (⌘+C), and paste (⌘+V) editing keys to cut, copy, and paste loops from place to place — both on the Timeline and from track to track. And you can click a loop and drag it anywhere.

Each track can be adjusted so that you can listen to the interplay between two or more tracks or hear how your song sounds without a specific track:

✔ Click the tiny speaker button under the track name in the list, and the button turns blue to indicate that the track is muted. To turn off the mute, click the speaker icon again.

✔ You can change the volume or balance of each individual track by using the mixer that appears next to the track name. This comes in handy if you want an instrument to sound louder or confine that instrument to the left or right speaker.

A track doesn't have to be filled for every second with one loop or another. Most of my songs have a number of repeating loops with empty space between them as different instruments perform solo.

Figure 15-7:
By repeating the bass loop, you can keep the thump flowing.

Using the Arrange track

GarageBand includes another method you can use to monkey with your music: The *Arrange track* can be used to define specific sections of a song, allowing you to reorganize things by selecting, moving, and copying entire sections. For example, you're probably familiar with the chorus (or refrain) of a song and how often it appears during the course of the tune. With the Arrange track, you can reposition the entire chorus within your song, carrying all the loops and settings within the chorus along with it! If you need another chorus, just copy that arrangement.

To use the Arrange track, display it by clicking Track➪Show Arrange Track. The Arrange track then appears as a thin strip at the top of the track list. Click the Add Region button in the Arrange track (which carries a plus sign) and you'll see a new, untitled region appear (as shown in Figure 15-8). You can drag the right side of the Arrangement region to resize it, or drag it to move it anywhere in the song.

Who wants an arrangement full of regions named "untitled"? To rename an Arrangement region, click the word *untitled* to select it (the Arrange track turns blue), and then click the title again to display a text box. Type a new name for the region and press Return.

Now, here's where Arrangement regions get *cool*:

✔ To move an entire Arrangement region, click the region's title in the Arrange track and then drag it anywhere you like in the song.

✔ To copy an Arrangement region, hold down the Option key and drag the desired region's title to the spot where you want the copy to appear.

✔ To delete an Arrangement region, select it and press ⌘+Option+Delete.

✔ To replace the contents of an Arrangement region with those of another Arrangement region, hold down the ⌘ key and drag the desired region's title on top of the offending region's title.

✔ To switch two Arrangement regions in your song — swapping the contents completely — drag one of the Arrangement region titles on top of the other and lift your finger from the mouse.

Figure 15-8:
I've just added a new region in my song's Arrange track.

Tweaking the settings for a track

You don't think that John Mayer or U2 just "play and walk away," do you? No, they spend hours after the recording session is over, tweaking their music in the studio and on the mixing board until every note sounds just as it should. You can adjust the settings for a track, too. The tweaks that you can perform include adding effects (pull a Hendrix and add echo and reverb to your electric guitar track) and kicking in an equalizer (for fine-tuning the sound of your background horns).

To make adjustments to a track, follow these steps:

1. **Click the desired track in the track list to select it.**

2. **Click the Track Info button (labeled in Figure 15-1).**

3. **Click the Edit tab to show the settings shown in Figure 15-9.**

4. **Click the button next to each effect you want to enable. (The button glows green when enabled.)**

Each of the effects has a modifier setting. For example, you can adjust the amount of echo to add by dragging its slider.

Figure 15-9:
Finesse
your tune
by tweaking
the sound
of a specific
track.

GarageBand offers a Visual Equalizer window that you can use to create a custom equalizer setting for each track. You can display the Visual EQ window by clicking the animated button next to the Visual EQ control on the Edit pane. To change the Bass, Low Mid, High Mid, or Treble setting for a track, click and drag the equalizer waveform in the desired direction. And yep, you can do this while your song is playing, so you can use both your eyes *and* ears to define the perfect settings!

5. **To save the instrument as a new custom instrument click the Save Instrument button.**

   Now you can use the instrument the next time you add a track.

6. **Click the Track Info button again to return to GarageBand.**

Join in and jam . . . or talk!

As I mention elsewhere in this chapter, GarageBand is even more fun if you happen to play an instrument! (And yes, I'm envious, no matter how much I enjoy the techno and jazz music that I create. After all, take away my iMac, and I'm back to playing the kazoo . . . at least until I absorb all the Learn to Play lessons for the guitar.)

Most musicians use MIDI instruments to play music on the computer. That pleasant-sounding acronym stands for *Musical Instrument Digital Interface.* A wide variety of MIDI instruments is available these days, from traditional MIDI keyboards to more exotic fun, such as MIDI saxophones. For example, Apple sells a 49-key MIDI keyboard from M-Audio for around $100; it connects to your iMac using a USB connection.

Most MIDI instruments on the market today use a USB connection. If you have an older instrument with traditional MIDI ports — they're round, so you'll never confuse them with USB connectors — you need a USB-to-MIDI converter. You can find this type of converter on the Apple Web site for around $50. (If you're recording your voice for a podcast, things are easier because you can use your iMac's built-in microphone; however, most podcasting professionals opt for an external microphone, which offers better fidelity and doesn't force you to sit directly in front of your screen to record.)

After your instrument is connected, you can record tracks using any software instrument. Create a new software instrument track as I demonstrate in this chapter, select it, and then play a few notes. Suddenly you're playing the instrument you chose! (If nothing happens, check the MIDI status light — which appears in the time display — to see whether it blinks with each note you play. If not, check the installation of your MIDI connection and make sure you've loaded any required drivers, as well as your MIDI settings within QuickTime and the input settings in the System Preferences Sound pane.)

Drag the playhead to a beat or two before the spot in the Timeline where you want your recording to start. This gives you time to match the beat. Then click the big red Record button and start jamming or speaking! When you're finished, click the Play button to stop recording.

Time for a Mark's Maxim:

Save your work often in GarageBand, just as you do in the other iLife applications. One power blackout, and you'll never forgive yourself. Press ⌘+S and enjoy the peace of mind.

Automatic Composition with Magic GarageBand

In a hurry? Too rushed to snag loops and tweak effects? Never fear, GarageBand '09 can even compose a song *automatically*! The Magic GarageBand feature provides a wide range of nine different genres of music to choose from — everything from blues to reggae to funk and rock.

To create a song automatically, follow these steps:

1. **Close all GarageBand windows.**

   If you're currently working on a song, GarageBand will prompt you to save it before closing the window.

2. **Click the Magic GarageBand button in the New Project dialog.**

3. **Click the desired genre button and click Choose.**

   Hover your cursor over a genre button to get a preview of the song for that genre.

4. **To hear the entire song with the default instruments, click Entire Song and press the Play button.**

   Alternatively, to hear a short sample of the song, click Snippet and press the Play button.

   As shown in Figure 15-10, you see each instrument on stage. To choose a different musical style for an instrument (or a variation of the instrument), click it and then select the desired sound from the menu below the stage.

   Click My Instrument (the empty space in the middle of the stage) to add your own voice or instrumental using a microphone or MIDI instrument.

5. **When the song fits like a glove, click Create Project to open the song as a project in GarageBand.**

Now you can edit and tweak the song to your heart's delight as you can any other GarageBand project, adding other software or real instrument tracks as necessary.

Figure 15-10:
Creating my
own arena-
rock classic
with Magic
GarageBand.

Sharing Your Songs and Podcasts

After you finish your song, you can play it whenever you like through
GarageBand. But then again, that isn't really what you want, is it? You want to
share your music with others with an audio CD or download it to your iPod
so that you can enjoy it yourself while walking through the mall!

iTunes to the rescue! As with the other iLife applications that I cover in this
book, GarageBand can share the music you make through the digital hub that
is your Mac.

Creating MP3 and AAC files and ringtones

You can create an MP3 or AAC file (or even an iPhone ringtone) from your
song or podcast project in just a few simple steps:

1. **Open the song that you want to share.**

2. **Choose Share⇨Send Song to iTunes.**

   GarageBand displays the settings you see in Figure 15-11.

   To create a ringtone and send it to iTunes, choose Share⇨Send
   Ringtones to iTunes.

3. **Click in each of the four text boxes to type the playlist, artist name, composer name, and album name for the tracks you create.**

   You can leave the defaults as they are, if you prefer. Each track that you export is named after the song's name in GarageBand.

4. **Click the Compress Using pop-up menu and choose the encoder GarageBand should use to compress your song file.**

   The default is AAC, but you can also choose MP3 encoding for wider device compatibility.

5. **Click the Audio Settings pop-up menu to select the proper audio quality for the finished file.**

   The higher the quality, the larger the file. GarageBand displays the approximate file size and finished file information in the description box.

6. **Click Share.**

After a second or two of hard work, your Mac opens the iTunes window and highlights the new (or existing) playlist that contains your new song.

Figure 15-11:
Tweaking
settings
for iTunes
song files.

Hey, GarageBand, teach me how to play!

Until the arrival of GarageBand '09, you were limited to creating music — and if you were a nonmusician like yours truly, GarageBand had no practical use as a tool for teaching yourself how to actually *play* an instrument.

Ah, but Apple's introduction of Learn to Play actually turns GarageBand into your private video tutor for basic piano and guitar! From the New Project dialog, click the Learn to Play heading to display your lessons. Right out of the box, you have an Introduction to both instruments, but you can download eight more free

lessons for each instrument from the Lesson Store — and they cover more advanced topics such as fingering and chords. Tim, your on-screen instructor, can even record what you play.

If you find the free Learn to Play lessons valuable, you can move up to the Artist lessons, which are actually taught by famous musicians (including favorites of mine such as John Fogerty and Sting, who actually teaches you how to play "Roxanne")! Each Artist lesson is $4.99 — well worth the price.

Sending a podcast to iWeb or iTunes

If you've prepared a new podcast episode in GarageBand, you can send it automatically to iWeb or iTunes by following these steps:

1. **Open the podcast that you want to export to iWeb.**

   Make sure that the Podcast track is displayed. If necessary, click Track⇨Show Podcast Track to display it.

2. **Choose Share⇨Send Podcast to iWeb (or Share⇨Send Podcast to iTunes).**

3. **Click the Compress Using pop-up menu and choose the encoder that GarageBand should use to compress your podcast file.**

   Your choices are AAC and MP3 format.

4. **Click the Audio Settings pop-up menu to select the proper audio quality for the finished file.**

5. **Click Share.**

Burning an audio CD

Ready to create a demo CD with your latest GarageBand creation? Follow these steps to burn an audio disc from within GarageBand:

1. **Open the song that you want to record to disc.**

2. **Choose Share⇨Burn Song to CD.**

3. **Load a blank disc into your optical drive.**

Chapter 16

Creating a Web Site with iWeb

. . . .

. . . .

I keep telling everyone who'll listen: The Web is *simple.* Or at least it *should* be.

Kids in preschool these days know how to use a browser. Millions of people contribute to Facebook pages, help to create the dynamic reference wonder that is Wikipedia, and correspond effortlessly through Web-based e-mail. Yet there's one untamed wilderness that many iMac owners haven't explored — or even set foot in! That's the jungle of *HTML,* the language used to create Web pages. Today's advanced Web page design is complex, and it's not particularly fun, either. Have you thrown up your hands and declared, "I guess I'll never get my own Web site on the Internet?"

Forget your Web site envy, fellow Mac enthusiast! With iWeb, Apple has provided a guide through that untamed wilderness . . . and suddenly it's as easy and fun to create a Web site as it is to make a movie or write a song with your iMac. In this chapter, you discover how to design a site, import your own photos, and add all sorts of different pages.

Soon, you'll proudly hold your head up high and declare to the world, "I am a Webmaster!"

Looking around the iWeb Window

All iWeb's major features and controls fit into a single window, naturally, just as it does in iPhoto and iMovie. (I agree with the Apple software designers: *Multiple windows* equals *confusing*.) Figure 16-1 illustrates the iWeb window, complete with a Web site in progress. The stuff to keep your eye on includes

- ✔ **Toolbar:** Located at the bottom of the window, the iWeb toolbar keeps all major controls one or two clicks away.

  The iWeb toolbar contains different buttons, depending on the chore you're handling at the moment. Figure 16-1 shows the set of toolbar buttons that you see when you're editing a page.

- ✔ **Layout:** You need elbow room to build a Web page, so the Layout section of the iWeb interface dominates the window. You create and edit your pages in the Layout display and then use it to preview and test-drive your finished site.

- ✔ **Site Organizer:** The strip to the left of the layout display is the Site Organizer, which allows you to organize your Web sites, add new pages to a site, and select an existing page for editing.

Figure 16-1:
The iWeb
window
holds every-
thing you
need to put
your mark
on the Web.

Before we get down to business, it's overview time. You essentially follow three phases to put your new site on the Web:

1. **Decide which pages you need.**

2. **Create a new site and build those pages.**

3. **Publish your site to your MobileMe account (or to a Web server using FTP).**

I go over each of these phases in order. (They taught me that in college . . . along with the history of the Aztecs and the wonders of FIFO accounting.)

Planning Your Pages

Every properly designed Web site has a purpose: to inform, to entertain, or to sell stuff. For example, if your site is a personal or informational site, it may contain downloads or contact information. The pages you add to your site should all reflect that common purpose.

iWeb focuses on creating personal sites for entertainment. It can produce the following types of pages for your site:

- **Welcome:** This is the default first page that iWeb adds to a site you create. The Welcome page familiarizes your visitor with the idea behind your site, and perhaps offers a snippet of the latest developments on the site in a "What's New" paragraph.

- **About Me:** This page provides a biography of you or another person, listing things like your age, favorite songs, and favorite foods. (After all, that's important stuff.) Links are provided to your photo album pages and other Web sites you want to share.

- **Photos:** Oh, this is good stuff here — iWeb makes it easy to add one of those cool online photo galleries for your snapshots, complete with a Web slideshow! You can add Events and albums from iPhoto, too.

- **My Albums:** You can organize all your Photos and Movie pages on a single My Albums page. Visitors click a thumbnail to jump to the corresponding Photos page or Movies page — it's a visual index done the *right* way.

- **Movie:** Got a QuickTime movie you've created with iMovie to share with others? This is the page that presents it to your adoring fans.

- ✔ **Blog:** Adding a *Blog* (or personal Web journal) page is a somewhat different beast: iWeb keeps track of each addition you make in an entry list so that you can quickly add or delete entries without requiring tons of scrolling, cutting, and pasting. A Blog page also includes an archive so that deleted entries aren't lost forever.

- ✔ **Podcast:** Consider a podcast as an audio (or audio/visual) blog — it's designed to be downloaded to a visitor's iPod or computer for later enjoyment. As does the Blog page, a Podcast page has an entry list and an archive list attached to it.

- ✔ **Blank:** Yep, an old-fashioned blank page, ready for you to fill with whatever you like.

Before you even launch iWeb, jot down on a piece of paper (or put in a Sticky) these important points:

- ✔ **What message do I want to communicate to visitors?**
- ✔ **What tone will I use — funny, informal, or businesslike?**
- ✔ **What stuff do I want to offer: photos, movies, or podcasts?**

Now you have the starting point for your site and you know what you want to include . . . so let's get down with the Web!

Adding a New Site

When you open iWeb for the first time, the application creates a new site for you, and you can rename and modify this default site to your heart's content. In fact, for many of us, one site is all we ever create — but iWeb can easily handle multiple Web sites, keeping them separate in the Site Organizer.

If there's at least one existing site in your Site Organizer, iWeb automatically displays the last site you were working on. Therefore, if you want to create an entirely new site, you have to perform a little manual labor. Here are a number of different ways to add a site:

- ✔ **Choose File⇨New Site.**
- ✔ **Press ⌘+Shift+N.**
- ✔ **Control-click (or right-click) in the Site Organizer and click New Site.**

iWeb leaps into action and displays the template sheet you see in Figure 16-2. Scroll through the template themes in the list at the left of the sheet until you find one that matches the tone you decided on in the previous section.

(Informal, formal, or silly, iWeb has templates that match every mood!) Click a template on the left, and the application automatically updates the page type thumbnails on the right.

Figure 16-2:
Choosing a template for a new site.

When you choose a template, iWeb automatically provides your pages with a common background, color scheme, and fonts so that your finished Web site has a common theme throughout.

After you find the right look and feel, click the desired template in the scrolling list at the left, click the Welcome page thumbnail, and then click the Choose button. iWeb creates a new site heading in the Site Organizer, complete with the default Welcome page. Figure 16-1, shown previously, illustrates the Welcome page from a new site I created with the Main Event template.

Adding a New Page

Time to add the pages you plan for your site! For example, I've decided to add Photo and About Me pages to the new site I've created. In the following section, I discuss how to edit these pages to personalize them . . . but for now, I just want you to add the pages.

If you have multiple sites in your Site Organizer list, click the top-level heading for the desired site to select it. You can add pages by

- ✔ **Clicking the Add Page button on the toolbar at the bottom of the iWeb window**
- ✔ **Choosing File⇨New Page**
- ✔ **Pressing ⌘+N**
- ✔ **Control-clicking or right-clicking the site header in the Site Organizer and clicking New Page**

Want to start with an existing page as a basis for a new page? Right-click that page entry in the Site Organizer and choose Duplicate. iWeb creates a new page with exactly the same contents and adds it to the site.

Pages are listed under the main site heading in outline format, making it easy to expand or collapse a site by clicking the familiar rotating triangle icon next to the site heading. (Apple calls these *disclosure triangles.* Wowzers!)

Deleting a page — or a whole site, for that matter — is easy in iWeb. Right-click the offending page or site heading in the Site Organizer and choose Delete Page/Delete Site. Note that iWeb doesn't prompt you for confirmation here, so these aren't commands to toy with.

Editing a Page

If you have your site framework complete, you can actually put your site on the Internet as-is! Of course, the photos would all be of good-looking strangers, and most of the text would read like Pig Latin nonsense. (Come to think of it, I've been on some real sites that aren't much better. Go figure.)

I think we both agree, however, that *you* want to personalize your pages with your *own* information. To begin editing a page, click it in the Site Organizer.

Modifying text

First, update the text with your own information by following these steps:

1. **Click the text you want to replace.**

   As do most desktop publishing applications, iWeb uses boxes to enclose text. When you click the text, the box appears, with handles that you can drag to resize the box.

2. Begin typing your text.

iWeb replaces the existing template text with the text you type, using the text formatting taken from the template. Don't forget that you can paste text from the Clipboard by pressing ⌘+V. To match the text style of the template, though, press Option+Shift+⌘+V.

Mistakes are *passé* in iWeb. To undo your last action, you can always press the familiar ⌘+Z keyboard shortcut or choose Edit⇨Undo.

3. Highlight and format your new text as necessary.

To make changes easier, click the Inspector button in the iWeb toolbar. The window you see in Figure 16-3 appears, allowing you to change text color, alignment, and spacing with aplomb. (You find more about the Inspector later.) You can click the Colors or Fonts buttons on the iWeb toolbar to display a Color Picker or Font Panel for the selected text.

4. Click outside the text box after you're satisfied with the text.

Because you're likely modifying everything on the template pages from the title to the last box on the page, repeat Steps 1–4 for each section of text you want to change.

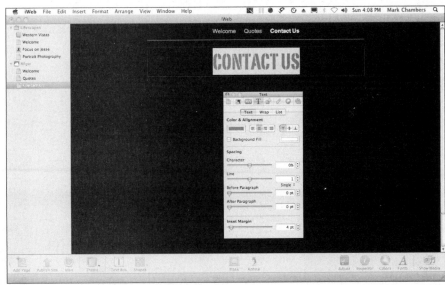

Figure 16-3:
Using the
Inspector
palette to
format text.

Replacing images

If your page includes photographs that you want to change, follow these steps:

1. **Click the image you want to replace.**

   As it does with a block of text, iWeb displays a box around the image, complete with resizing handles.

2. **Drag an image to the image box from a Finder window.**

   Alternatively, you can click the Show Media button in the toolbar, which displays the Media Browser you see in Figure 16-4. From this window, you can click the Photos tab to choose an image from your iPhoto library.

   You can hide the Media Browser to make more room for your page layout. Just click the Hide Media button in the toolbar.

3. **Adjust your new image if necessary.**

   Click the Adjust button, and iWeb displays a cool, semi-opaque dialog that allows you to tweak image settings, such as tint, brightness, and sharpness (see Figure 16-5). Click Enhance to allow iWeb to choose the settings it considers best for the image or click Reset Image to restore the photo to its original appearance. When you're satisfied with the image, click the Close button on the dialog to return to the image box.

4. **Click outside the image box (usually the page background) after you're satisfied with the photo.**

Again, lather/rinse/repeat for each image you want to change on your page.

Figure 16-4:
Browsing my iPhoto library for the right image.

Figure 16-5:
Adjusting
an image in
iWeb.

Adding new elements

iWeb also makes it easy to add new items to a page. The list of extras includes

- **Audio:** You can add a song (complete with volume control, Play/Pause button, and progress slider) to your page! Either drag an audio file from a Finder window to your page, or click the Audio tab in the Media Browser to select a song from your iTunes or GarageBand collections. You can drag any image to the player that appears. (How about a photo of your daughter instead of album art?)

- **Photos:** To add a new image box to your page, drag a photo from a Finder window to the iWeb layout section. Or, click the Photos tab in the Media Browser to choose an image from your iPhoto library, or throw caution to the wind and drag an entire Event or an album to your new page! iWeb takes care of all the details.

- **Movies:** Yep, you guessed it: You can drag a movie clip from a Finder window to your page, or click the Movies tab in the Media Browser to choose a movie from iMovie or your Movies folder.

- **Text:** Choose Insert⇔Text or click the Text button in the toolbar.

- **Shapes:** Click the Shape button in the toolbar to display the pop-up menu and then click the desired shape. (Don't forget to resize it as you desire with the box handles.)

✔ **Widgets:** Click this tab in the Media Browser to insert a *widget* (a Web applet) to your page. For example, HTML Snippet allows you to type HTML code directly into place on the page, or paste HTML code that you've copied from another Web site. You can also insert interactive Google Adsense advertisements or a Google Map. To populate the page with a MobileMe Gallery, choose the MobileMe Gallery widget and select a Gallery you've created using the iPhoto MobileMe Gallery feature. (For the complete scoop on iPhoto, cruise over to Chapter 12.) Other widgets include a countdown timer and YouTube videos.

You can move a widget anywhere on a page by dragging it, and it can be resized just as a text box can.

✔ **Links:** If you're editing text and you want to insert a Web link, choose Insert⇨Hyperlink and choose from the menu that appears. You can choose to link to another Web page or insert a link that automatically sends an e-mail message to the mail address you provide. You can also offer a file for downloading.

iWeb can automatically detect e-mail and Web addresses that you type in a text box, so you don't have to use the Links menu. To enable this feature, choose iWeb⇨Preferences and click the Automatically Detect Email and Web Addresses check box to select it.

✔ **Button:** Your Web page can include buttons that allow your visitors to e-mail you or display the number of hits (visits) your page has received. Choose Insert⇨Button and click an option to add or remove a specific button. (If the menu option is selected, the button appears on your page.) Blog and Podcast pages can also offer *RSS feeds* (for automated retrieval of new entries within a Web browser), subscriptions to your podcasts, and slideshows.

With these tools, you can use the Blank page template to create your own new pages. Personally, I prefer to use the professionally designed templates offered by Apple as starting points, removing whatever I don't need and adding new content.

Most Web designers would strongly recommend that you use a common theme for all the pages within a site (to lend continuity). Of course, you can also stick your tongue out at those very same Web designers and select a different theme for every page! To select a different theme for a page, open the page in iWeb and click the Theme button in the toolbar; then click the desired thumbnail from the pop-up menu. Nothing's lost but the old look of the page, so feel free to experiment to your heart's content.

Ready to offer a slideshow on your Web site? Add a Photo page to your site and notice that the Start Slideshow button is already in place at the top of the page. Simply add the photos to the page using the Media Browser or by dragging them from a Finder window. When your visitors click the Start Slideshow button, all the photos on the page are displayed in a pop-up window. (Other Mac and PC owners using Safari can enjoy the show, but older versions of Internet Explorer and Firefox can't handle it.)

Tweaking with the Inspector

Earlier, you used the Inspector to change text formatting attributes — but this star performer can do much more than just that! To modify page characteristics, click the page in the Site Organizer, display the Inspector, and click the Page Inspector button, which carries a document icon. These settings allow you to change the name of a page; you can also elect to include or exclude this page from the site menu, or to drop the site menu from this page.

If your site contains a Blog or Podcast page, you can click the RSS button to provide an automated RSS *(RDF Site Summary)* feed to your visitors. (For more information on RSS and how it works in Safari, see Chapter 8.)

Publishing Your Web Site

After you finish with a new site — or you're satisfied with the edits you make to existing pages — it's time to get your masterpiece on the Web! Even the best Web site design is worth next to nil if it isn't available on the Internet, and in this last section, I demonstrate how to publish your Web site to your MobileMe account or to a separate server maintained by a third party (perhaps your ISP, your company, or Dave down the street).

You specify where your iWeb site will be published from the Site Publishing Settings screen.

To make global changes to a site, click the site name in the Site Organizer. iWeb switches to the Site Publishing Settings screen (Figure 16-6), where you can change the name of the site, your contact e-mail, where the site is published, and password protection for MobileMe sites.

Click the site name in the Site Organizer to display the Publish To pop-up menu (Figure 16-6). iWeb offers the following publishing options:

  ✔ **Publish to MobileMe:** Your site is hosted by Apple as part of your MobileMe subscription. The application takes care of everything, uploading any changed pages or media.

✔ **Publish to FTP Server:** This publishing option provides you with a completely different collection of settings on the Site Publishing Settings screen. You'll need to furnish iWeb with your Web server's FTP settings (which should be furnished to you by the host) and your site's address (or *URL*).

✔ **Publish to a Local Folder:** The final publishing option creates a folder on your hard drive that contains all the files to display your Web site. This is the option to choose if you're not a MobileMe subscriber and you don't use a third-party hosting service. You can add these files directly to your home or business Web server. Once again, you must supply the site URL as it will appear on the Internet after you copy or upload the site files to the server.

After you've set the type of publishing the site will use, it's time to take care of business! Click the site to select it in the Site Organizer and then click the Publish Site button on the toolbar. The application takes care of everything else, automatically uploading all pages and media (if you choose MobileMe or FTP publishing) or saving them on your hard drive (if you chose the Local Folder option).

In a hurry? You can elect to publish just the changes necessary to update your site: Instead of clicking the Publish Site button on the toolbar, click the File menu and choose Publish Site Changes.

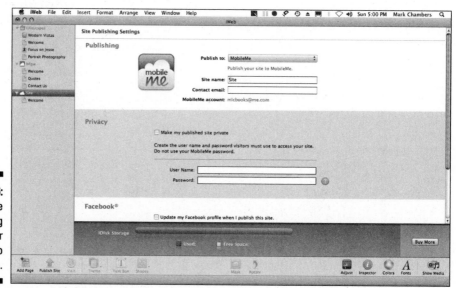

Figure 16-6:
Setting the
publishing
method for
an iWeb
site.

Part V
Getting Productive with iWork and Other Tools

The 5th Wave   By Rich Tennant

JERRY AND LYLE ATTEMPT TO LOAD THE NEWEST VERSION OF "TOAST", CD BURNING SOFTWARE

Okay, I've got the Sunbeam firewired to the iMac. Try putting the CD in the slot again.

In this part . . .

Who needs that *other* office productivity suite? If you've invested in Apple's iWork '09, these chapters will provide all the basics you need to use Pages, Numbers, and Keynote to produce eye-popping printed documents, spreadsheets, and professional-grade presentations! And if you're ready to share your iMac among all the members of your family, you can build a wireless home network. I show you how to provide others with access to your documents and data — securely, mind you, and with the least amount of hassle.

Chapter 17

Desktop Publishing with Pages

. . . .

. . . .

*W*hat's the difference between word processing and desktop publishing? In a nutshell, it's in how you *design* your document. Most folks use a word processor like an old-fashioned typewriter. (Yawn.)

A desktop publishing application allows far more creativity in choosing where to place text, how to align graphics, and how to edit formats. In this chapter, I show you how to set your inner designer free from the tedious constraints of word processing! Whether you need a simple letter, a stunning brochure, or a multipage newsletter, Pages '09 can handle the job with ease — and you'll be surprised at how simple it is to use.

Creating a New Pages Document

To create a new Pages document from scratch, follow these steps:

1. **Double-click your hard drive icon and click the Applications entry in the Finder window sidebar. Double-click the iWork folder to open it.**

2. **Double-click the Pages icon.**

   Pages displays the Template Chooser window that you see in Figure 17-1.

3. **Click the type of document you want to create in the list to the left. The thumbnails on the right are updated with templates that match your choice.**

4. **Click the template that most closely matches your needs.**

5. **Click Choose to create a new document using the template you selected.**

Open an Existing Pages Document

Of course, you can always open a Pages document from a Finder window — just double-click the document icon. However, you can also open a Pages document from within the program. Follow these steps:

1. **Double-click the Pages icon to run the program.**

2. **Press ⌘+O to display the Open dialog.**

   The Open dialog operates much the same as a Finder window in icon, list, or column view mode.

3. **Click the desired drive in the Devices list at the left of the dialog and then click folders and subfolders until you've located the Pages document. (You can also click in the Search box at the top of the Open dialog and type in a portion of the document name or its contents.)**

4. **Double-click the filename to load it.**

If you want to open a Pages document that you've edited in the recent past, things get even easier! Just click File⇨Open Recent, and you can open the document with a single click from the submenu that appears.

Saving Your Work

To save a Pages document after you finish it (or to take a break while designing), follow these steps:

1. **Press ⌘+S.**

   If you're saving a document that hasn't yet been saved, the familiar Save As sheet appears.

2. **Type a filename for your new document.**

3. **Click the Where pop-up menu and choose a location to save the document.**

   Alternatively, click the button sporting the down arrow to expand the Save As sheet. This allows you to navigate to a different location, or to create a new folder to store this Pages project.

4. **Click Save.**

Touring the Pages Window

Before we dive into any real work, let me show you around the Pages window! You'll find the following major components and controls, as shown in Figure 17-2:

✔ **Pages list:** This thumbnail list displays all the pages you've created within your document. (For a single-page document, of course, the Page list will contain only a single thumbnail.) You can switch instantly between different pages in your document by clicking the desired thumbnail in the list.

✔ **Layout pane:** This section takes up most of the Pages window — it's where you design and edit each page in your document.

✔ **Toolbar:** Yep, Pages has its own toolbar. The toolbar keeps all the most common application controls within easy, one-click reach.

✔ **Styles Drawer:** This window extension allows you to quickly switch the appearance of selected paragraphs, characters, and lists. You can hide and display the Styles Drawer from the View menu or from the View drop-down menu on the toolbar.

✔ **Format Bar:** This button strip runs under the Pages toolbar. Use it to format selected text, paragraphs, and lists on the fly.

Format Bar

Toolbar

Figure 17-2:
The major points of interest in the Pages window.

Entering and Editing Text

If you've used a modern word processing program, you'll feel right at home typing within Pages. To enter text, simply begin typing. To edit existing text in your Pages document, select and highlight the text. You can delete text by pressing Delete.

Using Text and Graphics Boxes

Within Pages, text and graphics appear in *boxes*, which can be resized by clicking and dragging on one of the handles that appear around the edges of the box. (Hover your cursor over one of the square handles and you'll see that it changes to a double-sided arrow, indicating that Pages is ready to resize the box.)

You can also move a box, including all the stuff it contains, to another location within the Layout pane. Click in the center of the box and drag the box to the desired spot. Note that Pages displays blue alignment lines to help you align the box with other elements around it (or with regular divisions of the page, such as the vertical center of a poster or flyer). Figure 17-3 illustrates a box containing text that I'm moving; note the vertical alignment line that automatically appears.

To select text or graphics within a box, you must first click the box to select it and then click again on the line of text or the graphic that you want to change.

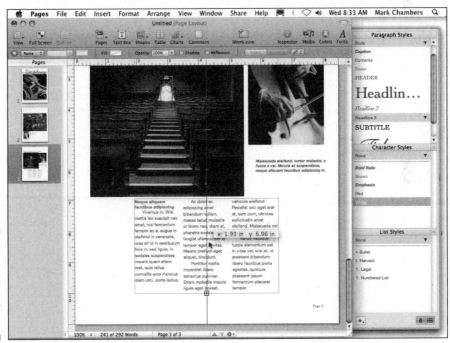

Figure 17-3:
Moving a
text box
within the
Layout
pane.

The Three Amigos: Cut, Copy, and Paste

"Hang on, Mark, you've covered moving stuff, but what if you want to *copy* a block of text or a photo to a second location? Or how about cutting something from a document open in another application?" Good questions, dear reader! That's when you can call on the power of the cut, copy, and paste features within Pages. The next few sections explain how you do these actions.

Cutting stuff

Cutting selected text or graphics removes it from your Pages document and places that material within your Clipboard. (Think of the Clipboard as a holding area for snippets of text and graphics that you want to manipulate.) To cut text or graphics, select some material and Choose Edit⇨Cut or press ⌘+X.

Copying text and images

When you copy text or graphics, the original selection remains untouched, but a copy of the selection is placed in the Clipboard. Select some text or graphics and Choose Edit⇨Copy or Press ⌘+C.

To copy selected items by dragging, hold down the Option key while you drag the items to their destination.

If you cut or copy a new selection into the Clipboard, it erases what was there. In other words, the Clipboard holds only the latest material you cut or copied.

Pasting from the Clipboard

Are you wondering what you can do with all that stuff that's accumulating in your Clipboard? Pasting the contents of the Clipboard places the material at the current location of the insertion cursor. You must paste the contents before you cut or copy again to avoid losing what's in the Clipboard.

To paste the Clipboard contents, click the insertion cursor at the location you want and Choose Edit⇨Paste or Press ⌘+V.

Formatting Text the Easy Way

If you feel that some (or all) of the text in your Pages document needs a face-lift, you can format that text any way you like. Formatting lets you change the color, font family, character size, and attributes as necessary.

After the text is selected, you can apply basic formatting in two ways:

- ✔ **Use the Format bar.** The Format bar appears directly underneath the Pages toolbar, as shown in Figure 17-2. Click to select a font control to display a pop-up menu and then click your choice. For example, click the Font Family button and you can change the font family from Arial to a more daring font. You can also select characteristics such as the font's background color (perfect for highlighting key information) or choose italicizing or bolding. The Format Bar also provides buttons for text alignment (Align Left, Center, Align Right, and Justify).

- ✔ **Use the Format menu.** Most controls on the Format Bar are also available from the Format menu. Click Format and hover the mouse cursor over the Font menu item, and you can then apply bolding, italicizing, and underlining to the selected text. You can also make the text bigger or smaller. To change the alignment from the Format menu, click Format and hover the mouse cursor over the Text menu item.

Adding a Spiffy Table

In the world of word processing, a *table* is a grid that holds text or graphics for easy comparison. You can create a custom table layout within Pages with a few simple mouse clicks.

Follow these steps:

1. **Click the insertion cursor at the location where you want the table to appear.**

2. **Click the Table button on the Pages toolbar.**

   Pages inserts a simple table and displays the Table Inspector. (Both are visible in Figure 17-4.)

   By default, Pages creates a table with three rows and three columns, with an extra row for headings at the top. You can change this layout from the Table Inspector — just click in the Body Rows or Body Columns box and type a number.

3. **Click within a cell in the table to enter text. The table cell automatically resizes and "wraps" the text you enter to fit.**

   You can paste material from the Clipboard into a table. See the earlier section "Pasting from the Clipboard" for details on pasting.

4. **To change the borders on a cell, click the cell to select it and then click one of the Cell Border buttons to change the border.**

   Select a range of multiple cells in a table by holding down Shift as you click. Hold down ⌘ and click to select multiple cells that aren't contiguous.

5. **To add a background color (or even fill cells with an image for a background), click the Cell Background pop-up menu and choose a type of background.**

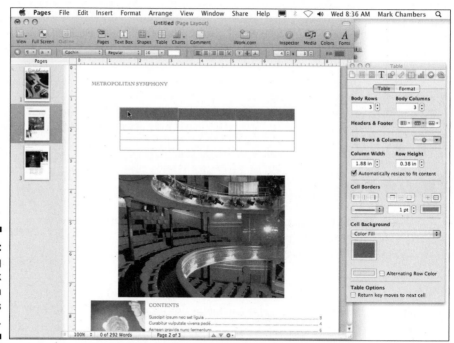

Figure 17-4:
Preparing
to tweak
a table in
my Pages
document.

Adding Alluring Photos

You can choose from two methods of adding a picture within your Pages document: as a *floating* object, meaning that you can place the image in a particular spot and it doesn't move, even if you make changes to the text; and as an *inline* object, which flows with the surrounding text as you make layout changes.

✔ **Add a floating object.** Drag an image file from a Finder window and place it at the spot you want within your document. Alternatively, you can click the Media button on the toolbar and click Photos, navigate to the location where the file is saved, and drag the image thumbnail to the spot you want in the document. Figure 17-5 illustrates the Media Browser in action.

Note that a floating object (such as a shape or image) can be sent to the *background*, where text will not wrap around it. To bring a background object back as a regular floating object, click the object to select it and click Arrange⇨Bring Background Objects to Front. (More about background objects later in this chapter.)

To resize an image object, click the image to select it and then drag one of the selection handles that appear along the border of the image. (They look like tiny squares.) The side-selection handles drag only that edge of the frame. The corner-selection handles resize both adjoining edges of the selection frame. Hold down the Shift key so that the vertical and horizontal proportions remain fixed.

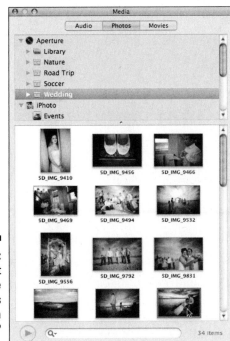

Figure 17-5:
Hey, isn't that the Pages Media Browser?

✔ **Add an inline object.** Hold down the ⌘ key as you drag an image file from a Finder window and place it where you want within your document. You can also click the Media toolbar button and click Photos to display the Media Browser. Navigate to the location where the file is saved, hold down the ⌘ key, and drag the image thumbnail to the spot where you want it in the document.

Adding a Background Shape

To add a shape (such as a rectangle or circle) as a background for your text, follow these steps:

1. **Click the insertion cursor in the location you want.**
2. **Click the Shapes button on the Pages toolbar and choose a shape.**

   The shape appears in your document.
3. **Click the center of the shape and drag it to a new spot.**

   Shapes can be resized or moved in the same manner as image boxes.
4. **Before you can type over a shape, remember to select it and choose Arrange⇨Send Object to Background.**

Are You Sure about That Spelling?

Pages can check spelling as you type (the default setting) or check it after you complete your document. If you find automatic spell-checking distracting, you should definitely pick the latter method.

To check spelling as you type, follow these steps:

1. **Click Edit and hover the cursor over the Spelling menu item.**
2. **Click Check Spelling As You Type in the submenu that appears.**

   If a possible misspelling is found, Pages underlines the word with a red, dashed line.
3. **Right-click the word to choose a possible correct spelling from the list, or you can ignore the word if it's spelled correctly.**

To turn off automatic spell checking, click the Check Spelling As You Type menu item again to deselect it.

To check spelling manually, follow these steps:

1. **Click within the document to place the text insertion cursor where the spell check should begin.**

2. **Click Edit and hover the mouse cursor over the Spelling menu item; then choose Check Spelling from the submenu that appears.**

3. **Right-click any possible misspellings and choose the correct spelling, or choose Ignore if the word is spelled correctly.**

Printing Your Pages Documents

Ready to start the presses? You can print your Pages document on real paper, of course, but don't forget that you can also save a tree by creating an electronic, PDF-format document instead of a printout — the you'll find the PDF button within the standard Snow Leopard Print dialog.

To print your Pages document on old-fashioned paper, follow these steps:

1. **Within Pages, click File and choose Print.**

   Pages displays the Print sheet.

2. **Click in the Copies field and enter the number of copies you need.**

3. **Select the pages to print.**

   - To print the entire document, select All.

   - To print a range of selected pages, select the From radio button and enter the starting and ending pages.

4. **Click the Print button to send the document to your printer.**

Sharing That Poster with Others

Besides printing — which is, after all, so passé — you can choose to share your Pages document electronically in a number of ways:

✔ **Sharing on iWork.com.** Apple provides a Web site, iwork.com, where you can invite others to view and comment on your Pages document. Click the iWork.com button on the Pages toolbar to get started, and the site will walk you through the rest of the process.

You'll need an Internet connection to use iWork.com (naturally), as well as an Apple ID and a working Apple Mail account. If you didn't create an Apple ID when setting up your iMac or installing Snow Leopard, you can save the day by clicking the Create New Account button on the iWork.com site.

✔ **Sharing through e-mail.** Click Share⇨Send via Mail, and you can choose to add your Pages document to a Mail message in three different formats: as a native Pages document file, as a Word format document, or as a PDF file. After you've selected a format, Pages obligingly launches Apple Mail for you automatically and creates a new message, ready for you to address and send! (Remember, most Internet Service Providers have a maximum message size, so if your document is too large it will likely be rejected by your mail server.)

✔ **Sharing through iWeb.** Again, click the Share menu, but this time choose Send to iWeb. Pages automatically opens the iWeb site you last edited and provides your Pages document as a native Pages document file or as a PDF file. (If your visitors may be using PCs or Linux, choose the PDF option.)

✔ **Exporting.** Don't forget that Pages can export your work in one of four different formats: a PDF document; a Word format document; an RTF (Rich Text Format) file; or even plain text. Click Share⇨Export, pick your format, click Next, and then select the location where Pages should save the file. Click Export and sit back while your favorite desktop publishing application does all the work.

To keep your document as close to how it appears in Pages as possible, I recommend either PDF or Word. Your document will retain far more of your original formatting than an RTF or plain-text document would.

Chapter 18

Creating Spreadsheets with Numbers

· ·

In This Chapter

▶ Opening, saving, and creating spreadsheets

▶ Selecting cells, entering data, and editing data

▶ Formatting cells

▶ Adding and removing rows and columns

▶ Creating simple calculations

▶ Adding charts to your spreadsheets

▶ Printing a Numbers spreadsheet

· ·

Are you downright afraid of spreadsheets? Does the idea of building a budget with charts and all sorts of fancy graphics send you running for the safety of the hall closet? Well, good iMac owner, Apple has once again taken something that everyone else considers super-complex and turned it into something that normal human beings can use! (Much as Apple did with video editing, songwriting, and Web site creation — heck, is there *any* type of software that Apple designers can't make intuitive and easy to use?)

In this chapter, I get to demonstrate how Numbers can help you organize data, analyze important financial decisions, and yes, even maintain a household budget! You'll soon see why the Numbers spreadsheet program is specifically designed with the home Mac owner in mind.

Before You Launch Numbers . . .

Just in case you're not familiar with applications like Numbers and Microsoft Excel — and the documents they create — let me provide you with a little background information.

A *spreadsheet* organizes and calculates numbers by using a grid system of rows and columns. The intersection of each row and column is a *cell,* and cells can hold either text or numeric values (along with calculations that are usually linked to the contents of surrounding cells).

Spreadsheets are wonderful tools for making decisions and comparisons because they let you "plug in" different numbers — such as interest rates or your monthly insurance premium — and instantly see the results. Some of my favorite spreadsheets that I use regularly include

✔ Car and mortgage loan comparisons

✔ A college planner

✔ My household budget (not that we pay any attention to it)

Creating a New Numbers Document

As does Pages, the desktop publishing application that's included in iWork '09, Numbers ships with a selection of templates that you can modify quickly to create a new spreadsheet. (For example, after a few modifications, you can easily use the Budget, Loan Comparison, and Mortgage templates to create your own spreadsheets.)

To create a spreadsheet project file, follow these steps:

1. **Open your Applications folder and double-click the iWork '09 folder to display its contents.**

2. **Double-click the Numbers icon.**

   Numbers displays the Template Chooser window you see in Figure 18-1.

3. **Click the type of document you want to create in the list to the left.**

   The document thumbnails on the right are updated with templates that match your choice.

4. **Click the template that most closely matches your needs.**

5. **Click Choose to open a new document using the template you selected.**

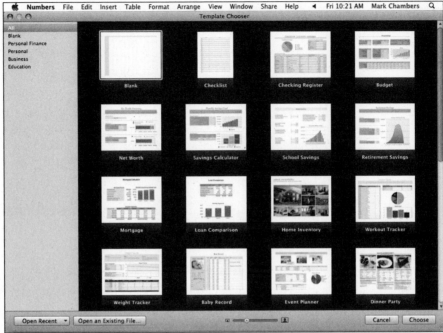

Figure 18-1:
Hey, these
templates
aren't
frightening
at all!

Opening an Existing Spreadsheet File

If a Numbers document appears in a Finder window, you can just double-click the Document icon to open it; Numbers automatically loads and displays the spreadsheet. However, it's equally easy to open a Numbers document from within the program. Follow these steps:

1. **Double-click the Numbers icon to run the program.**

2. **Press ⌘+O to display the Open dialog.**

3. **Click the desired drive in the Devices list at the left of the dialog and then click folders and subfolders until you've located the desired Numbers document.**

   If you're unsure of where the document is, click in the Search box at the top of the Open dialog box and type in a portion of the document name, or even a word or two of text it contains.

4. **Double-click the spreadsheet to load it.**

If you want to open a spreadsheet you've been working on over the last few days, click File ⇨ Open Recent to display Numbers documents that you've worked with recently.

Save Those Spreadsheets!

If you're not a huge fan of retyping data, I always recommend that you save your spreadsheets often (just in case of a power failure or a co-worker's mistake). Follow these steps to save your spreadsheet to your hard drive:

1. **Press ⌘+S.**

   If you're saving a document that hasn't yet been saved, the Save As sheet appears.

2. **Type a filename for your new spreadsheet.**

3. **Click the Where pop-up menu and choose a location to save the file.**

   This allows you to select common locations, such as your desktop, Documents folder, or Home folder.

   If the location you want isn't listed in the Where pop-up menu, you can also click the down-arrow button next to the Save As text box to display the full Save As dialog. Click the desired drive in the Devices list at the left of the dialog and then click folders and subfolders until you reach the desired location. You can also create a new folder in the full Save As dialog.

4. **Click Save.**

After you've saved the file the first time, you can simply press ⌘+S in the future and your changes are saved.

Exploring the Numbers Window

Apple has done a great job of minimizing the complexity of the Numbers window. Figure 18-2 illustrates these major points of interest:

✔ **Sheets list:** Because a Numbers project can contain multiple spreadsheets, they're displayed in the Sheets list at the left of the window. To switch between spreadsheets in a project, click the top-level headings (each of which has a spreadsheet icon).

✔ **Sheet canvas:** Numbers displays the rows and columns of your spreadsheet in this section of the window; you enter and edit cell values within the sheet canvas.

✔ **Toolbar:** The Numbers toolbar keeps the most common commands you'll use within easy reach.

✔ **Formula Box:** You'll use the Formula Box to enter formulas into a cell, allowing Numbers to automatically perform calculations based on the contents of other cells.

✔ **Format Bar:** Located directly under the toolbar, the Format Bar displays editing controls for the object that's currently selected. (If you enter an equal sign into the Formula Box, the Format Bar changes into the Formula Bar. No, I'm not making this up.) My goodness, this is starting to sound like that classic movie about the chocolate tycoon and those kids!

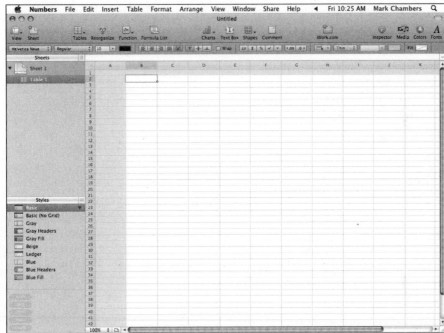

Figure 18-2:
The Numbers window struts its stuff.

Navigate and Select Cells in a Spreadsheet

You can use the scroll bars to move around in your spreadsheet, but when you enter data into cells, moving your fingers from the keyboard is a hassle. For this reason, Numbers has various movement shortcut keys that you can use to navigate, and I list them in Table 18-1. After you commit these keys to memory, your productivity shoots straight to the top.

Table 18-1	Movement Shortcut Keys in Numbers
Key or Key Combination	*Where the Cursor Moves*
Left arrow (←)	One cell to the left
Right arrow (→)	One cell to the right
Up arrow (↑)	One cell up
Down arrow (↓)	One cell down
Home	To the beginning of the active worksheet
End	To the end of the active worksheet
Page Down	Down one screen
Page Up	Up one screen
Return	One cell down (also works within a selection)
Tab	One cell to the right (also works within a selection)
Shift+Enter	One cell up (also works within a selection)
Shift+Tab	One cell to the left (also works within a selection)

You can use the mouse to select cells in a spreadsheet:

✔ To select a *single* cell, click it.

✔ To select a *range* of multiple adjacent cells, click a cell at any corner of the range you want and then drag the mouse in the direction you want.

✔ To select a *column* of cells, click the alphabetic heading button at the top of the column.

✔ To select a *row* of cells, click the numeric heading button on the far left side of the row.

Entering and Editing Data in a Spreadsheet

After you navigate to the cell in which you want to enter data, you're ready to type your data. Follow these steps to enter That Important Stuff:

1. **Either click the cell or press the spacebar.**

   A cursor appears, indicating that the cell is ready to hold any data you type.

2. **Type in your data.**

   Spreadsheets can use both numbers and text within a cell — either type of information is considered data in the Spreadsheet World.

3. **To edit data, click within the cell that contains the data to select it and then click the cell again to display the insertion cursor. Drag the insertion cursor across the characters to highlight them and then type the replacement data.**

4. **To simply delete characters, highlight the characters and press Delete.**

5. **When you're ready to move on, press Return (to save the data and move one cell down) or press Tab (to save the data and move one cell to the right).**

Selecting the Right Number Format

After your data has been entered into a cell, row, or column, you still might need to format it before it appears correctly. Numbers gives you a healthy selection of formatting possibilities. *Number formatting* determines how a cell displays a number, such as a dollar amount, a percentage, or a date.

Characters and formatting rules, such as decimal places, commas, and dollar and percentage notation, are included in number formatting. So, if your spreadsheet contains units of currency, such as dollars, format it as such. Then all you need to do is type the numbers, and the currency formatting is applied automatically.

To specify a number format, follow these steps:

1. **Select the cells, rows, or columns you want to format.**

2. **Click the Inspector toolbar button.**

3. **Click the Cells Inspector button in the Inspector toolbar to display the settings you see in Figure 18-3.**

4. **Click the Cell Format pop-up menu and click the type of formatting you want to apply.**

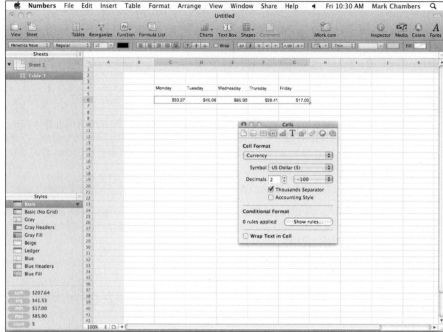

Figure 18-3:
You can format the data you've entered from the Inspector.

Aligning Cell Text Just So

You can also change the alignment of text in the selected cells. (The default alignment for text is flush left and for numeric data, flush right.) Follow these steps:

1. **Select the cells, rows, or columns you want to format.**

   See "Navigate and Select Cells in a Spreadsheet," earlier in this chapter, for tips on selecting stuff.

2. **Click the Inspector toolbar button.**

3. **Click the Text Inspector button in the Inspector toolbar to display the settings you see in Figure 18-4.**

4. **Click the corresponding alignment button to choose the type of formatting you want to apply.**

   You can choose left, right, center, justified, and text left and numbers right. Text can also be aligned at the top, center, or bottom of a cell.

You can also select the cells you want to align and click the appropriate alignment button in the Format Bar.

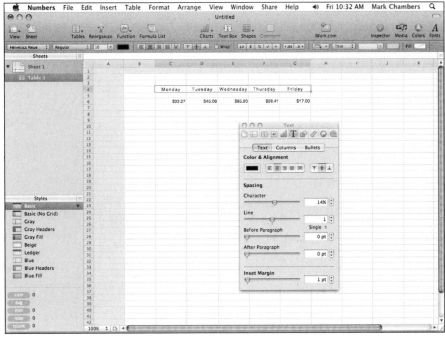

Figure 18-4:
Using the
Inspector to
change text
alignment
within a cell.

Do you need to set apart the contents of some cells? For example, you might need to create text headings for some columns and rows or to highlight the totals in a spreadsheet. To change the formatting of the data displayed within selected cells, select the cells, rows, or columns you want to format and then click the Font Family, Font Size, or Font Color buttons on the Format Bar.

Format with Shading

Shading the contents of a cell, row, or column is helpful when your spreadsheet contains subtotals or logical divisions. Follow these steps to shade cells, rows, or columns:

1. **Select the cells, rows, or columns you want to format.**

2. **Click the Inspector toolbar button.**

3. **Click the Graphic Inspector button in the Inspector toolbar.**

   Numbers displays the settings you see in Figure 18-5.

4. **Click the Fill pop-up menu to select a shading option.**

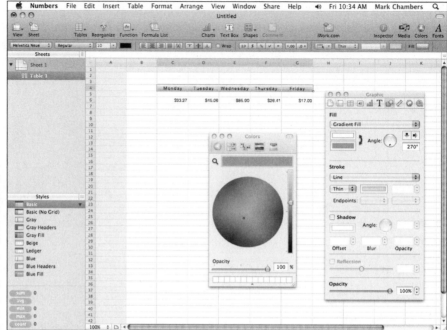

Figure 18-5:
Adding
shading
and colors
to cells,
rows, and
columns
is easy in
Numbers.

5. **Click the color box to select a color for your shading.**

   Numbers displays a color picker (also shown in Figure 18-5).

6. **Click to select a color.**

7. **After you achieve the right effect, click the Close button in the color picker.**

8. **Click the Inspector's Close button to return to your spreadsheet.**

The Fill function is also available on the Format Bar.

Insert and Delete Rows and Columns

What's that? You forgot to add a row and now you're three pages into your data entry? No problem. You can easily add or delete rows and columns. First, select the row or column that you want to delete or that you want to insert a row or column next to, and do one of the following:

✔ **For a row:** Right-click and choose Add Row Above, Add Row Below, or Delete Row from the shortcut menu that appears.

✔ **For a column:** Right-click and choose Add Columns Before, Add Columns After, or Delete Column from the shortcut menu that appears.

You can also insert rows and columns using the Table menu.

The Formula Is Your Friend

Sorry, but it's time to talk about *formulas.* These equations calculate values based on the contents of cells you specify in your spreadsheet. For example, if you designate cell A1 (the cell in column A at row 1) to hold your yearly salary and cell B1 to hold the number 12, you can divide the contents of cell A1 by cell B1 (to calculate your monthly salary) by typing this formula into any other cell:

=A1/B1

By the way, formulas in Numbers always start with an equal sign (=).

"So what's the big deal, Mark? Why not use a calculator?" Sure, but maybe you want to calculate your weekly salary. Rather than grab a pencil and paper, you can simply change the contents of cell B1 to 52, and — boom! — the spreadsheet is updated to display your weekly salary.

That's a simple example, of course, but it demonstrates the basis of using formulas (and the reason that spreadsheets are often used to predict trends and forecast budgets). It's the "what if?" tool of choice for everyone who works with numeric data.

To add a simple formula within your spreadsheet, follow these steps:

1. **Select the cell that will hold the result of your calculation.**

2. **Click inside the Formula Box and type = (the equal sign).**

   The Formula Box appears to the right of the Sheets heading, directly under the Button bar. Note that the Format Bar changes to show a set of formula controls (a.k.a. the Formula Bar).

3. **Click the Function Browser button, which bears the *fx* label. (It appears next to the red Cancel button on the Formula Bar.)**

4. **In the window that appears, as shown in Figure 18-6, click the desired formula and click Insert to add it to the Formula Box.**

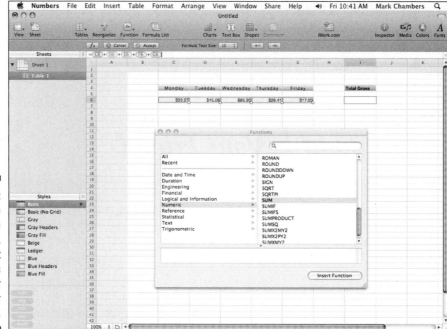

Figure 18-6:
If you have
to use
formulas,
at least
Numbers
can enter
them for
you.

5. **Click an argument button in the formula and click the cell that contains the corresponding data.**

   Numbers automatically adds the cell you indicated to the formula. Repeat this for each argument in the formula.

6. **After you finish, click the Accept button to add the formula to the cell.**

That's it! Your formula is now ready to work behind the scenes, doing math for you so that the correct numbers appear in the cell you specified.

To display all the formulas that you've added to a sheet, click the Formula List button in the toolbar.

Adding Visual Punch with a Chart

Sometimes you just have to see something to believe it — hence the ability to use the data you add to a spreadsheet to generate a professional-looking chart! Follow these steps to create a chart:

1. **Select the adjacent cells you want to chart by dragging the mouse.**

   To choose individual cells that aren't adjacent, you can hold down the ⌘ key as you click.

2. **Click the Charts button on the Numbers toolbar. The Charts button bears the symbol of a bar graph.**

   Numbers displays the thumbnail menu you see in Figure 18-7.

3. **Click the thumbnail for the chart type you want.**

   Numbers inserts the chart as an object within your spreadsheet so that you can move the chart. You can drag using the handles that appear on the outside of the object box to resize your chart. Figure 18-8 illustrates the 3-D chart I generated with just a couple of mouse clicks.

   Click the Inspector toolbar button and you can switch to the Chart Inspector dialog, where you can change the colors and add (or remove) the chart title and legend.

4. **To change the default title, click the title box once to select it; click it again to edit the text.**

After you've added your chart to the sheet, you'll note that it appears in the Sheets list, as also shown in Figure 18-8. To edit the chart at any time, just click on the corresponding entry in the Sheets list.

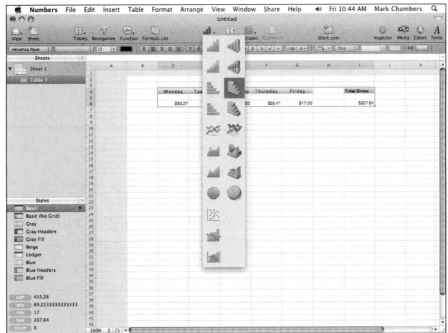

Figure 18-7:
Numbers displays the range of chart styles you can use.

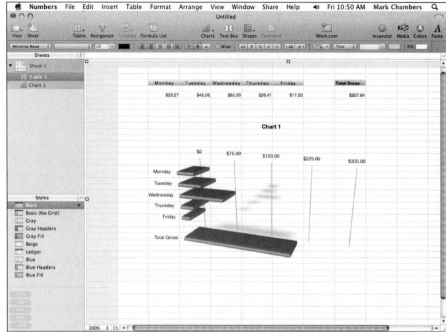

Figure 18-8:
My finished
chart looks
like some-
one with
talent drew
it for me!

Chapter 19

Building Presentations with Keynote

*I*t seems like only yesterday that I was giving business presentations with a clunky overhead projector and black-and-white acetate transparencies. Fancy color gradients and animation were unheard of, and the only sound my presentations made was the droning of the projector's fan. I might as well have been using tree bark and chalk.

Thank goodness those days are gone forever, because cutting-edge presentation software like Keynote makes slide creation easy and — believe it or not — *fun*! This is the application that Steve Jobs once used for his Macworld keynotes every year, and there's so much visual candy available that you'll never need to shout to wake your audience again.

In this chapter, I demonstrate how simple it is to build a stunning Keynote presentation, and how to start and control your slide display from your keyboard (or even your iPhone or iPod touch). Heck, we'll even print your slides and notes so that your audience can keep a copy of your brilliant work!

Creating a New Keynote Project

As do the other applications in the iWork '09 suite, Keynote begins the document creation process with a Template Chooser window. To create a new presentation project, follow these steps:

1. **Double-click your hard drive icon and click the Applications entry in the Finder window sidebar. Double-click the iWork folder to open it.**

   If presentations are your bread and butter, allow the iWork installation program to add a Keynote icon to your Dock. Your clicking finger will thank you.

2. **Double-click the Keynote icon.**

   The Template Chooser window that you see in Figure 19-1 appears. (I have to say that these are probably the most stunning visual building blocks I've ever seen in a presentation application.

3. **Click the Slide Size pop-up menu at the bottom of the screen to select the resolution for your completed slides.**

Figure 19-1: Selecting a template from the Template Chooser window.

Although you don't necessarily need to select an exact match for the screen resolution of your iMac, it's a good idea to select the closest value to the maximum resolution of your projector. (If someone else is providing the projector, the default value of 1024 x 768 is a good standard to use.)

4. **Click the template that most closely matches your needs.**

5. **Click Choose to open a new document by using the template you selected.**

Opening a Keynote Presentation

If an existing Keynote presentation file is visible in a Finder window, you can double-click the document icon to open the project. If Keynote is already running, however, follow these steps to load a project:

1. **Press ⌘+O to display the Open dialog.**

2. **Click the desired drive in the Devices list at the left of the dialog; then click folders and subfolders until you've located the Keynote project. (You can also use the Search box at the top of the Open dialog to locate the document by name or by some of the text it contains.)**

3. **Double-click the filename to load it.**

If you want to open a Keynote document that you've edited in the recent past, things get even easier! Just click File⇨Open Recent and you can open the document with a single click from the submenu that appears. (Note that the Template Chooser window has both Open Recent and Open Existing File buttons as well.)

Saving Your Presentation

When you're done working on a Keynote presentation (or if you'd simply like to safeguard your work in a world of power failures), follow these steps:

1. **Press ⌘+S.**

If you're saving a document that hasn't yet been saved, the familiar Save As sheet appears.

2. **Type a filename for your new document.**

3. **Click the Where pop-up menu and choose a location to save the document.**

   To select a location not on the Where pop-up menu, click the button with the down arrow symbol to expand the sheet. You can also create a new folder from the expanded sheet.

4. **Click Save.**

Putting Keynote to Work

Ready for the 5-cent tour of the Keynote window? Launch the application and create or load a project, and you'll see the tourist attractions shown in Figure 19-2:

Toolbar

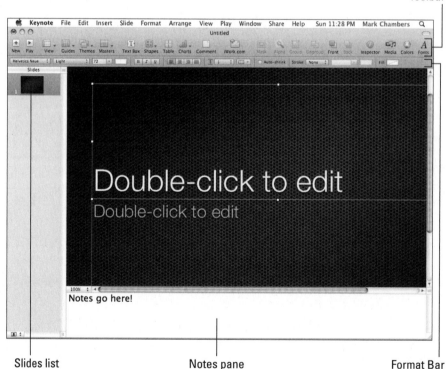

Figure 19-2:
The Keynote window is dominated by the Layout pane.

Slides list

Notes pane

Format Bar

✔ **Slide list:** Use this thumbnail list of all the slides in your project to help you navigate quickly. Click a thumbnail to switch instantly to that slide.

The Slide list can also display your project in outline format, allowing you to check all your discussion points. (This is a great way to ferret out any "holes" in your presentation's flow.) While in outline mode, you can still jump directly to any slide by clicking the slide's title in the outline. To display the outline, click View⇨Outline. You can switch back to the default Navigator Slide list by clicking View⇨Navigator.

✔ **Layout pane:** Your slide appears in its entirety in this pane. You can add elements and edit the content of the slide from the Layout pane.

✔ **Toolbar:** As does the toolbar in Pages and Numbers, Keynote's toolbar makes it easy to find the most common controls you'll use while designing and editing your slides. Clicking an icon in the toolbar performs an action, just as selecting a menu item does.

✔ **Notes pane:** If you decide to add notes to one or more slides (either for your own use or to print as additional information for your audience), click View⇨Show Presenter Notes to open the Notes pane. This text box appears under the Layout pane.

✔ **Format Bar:** Keynote displays this button strip underneath the Keynote toolbar, allowing you to format selected text, paragraphs and lists on the fly.

Adding Slides

Sure, Keynote creates a single Title slide when you first create a project, but not many presentations are complete with just a single slide! To add more slides to your project, use one of these methods:

✔ Click the New button on the Keynote toolbar.

✔ Choose New Slide from the Slide menu.

✔ Press ⌘+Shift+N.

✔ Right-click (or Control-click) in the Slides list and choose New Slide from the menu.

Keynote adds the new slide to your Slides list and automatically switches to the new slide in the Layout pane.

Need a slide that's very similar to an existing slide you've already designed? Right-click the existing slide and choose Duplicate to create a new slide just like it. (Consider it cloning without the science.)

To move slides to different positions in the Slides list (and therefore a different order in your Keynote slideshow), drag each slide thumbnail to the desired spot in the list.

Working with Text and Graphics Boxes

You've probably noticed that all the text within your first Title slide appears within boxes. Keynote uses boxes to manipulate text and graphics. You can resize a box (and its contents) by clicking and dragging one of the handles that appear around the edges of the box. (Your mouse cursor will change into a double-sided arrow when you're "in the zone.") The side-selection handles drag only that edge of the frame, whereas the corner-selection handles resize both adjoining edges of the selection frame.

To keep the proportions of the box constrained, hold down Shift while dragging the corner handles.

Boxes make it easy to move text and graphics together (as a single unit) to another location within the Layout pane. Click in the center of the box and drag the box to the desired spot; Keynote displays alignment lines to help you align the box with other elements around it (or with regular divisions of the slide, like horizontal center). As you can see in Figure 19-3, I'm moving a box on the slide to a new location, and Keynote has supplied alignment lines to help me place it correctly.

To select text or graphics within a box, you should double-click the box.

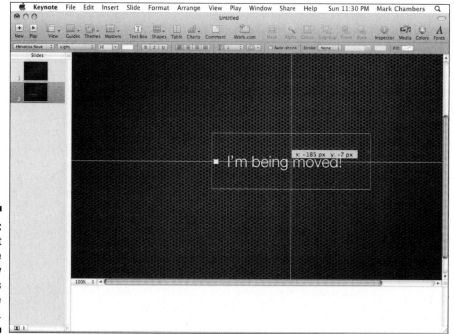

Figure 19-3:
Alignment lines are provided by Keynote as you move boxes.

If you're resizing a photo in a box, don't forget to hold down the Shift key as you drag the frame. Doing so specifies that Keynote should preserve the aspect ratio of the image so that the vertical and horizontal proportions remain fixed. You can also flip images horizontally or vertically from the Arrange menu.

Adding and Editing Slide Text

As with Pages and Numbers, which also use boxes for text layout, Keynote allows you to add or edit text with ease. For example, double-click in a box with the text `Double-click to edit`, and the placeholder text disappears, leaving the field ready to accept new text. Any new text you type appears at the blinking cursor within the box.

To edit existing text in your Keynote document, click using the bar-shaped cursor to select just the right spot in the text, and drag the insertion cursor across the characters to highlight them. Type the replacement text, and Keynote obligingly replaces the text that was there with the text you type.

If you want to delete existing text, click and drag across the characters to highlight them; then press Delete. You can also delete an entire box and all its contents: Right-click (or Control-click) the offending box and choose Delete from the menu that appears.

When the contents of a box are just right and you're finished entering or editing text, click anywhere outside the box to hide it from view. You can always click the text again to display the box later.

Formatting Slide Text for the Perfect Look

Keynote doesn't restrict you to the default fonts for the theme you chose. It's easy to format the text in your slides — you can choose a different font family, font color, text alignment, and text attributes such as bolding and italicizing on the fly, whenever you like.

Select the desired text by double-clicking a box and then dragging the text cursor to highlight the characters. Now apply your formatting using one of these two methods:

✔ **The Format Bar:** The font controls on the Format Bar work just as the controls on the toolbar do: Either click a font control to display a pop-up menu or click a button to immediately perform an action. Clicking the Font Size pop-up menu, for example, displays a range of sizes for the selected text — with a single click on the B (bold) button, you'll add the bold attribute to the highlighted characters.

✔ **The Format menu:** The controls on the Format menu generally mirror those on the Format Bar. To change the alignment from the Format menu, click Format and hover the mouse cursor over the Text menu item. To change text attributes, click Format and hover your mouse over the Font menu.

Using Presenter's Notes in Your Project

As I mention earlier, you can type text notes in the Notes pane — I use them for displaying alternate topic points while presenting my slideshow. However, you can also print the notes for a project along with the slides, so presenter's notes are also great for including reminders and To Do points for your audience in handouts.

To type your notes, just click within the Notes pane; if it's hidden, click View⇨Show Presenter Notes. When you're done adding notes, click in the Slide list or the Layout pane to return to editing mode.

To display your notes while practicing, use Keynote's Rehearsal feature. Click Play and choose Rehearse Slideshow, and you can scroll through the notes while the slideshow runs. (More on slideshows in a second.)

Every Good Presentation Needs Media

Adding audio, photos, and movies to a slide is drag-and-drop easy in Keynote! Simply drag an image, audio, or movie file from a Finder window and place it at the spot you want within your document.

You can also use the Media Browser — click the Media button on the toolbar and click the Audio, Photos, or Movies button to select the desired type. Keynote displays the contents of your various media collections — like your iPhoto and iTunes libraries — or you can also navigate to the file's location on your hard drive, or type in a filename in the Search box at the bottom of the browser. When you've found the file you want to add, drag it to the spot you want in the document. Figure 19-4 illustrates the Media Browser in action.

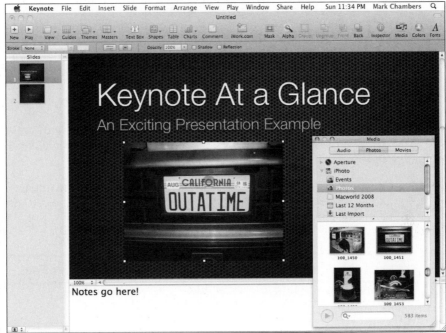

Figure 19-4: It's not just photos — you can add audio and movie clips to a slide, too!

Adding a Background Shape

Text often stands out on a slide when it sits on top of a background shape. To add a shape (such as a rectangle or circle) as a background for your text, follow these steps:

1. **Click the insertion cursor in the location you want.**

2. **Click the Shapes button on the Keynote toolbar and choose a shape.**

   The shape appears in your document.

3. **Click the center of the shape and drag it to a new spot.**

   Like image boxes, shapes can be resized or moved.

4. **When the shape is properly positioned and sized, select it and choose Arrange⇨Send to Back.**

Creating Your Keynote Slideshow

The heart of a Keynote presentation is the slideshow that you build from the slides you've created. A Keynote slideshow is typically presented as a full-screen presentation, with slides appearing in linear order as they are sorted in the Slides list.

In its simplest form, you can always run a slideshow from a Keynote project by clicking the Play button in the toolbar, or by choosing Play⇨Play Slideshow from the menu. You can advance to the next slide by clicking your mouse, or by pressing the right bracket key, which looks like this:].

Of course, other controls are available besides just the ones that advance to the next slide! Table 19-1 illustrates the key shortcuts you'll use most often during a slideshow.

Keynote offers a number of settings that you can tweak to fine-tune your slideshow. To display these settings, choose Keynote⇨Preferences and click the Slideshow button in the Preferences window.

Table 19-1	Keynote Slideshow Shortcut Keys
Key or Key Combination	*Action*
] (right bracket)	Next slide
P	Previous slide
Home	Jump to first slide
End	Jump to last slide
C	Show or hide the pointer
(number)	Jump to the corresponding slide in the Slide list
U	Scroll notes up
D	Scroll notes down
N	Show current slide number
H	Hide slideshow and display last application used (the presentation appears as a minimized icon in the Dock)
B	Pause slideshow and display a black screen (press any key to resume the slideshow)
Esc	Quit

If you have an iPhone or iPod touch handy and you've installed the Apple Keynote Remote application on your device, display the Preferences window and click the Remote button to link your iPhone or iPod touch to your iMac and Keynote. Now you can use your handheld device as a remote and use it during your slideshow!

Printing Your Slides and Notes

Okay, I'll be honest: I don't always print handouts for every presentation I give, just because some of the slideshows I run are short introductions to hands-on demonstrations. However, if you're presenting a lengthy slideshow with plenty of information that you'd like your audience to remember, nothing beats handouts that include scaled-down images of your slides (and, optionally, your presenter's notes).

You're not limited to just paper, though! You can also use Keynote to create an electronic PDF-format document instead of a printed handout, which your audience members can download from your Web site. Or, if you're an educator with access to an interactive whiteboard (such as the SMARTBoard), you can use this new technology with Keynote.

To print your slides and notes, follow these steps:

1. **Within Keynote, click File and choose Print.**

   Keynote displays the Print sheet you see in Figure 19-5. (Note that some printer-specific features may be different on your screen.)

2. **Click the desired format.**

   - To print each slide on a separate page at full size, click Individual Slides.

   - To print each slide on a separate page with the presenter's notes for that slide, click Slides with Notes.

   - To print the contents of your Slides list in Outline view, click Outline.

   - To print a handout with multiple slides per page (and, optionally, with presenter's notes), click Handout. Click the Slides per Page pop-up menu to specify the number of slides that Keynote should print on each page.

3. **Select the pages to print.**

   • To print the entire document, select All.

   • To print a range of selected slides, select the From radio button and enter the starting and ending pages.

4. **Select or deselect specific options from the Options column.**

   You can include elements such as the date, borders around each slide, and the slide number as part of each page of the hardcopy.

5. **Click the Print button to send the job to your printer.**

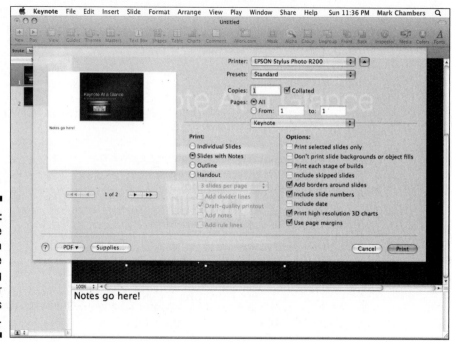

Figure 19-5:
Keynote
offers a
wide range
of printing
options for
your slides
and notes.

Chapter 20

Creating a Multiuser iMac

. . . .

In This Chapter

▶ Enjoying the advantages of a multiuser iMac

▶ Understanding access levels

▶ Adding, editing, and deleting user accounts

▶ Restricting access for managed accounts

▶ Configuring your login window

▶ Sharing files with other users

▶ Securing your stuff with FileVault

. . . .

*E*verybody wants a piece. (Of your iMac, that is.)

Perhaps you live in a busy household with kids, significant others, grandparents, and a wide selection of friends — all of them clamoring for a chance to spend time on the Internet, take care of homework, or enjoy a good game.

On the other hand, your iMac might occupy a classroom or a break room at your office — someplace public, yet everyone wants his own Private iDaho on the iMac, complete with a reserved spot on the hard drive and his own hand-picked attractive Desktop background.

Before you throw your hands up in the air in defeat, read this chapter and take heart! Here you find all the step-by-step procedures, explanations, and tips to help you build a *safe* multiuser iMac that's accessible to all.

(Oh, and you still get to use it, too. That's not being selfish.)

Once Upon a Time (An Access Fairy Tale)

Okay, so you don't have Cinderella, Snow White, or that porridge-loving kid with the trespassing problem. Instead, you have your brother Bob.

Every time Bob visits your place, it seems he needs to do "something" on the Internet, or he needs a moment with your iMac to bang out a quick message, using his Web-based e-mail application. Unfortunately, Bob's forays onto your iMac always result in stuff getting changed, like your Desktop settings, Address Book, and Safari bookmarks.

What you need, good reader, is a visit from the Account Fairy. Your problem is that you have but a single user account on your system, and Snow Leopard thinks that Bob is *you*. By turning your iMac into a multiuser system and giving Bob his own account, Snow Leopard can tell the difference between the two of you, keeping your druthers separate!

With a unique user account, Snow Leopard can track all sorts of things for Bob, leaving your computing environment blissfully pristine. A user account keeps track of stuff such as

- Address Book contacts
- Safari bookmarks and settings
- Desktop settings (including background images, screen resolutions, and Finder tweaks)
- iTunes libraries, just in case Bob brings his own music (sigh)
- Web sites that Bob might ask you to host on your computer (resigned sigh)

Plus, Bob gets his own reserved Home folder on your iMac's hard drive, so he'll quit complaining about how he can't find his files. Oh, and did I mention how user accounts keep others from accessing *your* stuff? And how you can lock Bob out of where-he-should-not-be, such as certain applications, iChat, Mail, and Web sites (including that offshore Internet casino site that he's hooked on)?

Naturally, this is only the tip of the iceberg. User accounts affect just about everything you can do in Snow Leopard and on your iMac. The moral of my little tale? A Mark's Maxim to the rescue:

Assign others their own user accounts, and let Snow Leopard keep track of everything. Then you can share your iMac with others and still live happily ever after!

Big-Shot Administrator Stuff

Get one thing straight right off the bat: *You* are the administrator of your iMac. In network-speak, an *administrator* (or *admin* for short) is the one with the power to Do Unto Others — creating new accounts, deciding who gets access to what, and generally running the multiuser show. In other words, think of yourself as the Monarch of Mac OS X (the ruler, not the butterfly).

I always recommend that you have only one (or perhaps two) accounts with administrator-level access on any computer. This makes good sense because you can be assured that no one can monkey with your iMac while you're away from the keyboard. So why might you want a second admin account? Well, if you're often away on business, you might need to assign a second administrator account to a *trusted* individual who knows as much about your iMac as you do. (Tell 'em to buy a copy of this book.) That way, if something breaks or an account needs to be tweaked in some way, the other person can take care of it whilst you're gone (but without giving that person access to your personal data).

In this section, I explain the typical duties of a first-class iMac administrator.

Deciding who needs what access

Snow Leopard provides three levels of individual user accounts:

- ✔ **Admin (administrator):** See the beginning of this section.
- ✔ **Standard level:** Perfect for most users, these accounts allow access to just about everything but don't let the user make drastic changes to Snow Leopard or create new accounts.
- ✔ **Managed with Parental Controls level:** These are standard accounts with specific limits that are assigned either by you or by another admin account.

Another Mark's Maxim is in order:

Assign other folks standard-level accounts and then decide whether each new account needs to be modified to restrict access as a managed account. *Never* **assign an account admin-level access unless you deem it truly necessary.**

Standard accounts are quick and easy to set up, and I think they provide the perfect compromise between access and security. You'll find that standard access allows your users to do just about anything they need to do, with a minimum of hassle.

Managed accounts (with Parental Controls) are highly configurable so you can make sure that your kids don't end up trashing the hard drive, sending junk mail, or engaging in unmonitored chatting. (*Note:* Parents, teachers, and those folks designing a single public access account for a library or organization — this means *you*.)

Snow Leopard also provides Group and Sharing Only accounts, but shy away from these advanced levels. Stick with the Big Three levels to ensure that everyone has the proper access to your iMac.

Adding users

All right, Mark, enough pregame jabbering — show this good reader how to set up new accounts! Your iMac already has one admin-level account set up for you (created during the initial Snow Leopard set-up process), and you need to be logged in with that account to add a user. To add a new account, follow these steps:

1. **Click the System Preferences icon on the Dock and then click the Accounts icon to display the Accounts pane that you see in Figure 20-1.**

2. **Click the New User button — the one with the plus sign at the bottom of the accounts list — to display the new user sheet shown in Figure 20-2.**

If your New User button is grayed out, your Accounts pane is locked. Remember that you can toggle the padlock icon at the lower-left corner of most of the panes in System Preferences to lock or allow changes. To gain access, do the following:

Figure 20-1: Add new user accounts here.

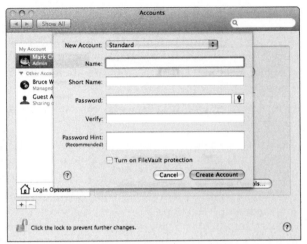

a. *Click the padlock icon to make changes to the Accounts pane.*

b. *When Snow Leopard prompts you for your admin account password (the account you're currently using), enter it.*

c. *Click OK.*

Now you can click the New User button.

3. **Click the New Account pop-up menu and specify the account level status.**

Choose from Administrator, Standard, or Managed with Parental Controls.

You should have only one or two administrator-level users, and your account is already an admin account.

4. **Type the name that you want to display for this account in the Name text box. Press Tab to move to the next field.**

Snow Leopard displays this name on the Login screen, so behave! (For example, Bob has only one "o" the last time I checked.)

5. **(Optional) Although Snow Leopard automatically generates the user's** *short name* **(for use in iChat, and for naming the user's Home folder), you can type a new one. (No spaces, please.) Press Tab again.**

6. **In the Password text box, type the password for the new account. Press Tab to move to the next field.**

Generally, I recommend a password of at least six characters, using a mixture of alpha and numeric characters.

Run out of password ideas? No problem! Click the key button (to the right of the Password text box) to display the Password Assistant, from which Snow Leopard can automatically generate password suggestions of the length you specify. Click the Suggestion pop-up menu, or type directly into the field, and Snow Leopard automatically adds the password you've generated into the Password field.

7. **In the Verify text box, retype the password you chose. Press Tab again to continue your quest.**

8. **(Optional) Snow Leopard can provide a password hint after three unsuccessful login attempts. To offer a hint, type a short question in the Password Hint text box.**

From a security standpoint, password hints are taboo. (Personally, I **never** use 'em. If someone is having a problem logging in to a computer I administer, you better believe I want to know *why*.) Therefore, despite the recommendation Snow Leopard shows here, I strongly recommend that you skip this field — and if you *do* offer a hint, **keep it vague!** Avoid hints like, "Your password is the name of the Wookie in Star Wars." *Geez.*

9. **(Optional) Click the Turn on FileVault protection check box to enable it.**

I'll discuss this security feature in more detail at the end of this chapter — it's A Good Thing, so I recommend using FileVault.

10. **Click the Create Account button.**

The new account shows up in the list at the left of the Accounts pane.

Each user's Home folder has the same default subfolders, including Movies, Music, Pictures, Sites, and such. A user can create new subfolders within his or her Home folder at any time.

Here's one more neat fact about a user's Home folder: No matter what the account level, most of the contents of a Home folder can't be viewed by other users. (Yes, that includes admin-level users. This way, everyone using your iMac gets her own little area of privacy.) Within the Home folder, only the Sites and Public folders can be accessed by other users — and only in a limited fashion. More on these folders later in this chapter.

Modifying user accounts

Next, consider the basic modifications that you can make to a user account, such as changing existing information or selecting a new picture to represent that user's unique personality.

To edit an existing account, log in with your admin account, display the System Preferences window, and click Accounts to display the account list. Then follow these steps:

1. **Click the account that you want to change.**

   Don't forget to unlock the Accounts pane if necessary. See the earlier section, "Adding users," to read how.

2. **Edit the settings that you need to change.**

   For example, you can reset the user's password, or (if absolutely necessary) upgrade the account to admin level.

3. **Click the Picture well and then click a thumbnail image to represent this user (as shown in Figure 20-3).**

Figure 20-3:
Pick the image that best represents a user.

An easy way to get an image is to use one from your hard drive. Click Edit Picture and then drag a new image from a Finder window into the Picture well. (Alternatively, you could click Edit Picture and then click the Snapshot button — which bears a tiny camera — to grab a picture from your iSight video camera. After you capture the essence of your subject as a photo, click Set to return to the Accounts pane.)

Using the default login settings, Snow Leopard displays this image in the Login list next to the account name.

4. **When everything is correct, press ⌘+Q to close the System Preferences dialog.**

   There's no need to save your changes (as a separate step) within System Preferences. Snow Leopard does that automatically when you close the System Preferences window.

Standard-level users have some control over their accounts — they're not helpless, ya know. Standard users can log in, open System Preferences, and click Accounts to change the account password or picture, as well as the *My Card* assigned to them in Snow Leopard Address Book. All standard users can also set up Login Items, which I cover later in this chapter. Note, however, that managed users might not have access to System Preferences at all, so they can't make changes. (Read about this in the upcoming section, "Managing access settings for an account.")

I banish thee, Mischievous User!

Not all user accounts last forever. Students graduate, co-workers quit, kids move out of the house (at last!), and Bob might even find a significant other who has a faster cable modem. We can only hope.

Anyway, no matter what the reason, you can delete a user account at any time. Log in with your admin account, display the Accounts pane in System Preferences, and then follow these steps to eradicate an account:

1. **Click the account that you want to delete.**

2. **Click the Delete User button (which bears the Minus Sign of Doom). Refer to Figure 20-1.**

   Snow Leopard displays a confirmation sheet, as shown in Figure 20-4. By default, the contents of the user's Home folder are saved in a disk image file — which you can restore with Disk Utility — in the Deleted Users folder. (This safety is a good idea if the user might return in the future, allowing you to retrieve their old stuff. However, this option is available only if you have enough space on your hard drive to create the Home folder image file.)

3. **To clean up completely, select the Delete the Home Folder radio button and then click OK.**

   Snow Leopard wipes everything connected with the user account off your hard drive.

4. **Press ⌘+Q to close the System Preferences dialog.**

Time once again for a Mark's Maxim:

> *Always* delete unnecessary user accounts. Otherwise, you're leaving holes in your iMac's security — and eating up disk space.

Figure 20-4:
This is your
last chance
to save the
stuff from a
deleted user
account.

Setting up Login Items and Parental Controls

Every account on your iMac can be customized. Understandably, some settings are accessible only to admin-level accounts, and others can be adjusted by standard-level accounts. In this section, I introduce you to the things that can be enabled (or disabled) within a user account.

Automating with Login Items

Login Items are applications or documents that can be set to launch or load automatically as soon as a specific user logs in — for example, Apple Mail or Address Book. In fact, a user must be logged in to add or remove Login Items. Even an admin-level account can't change the Login Items for another user.

A user must have access to the Accounts pane within the System Preferences window in order to use Login Items. As you can read in the following section, a user can be locked out of System Preferences, which makes it more difficult for Login Items to be added or deleted for that account. (Go figure.)

To set Login Items for your account, follow these steps:

1. **Click the System Preferences icon on the Dock and then click the Accounts icon.**

2. **Click the Login Items tab to display the settings that you see in Figure 20-5.**

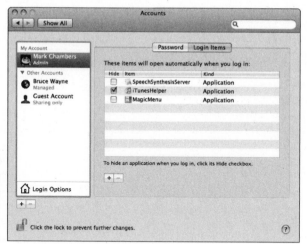

Figure 20-5:
Add apps to
your Login
Items list.

3. **Click the Add button (with the plus sign) to display a file selection sheet.**

4. **Navigate to the application you want to launch each time you log in, click it to select it, and then click Add.**

   If you're in the mood to drag and drop, just drag the applications you want to add from a Finder window and drop them directly into the list.

5. **Press ⌘+Q to quit System Preferences and save your changes.**

Login Items are launched in the order that they appear in the list, so feel free to drag the items into any order you like.

Managing access settings for an account

A standard-level account with restrictions is a managed account. (You can read about these accounts earlier in this chapter.) With these accounts, you can restrict access to many different places within Snow Leopard and your iMac's applications via *Parental Controls*. (Naturally, admin-level accounts don't need Parental Controls because an admin account has no restrictions.)

In short, Parental Controls come in handy in preventing users — family members, students, co-workers, friends, or the public at large — from damaging your computer, your software, or Snow Leopard itself to accessing inappropriate material on the Internet (or even just using your iMac after bedtime). If an account has been restricted with Parental Controls, the account description changes from Standard to Managed in the Accounts list.

To display the Parental Controls for a standard account, start here:

1. **Log in with an admin-level account.**

2. **Open System Preferences and then click Accounts.**

3. **Click the Standard account in the list and then select the Enable Parental Controls check box.**

Now click the Open Parental Controls button to display the specific category tabs that you see in Figure 20-6:

- ✔ **System:** These settings (which I discuss in more detail in a second) affect what the user can do within Snow Leopard as well as what the Finder itself looks like to that user.

- ✔ **Content:** These settings control the Dictionary and Safari applications. If you prefer that profane terms be hidden within the Dictionary for this user, select the Hide Profanity in Dictionary check box to enable it. Snow Leopard also offers three levels of control for Web sites:

  - *Allow Unrestricted Access:* Select this radio button to allow unfettered access for this user.

  - *Try to Limit Access:* You can allow Safari to automatically block Web sites that it deems "adult." To specify particular sites that Safari should allow or deny, click the Customize button.

  - *Allow Access to Only These Websites:* Select this radio button to specify which Web sites that the user can view. To add a Web site, click the Add button (which bears a plus sign); Snow Leopard then prompts you for a title and the Web site address.

- ✔ **Mail & iChat:** Select the Limit Mail and the Limit iChat check boxes to specify the e-mail and instant-messaging addresses that this user can communicate with. To add an address that the user can e-mail or chat with, click the Add button.

  If you want a notification if the user is attempting to send an e-mail to someone not in the list, select the Send Permission Requests To check box to enable it and then type your e-mail address in the text box.

- ✔ **Time Limits:** Parents, click the Time Limits button, and you'll shout with pure joy! You can limit an account to a certain number of hours of usage per weekday (Weekday Time Limits), limit to a specified number of hours of usage per weekend day (Weekend Time Limits), and set a bedtime computer curfew time for both weekdays and weekend days.

- ✔ **Logs:** Snow Leopard keeps a number of different types of *text log files* (which track where the user goes on the Internet, which applications are launched by the account, and the contents of any iChat conversations where the user was a participant). From this central pane, you can monitor all the logs for a particular account. Note that these logs are enabled or disabled from other locations within Snow Leopard: For example, the log showing the Web sites visited and blocked is enabled from the Content panel that I describe a little earlier, whereas the applications log is enabled from the System panel. iChat logging is turned on from the Preferences dialog within the iChat application.

Figure 20-6:
You don't have to be a parent to assign Parental Controls!

You can always tell whether an account has been assigned Parental Controls because the account description changes from Standard to Managed in the Accounts list.

Of particular importance are the System controls. Click the System tab to modify these settings:

- **Use Simple Finder:** The Simple Finder is a great idea for families and classrooms with smaller children. For the ultimate in restrictive Snow Leopard environments — think public access or kiosk mode — you can assign the Simple Finder to an account. Even the Dock itself is restricted, sporting only the Finder icon, Trash, the Dashboard, and those folders that allow users to access their documents and applications.

- **Only Allow Selected Applications:** When this option is enabled, you can select the specific applications that appear to the user. These restrictions are in effect whether the user has access to the full Finder or just the Simple Finder.

- *To allow access to all the applications of a specific type:* Select the check box next to the desired group heading to enable it. This includes iLife, iWork, Internet, Widgets, Other, and Utilities.

- *To restrict access to all applications within a group:* If a group heading check box is enabled and you want to deny access to all the applications in that group, clear the check box next to the heading to disable it.

- *To toggle restriction on and off for specific applications within these groups:* Click the triangle icon next to each group heading to expand its list and then either mark or clear the check box next to the desired applications. Snow Leopard denotes partial access within a group — a mixture of full and restricted applications — with a dash mark in the group heading check box.

  To locate a specific application, click in the Search box and type the application name.

- *To add a new application to the Allow list:* Drag its icon from the Finder and drop it in the list within the Other group. After you add an application, it appears in the Other group, and you can toggle access to it on and off like the applications in the named groups.

✔ **Can Administer Printers:** With this check box enabled, the user can modify the printers and printer queues within the Print & Fax pane in System Preferences. If disabled, the user can still print to the default printer and switch to other assigned printers, but can't add or delete printers.

✔ **Can Burn CDs and DVDs:** Disable this check box to prevent the user from recording CDs or DVDs via the built-in disc recording features in Mac OS X. (*Note:* If you load a third-party recording program, such as Toast, the user can still record discs with it, so you probably want to disallow Toast access for the user in question.)

✔ **Can Change Password:** Enable this check box to allow the user to change the account password.

If you're creating a single standard-level account for an entire group of people to use — for example, if you want to leave the machine in kiosk mode in one corner of the office or if everyone in a classroom will use the same account on the machine — I recommend disabling the ability to change the account password. (Oh, and please do me a favor . . . *don't* create a system with just one admin-level account that everyone is supposed to use! Instead, keep your one admin-level account close to your bosom and create a standard-level account for the Unwashed Horde.)

✔ **Can Modify the Dock:** Enable this check box, and the user can add or remove applications, documents, and folders from the Dock in the full Finder.

Multiuser Rules for Everyone

After you're hip on user accounts and the changes you can make to them, turn to a number of topics that affect all users of your iMac — things like how they log in, how a user can share information with everyone else on the computer, and how each user account can be protected from unscrupulous outsiders with state-of-the-art encryption. (Suddenly you're James Bond! I told you Snow Leopard would open new doors for you.)

Logging on and off in Snow Leopard For Dummies

Hey, how about the login screen itself? How do your users identify themselves? Time for another of my "Shortest books in the *For Dummies* series" special editions. (The title's practically longer than the entire book.)

Snow Leopard offers four methods of logging folks in to your multiuser iMac:

- **The username and password login:** This is the most secure type of login screen you'll see in Snow Leopard because you have to actually type your account username and your password. (A typical hacker isn't going to know all the usernames on your iMac.) Press Return or click the Log In button to compete the process.

    When you enter your username and password, you see bullets instead of your password because Snow Leopard displays bullet characters to ensure security. Otherwise, someone could simply look over your shoulder and see your password.

- **The list login:** This login screen offers a good middle of the road between security and convenience. Click your account username in the list and type your password when the login screen displays the password prompt. Press Return or click the Log In button to continue.

- **Fast User Switching:** This feature, as shown in Figure 20-7, allows another user to sit down and log in while the previous user's applications are still running in the background. This is perfect for a fast e-mail check or a scan of your eBay bids without forcing someone else completely off the iMac. When you turn on Fast User Switching, Snow Leopard displays the currently active user's name at the right side of the Finder menu bar.

To switch to another account

a. *Click the current user's name in the Finder menu (refer to Figure 20-7).*

b. *Click the name of the user who wants to log in.*

Snow Leopard displays the login window, just as if the iMac had been rebooted.

The previous user's stuff is still running, so you definitely shouldn't reboot or shut down the iMac!

To switch back to the previous user

a. *Click the username again in the Finder menu.*

b. *Click the previous user's name.*

For security, Snow Leopard prompts you for that account's login password.

✔ **Auto login:** This is the most convenient method of logging in but offers no security whatsoever. Snow Leopard automatically logs in the specified account when you start or reboot your iMac.

Figure 20-7:
The Fast
User
Switching
menu,
unfurled for
all to see.

I *strongly recommend* that you use auto login only if

- Your iMac is in a secure location.
- You are the only one using your iMac.
- You're setting up a public-access iMac, in which case you want your iMac to immediately log in with the public account.

Working in a public environment? *Never* set an admin-level account as the auto login account. This is the very definition of ASDI, or *A Supremely Dumb Idea.*

To set up a username/password or list login, open System Preferences, click the Accounts icon, and then display the Login Options settings (see Figure 20-8). Select the List of Users radio button for a list login screen, or select the Name and Password radio button to require your users to type their full user-name and password.

To enable Fast User Switching, mark the Enable Fast User Switching check box (as shown in Figure 20-8).

To set Auto Login, choose the account that Snow Leopard should use from the Automatic Login pop-up menu (as shown by the now-legendary Figure 20-8).

Figure 20-8: Configure your login settings from the Login Options pane.

Logging out of Snow Leopard all the way (without Fast User Switching) is a cinch. Just click the Apple menu (⌘) and then choose Log Out. (From the keyboard, press ⌘+Shift+Q.) A confirmation dialog appears that will auto-matically log you off in one minute — but don't forget that if someone walks up and clicks Cancel, he'll be using your iMac with your account! Your iMac returns to the login screen, ready for its next victim. Heed this Mark's Maxim:

Always **click the Log Out button on the logout confirmation dialog before you leave your iMac.**

Interesting stuff about sharing stuff

You might wonder where shared documents and files reside on your iMac. That's a good question. Like just about everything in Snow Leopard, there's a simple answer. The Users folder on your iMac has a *Shared* folder within it. To share a file or folder, it should be placed in the Shared folder.

You don't have to turn on File Sharing in the Sharing pane of System Preferences to use Shared folders on your iMac. Personal File Sharing affects only network access to your machine by users of other computers.

Each user account on your iMac also has a *Public* folder within that user's Home folder. This is a read-only folder that other users on your iMac (and across the network) can access: They can only open and copy the files that it contains. (Sorry, no changes to existing documents from other users, or new documents from other users.) Every user's Public folder contains a *Drop Box* folder, where other users can copy or save files but can't view the contents. Think of the Drop Box as a mailbox where you drop off stuff for the other user.

Encrypting your Home folder can be fun

Allowing others to use your iMac always incurs a risk — especially if you store sensitive information and documents on your computer. Although your login password should ensure that your Home folder is off limits to everyone else, consider an extra level of security to prevent even a dedicated hacker from accessing your stuff.

To this end, Snow Leopard includes *FileVault,* which automatically encrypts the contents of your Home folder. Without the proper key (in this case, either your login password or your admin's master password), the data contained in your Home folder is impossible for just about anyone to read. (I guess the FBI or NSA would be able to decrypt it, but they're not likely a worry at your place!)

The nice thing about FileVault is that it's completely transparent to you and your users. In other words, when you log in, Snow Leopard automatically takes care of decrypting and encrypting the stuff in your Home folder for you. You literally won't know that FileVault is working for you — which is how computers are *supposed* to work.

To turn on FileVault protection for a specific account, follow these steps:

1. **Click the System Preferences icon on the Dock and then click the Security icon.**

2. **Click the FileVault button.**

3. **If necessary, click Set Master Password to create a master password.**

You need to be logged in with an admin-level account to set a master password. However, this needs to be done only once, no matter how many accounts you're hosting on your iMac. Using this master password, any admin-level user can unlock any Home folder for any user.

Before you move to Step 4, note that you must be logged in using the account that requires the FileVault protection. (Therefore, if you had to log in using your admin-level account to set a master password, you have to log out and log in again using the account you want to protect. Arrgh.)

4. **Click the Turn on FileVault button.**

5. **Enter your account's login password when prompted and then click OK.**

6. **Click the Turn on FileVault button on the confirmation screen.**

7. **After Snow Leopard encrypts your Home folder and logs you out, log in again normally.**

You're done!

Remember those passwords. Again, **do not forget** your account login password, and make doggone sure that your admin user never forgets the master password! If you forget these passwords, you can't read anything in your Home folder, and even the smartest Apple support technician will tell you that nothing can be done.

Chapter 21

Building (Or Joining) a Network

*I*n my book, network access ranks right up there with air conditioning and the microwave oven. Like other "I can't imagine life without them" kinds of technologies, it's hard to imagine sharing data from your iMac with others around you without a network. Sure, I've used a *sneakernet* (the old-fashioned term for running back and forth between computers with a floppy disk), but these days, Apple computers don't even *have* floppy drives.

Nope, networking is here to stay. Whether you use it to share an Internet connection, challenge your friends to a nice relaxing game of WWII battlefield action, or stream your MP3 collection to other computers that use iTunes, you'll wonder how you ever got along without one. In this chapter, I fill you in on all the details you need to know to get your iMac hooked up to a new (or an existing) network.

What, Exactly, Is the Network Advantage?

If you have other family members with computers or if your iMac is in an office with other computers (including those rascally PCs), here's just a sample of what you can do with a network connection:

✔ **Share an Internet connection.** This is *the* major reason why many families and most small businesses install a network. Everyone can simultaneously use the same digital subscriber line (DSL) or cable Internet connection on every computer on the network.

✔ **Share a printer.** You say your fellow employee — or even worse, your big sister — has a great printer connected to their computer? Luckily, that printer can be shared with anyone across your network.

✔ **Copy and move files of all sizes.** Need to get a large iDVD project from one Mac to another? With a network connection, you can accomplish this task in just minutes. Otherwise you'd have to burn that file to a DVD-R or use a Flash drive. A network connection makes copying as simple as dragging the project folder from one Finder window to another.

✔ **Share documents across your network.** Talk about a wonderful collaboration tool. For example, you can drop a Word document or Keynote presentation file in your Public folder and ask for comments and edits from others in your office.

✔ **Stream music and video.** With iTunes, you can share your audio and video media collection on your iMac with other Macs and PCs on your network. Your eyes and ears can't tell the difference!

✔ **Play multiplayer games.** Invite your friends over and tell 'em that you're hosting a *LAN party* (the techno-nerd term for a large gathering of game players, connected through the same network, all playing the same multiplayer game. (Suddenly you'll see firsthand just how devious a human opponent can be.) Each participant needs to buy a copy of the same game, naturally, but the fun you'll have is worth every cent you spend. Don't forget the chips!

If your iMac isn't within shouting distance of an existing network or you don't plan on buying any additional computers, stop right here — a lone iMac hanging out in your home with no other computers around won't need a network.

If you have just your iMac and an Internet connection and you have no plans to add another computer or a network printer, a network isn't necessary.

The Great Debate: Wired versus Wireless

After you decide that you indeed need a network for your home or office, you have another decision to make: Should you install a *wired* network (running cables between your computers) or a *wireless* network? Heck, should you throw caution completely to the wind and build a combination network with both wireless and wired hardware?

Your first instinct is probably to choose a wireless network for convenience. After all, this option allows you to eliminate running cables behind furniture (or in the ceiling of your office building). Ah, but I must show you the advantages to a wired network as well. Table 21-1 shows the lowdown to help you make up your mind.

Table 21-1	Network Decision Making	
Factor	*Wireless Networks*	*Wired Networks*
Speed	Moderate	Much faster
Security	Moderate	Better
Convenience	Better	Worse
Compatibility	Confusing standards	Easier to understand
Cables	Few (or none)	Required

As I call it, here are the advantages of choosing a wired or a wireless network setup:

✔ **Wired:** Using a wired network offers two significant perks over a wireless network:

- *Faster speeds:* In general, wired networks that are compatible with your iMac are many times faster than the fastest 802.11n wireless connections.

  The performance of a wireless connection can be compromised by interference (from impeding structures, such as concrete walls; and from household appliances, such as some wireless phones and microwave ovens) and by distance.

- *Better security:* A wired network doesn't broadcast a signal that can be picked up outside your home or office, so it's more secure.

  Hackers can attack through your Internet connection. Always use a firewall. I subtly emphasize this point in the section, "USE YOUR FIREWALL!," later in this chapter.

✔ **Wireless:** A wireless connection really has only one advantage, but it's a big one: *convenience* (which, in this case, is another word for *mobility* for all your networked devices).

Accessing your network anywhere within your home or office — without cables — is so easy. You can also easily connect a wireless printer. And when using an AirPort Express mobile Base Station, even your home stereo can get connected to your MP3 collection on your iMac. Read more about Base Stations later on.

Sharing Internet Access

Time to see what's necessary to share an Internet connection. In this section, I cover two methods of connecting your network to the Internet. (And before you open your wallet, keep in mind that you might be able to use your iMac to share your broadband connection across your network!)

Using your iMac as a sharing device

Figure 21-1 illustrates how you can use your iMac to provide a shared Internet connection across a simple wireless network, using either

- **A broadband DSL or cable connection**
- **An external USB dialup modem**

I recommend sharing a dialup modem Internet connection *only* if you have no other option. A dialup modem connection really can't handle the data transfer speeds for more than one computer to access the Internet comfortably at one time. (In plain English, an external USB modem that you add to your iMac isn't fast enough for both you and your significant other to surf the Web at the same time.) Sharing a dialup connection just isn't practical.

In either configuration, your iMac uses the Mac OS X Snow Leopard built-in Internet connection sharing feature to get the job done, *but your iMac must remain turned on to allow Internet sharing*. I show you how to do this in the upcoming section, "Network Internet connections," later in this chapter.

Using a dedicated Internet sharing device

Figure 21-2 illustrates how a broadband connection works if you use a dedicated Internet sharing device (often called an *Internet router*) to connect to your cable or DSL modem. You have to buy this additional hardware, but your iMac doesn't have to remain turned on just so everyone can get on the Internet.

Internet routers usually include either wired or wireless network connections — and many include both.

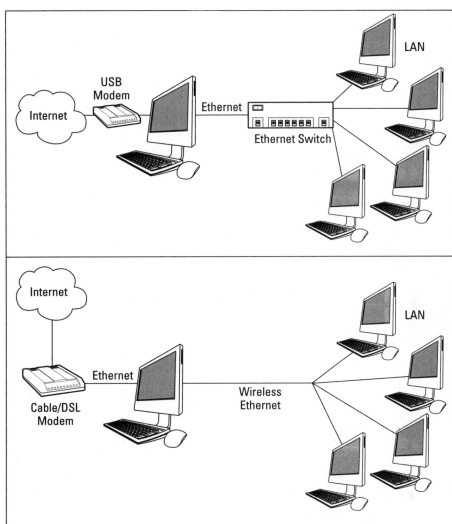

Figure 21-1:
Share an
Internet
connection
wirelessly
via your
iMac.

Setting up an Internet router is usually a pretty simple matter, but the
configuration depends on the device manufacturer and usually involves a
number of different settings in System Preferences that vary according to the
model of router you're installing. Grab a diet cola, sit down with the router's
manual, and follow the installation instructions you'll find there. (In some
cases, you may need to set up your cable or DSL modem as a *bridge* between
your ISP and your router, which should be covered in your modem and
router manuals as well.)

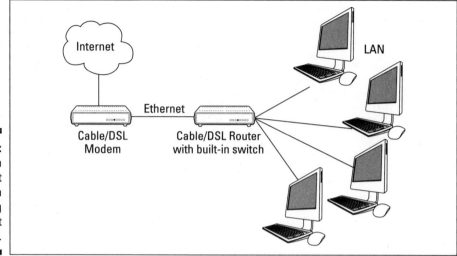

Figure 21-2:
Share an
Internet
connection
by using
an Internet
router.

Most Internet routers offer a DHCP (Dynamic Host Configuration Protocol) server, which automatically assigns Internet protocol (IP) addresses, and I *strongly* recommend that you turn on this feature!

What Do You Need to Connect?

Most *normal* folks — whom I define as those who have never met a network system administrator, and couldn't care less — think that connecting to a network probably involves all sorts of arcane chants and a mystical symbol or two. In this section, I provide you with the shopping list that you need to set up a network — or connect to a network that's already running.

Wireless connections

Today's iMacs come complete with built-in AirPort Extreme wireless hardware, so if you already have an AirPort Extreme or Express Base Station, you're set to go. Otherwise, hold on tight while I lead you through the hardware requirements for wireless networking. (Kinda ironic, don't you think?)

The maximum signal range — and effectiveness — of any wireless network can be impeded by intervening walls or by electrical devices, such as microwave ovens and some wireless phones, all of which can generate interference.

Connecting an iMac to an existing wireless network

Connecting an Intel iMac to an existing wireless network requires no extra hardware because your hardware is already built in. (Whew. That was easy!)

Using a base station to go wireless

If you decide that you want to build your own wireless network, you eschew cables, or you want to add wireless support to your existing wired network, you need a *base station*. The base station can act as a bridge between computers using wireless and your existing wired network. Such a wireless base station will have either

- ✔ A port that can connect to your existing wired network's switch
- ✔ A full built-in switch for wired connectivity (which means you can sell your old wired Ethernet switch to your sister in Tucson)

And, of course, a base station can simply act as a central switch for your wireless network (with no support for a wired network at all).

You can use either a cool Apple Base Station or a boring 802.11n generic wireless base station; however, the Apple hardware requires less configuration and tweaking. (Sounds like a Mark's Maxim!)

If you don't want the hassle of tweaking PC hardware to accommodate your aluminum iMac, buy Apple hardware and software.

Apple Base Station models

As listed in Table 21-2, your iMac can work with three different Apple Base Station models for wireless networking:

- ✔ **AirPort Extreme**

  I recommend using AirPort Extreme if your network needs an enhanced antenna, which provides greater range. You can read about connectivity ranges in the upcoming Table 21-2. The Extreme is also a good pick if you need wired connectivity on your network.

- ✔ **AirPort Express (as shown in Figure 21-3)**

Figure 21-3:
The AirPort Express portable Base Station.

I recommend using AirPort Express if you want to

- *Carry your wireless base station with you.* Express is much smaller than the other Apple Base Station models. (Think "party on the patio" or a LAN gaming get-together at a friend's house.)

- *Connect your home stereo for wireless music streaming.* You can use the AirTunes sharing feature in iTunes.

✔ **Time Capsule**

Apple's Time Capsule unit isn't just a wireless remote hard drive: It can also act as a full AirPort Extreme Base Station. In fact, the wireless specifications for a Time Capsule unit and an AirPort Extreme Base Station are almost identical.

The 802.11n standard used by the AirPort Extreme, Time Capsule, and AirPort Express Base Stations delivers a connection that's several times faster than the old AirPort Base Station's 802.11b/802.11g standards. 802.11n is also compatible with *all* the older standards — 802.11b/a/g — so I highly recommend that you stick with 802.11n in the future. It plays well with others, and at warp speed, to boot!

Table 21-2	Apple Wireless Network Base Stations	
Feature	*AirPort Extreme/Time Capsule*	*AirPort Express*
Price	$180/$299	$99
Users (maximum)	50	10
802.11n support	Yes	Yes
802.11g support	Yes	Yes
802.11b support	Yes	Yes
LAN Ethernet jack (high-speed Internet connection)	Yes	Yes
WAN Ethernet jack (wired computer network)	Yes	No
Stereo mini-jack	No	Yes
USB printer port	Yes	Yes
Maximum signal range (approximate)	150 feet (standard) 250 feet (with add-on antenna)	150 feet
AC adapter	Separate on AirPort Extreme/ built-in on Time Capsule	Built-in

The names of the Apple Base Stations are irritatingly similar; Apple usually does a better job differentiating their product names. Jot down the name of your model on a sticky note and stick it on your iMac's Desktop just so you don't get confused.

Installing an Apple Base Station is simple:

1. **If you have a DSL or cable modem, connect it to the Ethernet LAN port on the Base Station with an Ethernet cable.**

2. **If you have an existing wired Ethernet computer network using a switch or router, connect it to the WAN (wide area network) port on the Base Station with an Ethernet cable.**

   Only the AirPort Extreme and Time Capsule stations have a WAN port.

3. **If you have a USB printer, connect it to the USB port on the Base Station.**

   I cover the steps to share a printer in the upcoming section, "Sharing a network printer."

4. **Connect the power cable from the AC power adapter.**

   The AirPort Express and Time Capsule units have a built-in AC adapter, so if you're using one of these models, just plug the device itself into the wall.

5. **Switch on your Base Station.**

6. **Run the installation software provided by Apple on your iMac.**

Using non-Apple base stations

If any company other than Apple manufactured your wireless base station, the installation procedure is almost certainly the same. (Naturally, you should take a gander at the manufacturer's installation guide just to make sure, but I added many different brands of these devices and used the same steps for each one.)

However, I should note that Apple wireless hardware uses a slightly different security encryption standard than most PC wireless hardware, which results in an extra hurdle when connecting to a non-Apple base station with your iMac. (More on this in the next section. For now, just remember that I recommend using Apple wireless hardware with your iMac whenever possible. It's just a little easier!)

Joining a wireless network

As far as I'm concerned, the only two types of base stations on the planet are Apple and non-Apple (which includes all 802.11n and 802.11g Base Stations and access points). In these two sections, I relate what you need to know to get onboard, using either type of hardware.

Apple AirPort Base Stations

To join a wireless network that's served by any flavor of Apple Base Station, follow these steps on each Mac with wireless support:

1. **Click the System Preferences icon on the Dock.**

2. **Click the Network icon.**

3. **From the Connection list on the left, click AirPort.**

4. **Mark the Show AirPort Status in Menu Bar check box.**

5. **Click the Apply button.**

6. **Press ⌘+Q to quit System Preferences and save your settings.**

7. **Click the AirPort status icon (which looks like a fan) on the Finder menu bar.**

8. **From the AirPort menu, choose an existing network connection that you'd like to join.**

   The network name is the same as the network name you chose when you set up your AirPort Base Station.

9. **If you set up a secure network, enter the password you assigned to the network during setup.**

By the way, security is always A Good Thing, and I strongly recommend that you enable the password encryption features of your Apple Base Station while installing it! (Luckily, the Apple Base Station setup application leads you through this very process.) In the words of an important Mark's Maxim:

Keep uninvited guests out of your network! Use your base station's security features and encrypt your data!

Some wireless networks might not appear in your AirPort menu list. These are *closed networks*, which can be specified when you set up your AirPort Base Station. You can't join a closed network unless you know the exact network name (which is far more secure than simply broadcasting the network name). To join a closed network, follow these steps:

1. **Select Join Other Network from the AirPort menu.**

   To open the menu, click the AirPort status icon (which looks like a fan) on the Finder menu bar.

2. **Type the name of the network.**

3. **If the network is secured with *WEP* or *WPA2* encryption — the two most popular security standards for protecting your data through encryption — click the Security pop-up menu and select which type of encryption is being used.**

4. **Enter the network password, if required.**

To disconnect from an AirPort network, click the AirPort menu and either

✔ **Choose Turn AirPort Off.**

✔ **Connect to another AirPort network.**

In other words, if you choose another available AirPort network from the AirPort menu, your iMac will automatically drop the previous connection. (You can only be connected to one wireless network at a time, which makes Good Sense.)

Using non-Apple Base Stations

If you're using your iMac to connect to a non-Apple base station, you might need to follow a specific procedure that takes care of the slightly different password functionality used by standard 802.11b/g/n hardware.

Snow Leopard can take care of many potential wireless "language barriers" caused by security encryption — the two most common forms are WEP and LEAP — so whether you need to massage your password to connect to your non-Apple base station depends on the specific hardware and encryption system that it uses.

To read or print the latest version of this procedure, fire up Safari and visit http://kbase.info.apple.com/index.html, searching on the number 106250. (This is the Apple Knowledge Base article number, which you can type in the first search field.) This article provides the details on how to convert a standard wireless encrypted password to a format that your AirPort Extreme hardware can understand.

Wired connections

If you're installing a wired network, your iMac already comes with most of what you need for joining your new cabled world. You just connect the hardware and configure the connection. Don't forget that you also need cables and an inexpensive Ethernet switch. (If you're using an Internet router or other hardware sharing device, it almost certainly has a built-in 4 or 8-port switch.)

Connecting iMac hardware to a wired network

Your Ethernet 10/100/1000 port (which looks like a slightly oversized modem port) is located in the line of ports on the back of your iMac, ready to accept a standard Ethernet Cat5/Cat5E/Cat6 cable with RJ-45 connectors. If you're connecting to an existing wired network, you need a standard Cat5/Cat5E/Cat6 Ethernet cable of the necessary length. I recommend a length of no more than 25 feet because cables longer than 25 feet are often subject to line interference (which can slow down or even cripple your connection). You also need a live Ethernet port from the network near your iMac. Plug the cable into your iMac, and then plug the other end into the network port.

Wired network hardware

If you don't know your switch from your NIC, don't worry. Here, I provide you with a description of the hardware that you need for your wired network.

Wired network components

If you're building your own wired network, you need

 ✔ **A switch:** This gizmo's job is to provide more network ports for the other computers in your network. They typically come in 4- and 8-port configurations.

   As I mention earlier in this chapter, most Internet routers (sometimes called *Internet sharing devices*) include a built-in switch, so if you've already invested in an Internet router, before you go shopping for a switch make doggone sure that the router doesn't already come equipped with the ports you need!

 ✔ **A number of Ethernet cables:** Exactly how many cables you need is determined by how many computers you're connecting. If you're working with a gigabit Ethernet system, you need Cat5E or Cat6 cables. Cat6 cables provide better performance, but they are more expensive.

Naturally, if you're using a broadband Internet connection, you also have a DSL or cable modem. These boxes always include a port for connecting to your wired Ethernet network. (If you have one of the new breed of *wireless* modems — which acts as a wireless base station — don't panic because it should also have a wired port for connecting to your existing switch.)

Wired network connections

After you assemble your cables and your router or switch, connect the Ethernet cables from each of your computers to the router or switch, and then turn on the device. (Most need AC power to work.) Check the manual that comes with your device to make sure that the lights you're seeing on the front indicate normal operation. (Colors vary by manufacturer, but green is usually good.)

Next, connect your cable or DSL modem's Ethernet port to the WAN port on your switch with an Ethernet cable. If your modem isn't already on, turn it on now and check for normal operation.

When your router or switch is powered on and operating normally, you're ready to configure Mac OS X for network operation. Just hop to the upcoming section, "Connecting to the Network." (How about that? Now you can add network technician to your rapidly growing computer résumé!)

Joining a wired Ethernet network

After all the cables are connected and your central connection gizmo is plugged in and turned on, you've essentially created the hardware portion of your network. Congratulations! (Now you need a beard and suspenders.)

With the hardware in place, it's time to configure Snow Leopard. In this section, I assume that you're connecting to a network with an Internet router or switch that includes a DHCP server.

Follow these steps on each Mac running Mac OS X that you want to connect to the network:

1. **Click the System Preferences icon on the Dock.**

2. **Click the Network icon (under Internet & Network).**

3. **From the Connection list on the left, click Ethernet.**

4. **Click the Configure pop-up menu (see Figure 21-4) and choose Using DHCP.**

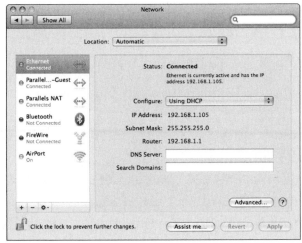

Figure 21-4:
All hail DHCP, the magical networking fairy!

5. **Click the Apply button.**

   The Apply button is grayed out in the figure because my Status (in this dialog) is Connected.

   Enjoy the automatic goodness as Mac OS X connects to the DHCP server to obtain an IP address, a subnet mask, a gateway router IP address, and a Domain Name System (DNS) address. (Without a DHCP server, you'd have to add all this stuff manually. Ugh.)

   A few seconds after clicking the Apply button, you should see the information come up. You might also notice that the DNS Server field is empty, but fear not because Mac OS X is really using DNS Server information provided by the DHCP server.

6. **Press ⌘+Q to quit System Preferences and save your settings.**

   You're on!

Connecting to the Network

All right! The hardware is powered up, the cables (if any) are installed and connected, and you configured Snow Leopard. You're ready to start (or join) the party. In this section, I show you how to verify that you're connected as well as how to share data and devices with others on your network.

Verifying that the contraption works

After you have at least two computers on a wired or wireless network, test whether they're talking to each other over the network by *pinging* them. (No, I didn't make up the term, honest.) Essentially, pinging another computer is like yelling, "Are you there?" across a crevasse.

To ping another computer on the same network from any Mac running Snow Leopard, follow these steps:

1. **Open a Finder window, click Applications, and then click Utilities.**

2. **Double-click the Network Utility icon to launch the application.**

3. **Click the Ping tab; see upcoming Figure 21-5.**

4. **In the Please Enter the Network Address to Ping text field, enter the IP address of the computer that you want to ping.**

- *If you're pinging another Mac running Mac OS X,* you can get the IP address of that machine by simply displaying its Network pane within System Preferences, which always displays the IP address.

- *If you're trying to ping a PC running Windows* and you don't know the IP address of that machine, follow these steps:

   a. *Click Start, right-click My Network Places (XP)/Network (Vista and Windows 7) and then choose Properties.*

   b. *From the Network Connections window, right-click your Local Area Network connection icon and then choose Status.*

   c. *Click the Support tab.*

   The IP address of that PC is proudly displayed.

5. **Select the Send Only x Pings radio button and enter** 2 **in the text field.**

6. **Click the Ping button.**

   - *Yay!:* If everything is working, you should see results similar to those shown in Figure 21-5, in which I'm pinging my Windows server at IP address 192.168.0.104, across my wired Ethernet network.

   - *Nay:* If you *don't* get a successful ping, check your cable connections, power cords, and Mac OS X settings. Folks using a wireless connection might have to move closer to the network base station to connect successfully, especially through walls.

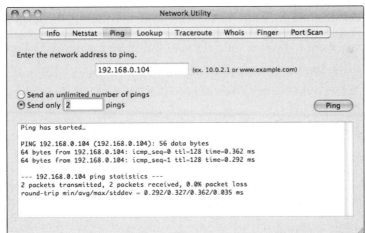

Figure 21-5:
Look, Ma,
I'm pinging!

Sharing stuff nicely with others

It works . . . by golly, it works! Okay, now what do you *do* with your all-new shining chrome network connection? Ah, my friend, let me be the first to congratulate you, and the first to show you around! In this section, I cover the most popular network perks. (And the good news is that these perks work with both wired and wireless connections.)

Network Internet connections

If your DSL or cable modem plugs directly into your iMac (rather than a dedicated Internet sharing device or Internet router), you might ponder just how the other computers on your network can share that spiffy high-speed broadband connection. If you're running a wireless network, it comes to the rescue!

Follow these steps to share your connection wirelessly:

1. **Click the System Preferences icon on the Dock.**

2. **Click the Sharing icon (under Internet & Network).**

3. **Click the Internet Sharing entry in the Services list to the left of the pane.**

4. **From the Share Your Connection From pop-up menu, choose Ethernet.**

5. **Mark the AirPort check box (in the To Computers Using list).**

   Snow Leopard displays a warning dialog stating that connection sharing could affect your Internet service provider (ISP) or violate your agreement with your ISP. I've never heard of this actually happening, but if you want to be sure, contact your ISP and ask the good folks there.

6. **Click Start in the warning dialog to continue.**

7. **Select the On check box next to the Internet Sharing entry in the Services list.**

8. **Click the Close button to exit System Preferences.**

Sharing an Internet connection (without an Internet router or dedicated hardware device) through Mac OS X requires your iMac to remain on continuously. This is no big deal if you're using your iMac as a Web server — and your iMac has absolutely no problem remaining on ad infinitum — but tell others in your office or your home that the svelte iMac must remain on, or they'll lose their Internet connection!

Don't forget that you won't need to configure Internet sharing if your DSL or cable modem connects to a dedicated sharing device or router. That snazzy equipment automatically connects your entire network to the Internet.

Network file sharing

You can swap all sorts of interesting files with other Macintosh computers on your network. When you turn on Personal File Sharing, Snow Leopard lets all Macs on the network connect to your iMac and share the files in your Public folder. (***Note:*** Sharing across a network is different from sharing a single computer betwixt several people. I cover that environment in Chapter 20.)

Follow these steps to start sharing files and folders with others across your network:

1. **Click the System Preferences icon on the Dock.**

2. **Click the Sharing icon.**

3. **Select the On check box next to the File Sharing service entry to enable the connections for Mac and Windows sharing.**

   Other Mac users can connect to your computer by clicking Go in the Finder menu and choosing the Network menu item. The Network window appears, and your iMac is among the choices. If the other Macs are running Snow Leopard, your iMac's shared files and folders appear in a Finder window, and they're listed under the Shared heading in the Sidebar.

   Windows XP users should be able to connect to your Mac from their My Network Places window, and Vista and Windows 7 users can use the Network window. Those lucky Windows folks also get to print to any shared printers you've set up. (The following section covers shared printers.)

4. **Click the Close button to exit System Preferences.**

Snow Leopard conveniently reminds you of the network name for your iMac at the bottom of the Sharing pane.

Sharing a network printer

Boy, howdy, do I love describing easy procedures, and sharing a printer on a Mac network ranks high on the list! You can share a printer that's connected to your iMac (or your AirPort Extreme, Time Capsule, or AirPort Express Base Station) by following these very simple steps:

1. **Click the System Preferences icon on the Dock.**

2. **Click the Sharing icon.**

3. Select the On check box next to the Printer Sharing service entry.

4. From the list at the right of the System Preferences window, select the printer you want to share.

5. Click the Close button to exit System Preferences.

A printer that you share automatically appears in the Print dialog on other Macs connected to your network.

Running a Web site from a network

Web jockeys tell you that Mac OS X is a great platform for running a Web site that you can access from either the Internet or your local network. In fact, it's ridiculously easy to engage the mind-boggling power of Snow Leopard's built-in Apache Web server. (Keep in mind, however, that your iMac must always be on and connected to the Internet, or your Web pages won't be available to your folks in Schenectady.)

To begin serving Web pages, follow these steps:

1. **Click the System Preferences icon on the Dock.**

2. **Click the Sharing icon.**

3. **Select the On check box next to the Web Sharing service entry.**

4. **Click the Close button to exit System Preferences.**

To check out the default HTML page that ships with Apache, open the System Preferences Sharing pane again and click the link that appears under the heading Your Computer's Website. Note that Snow Leopard also creates a personal Web site under your username, which is different from the default Web site created by Apache. Click the link under the heading Your Personal Website to display this page.

To add pages to your Web server, navigate to the Sites folder that resides in your Home folder. Because this is the root of your Apache Web server, the files that you add to this folder are accessible from your Web server.

Don't forget that folks connecting to your Web site across the Internet must use your public IP address! Your iMac's IP address appears in the Built-in Ethernet description on the Network pane in System Preferences. If you're using an Internet router or Internet connection sharing device, your *public* IP address might be different, so the links on the Web Sharing pane might not work for folks outside your local network. Check the documentation for the device to determine how to find your actual public IP address. Also, your router or sharing device might require you to specify which computer on your network is to receive HTTP (Web) page requests and send the pages. Again, this should be covered in the device manual.

USE YOUR FIREWALL!

Yep. That's the only heading in this entire book that's all uppercase. It's that important.

The following Mark's Maxim, good reader, isn't a request, a strong recommendation, or even a regular Maxim — consider it an absolute commandment (right up there with *Get an antivirus application now*).

Turn on your firewall *now.*

When you connect a network to the Internet, you open a door to the outside world. As a consultant to several businesses and organizations in my hometown, I can tell you that the outside world is chock-full of malicious individuals who would *dearly love* to inflict damage on your data or take control of your iMac for their own purposes. Call 'em hackers, call 'em delinquents, or call 'em something I can't repeat, but *don't let them in!*

Snow Leopard comes to the rescue again with the built-in firewall within Mac OS X. When you use this, you essentially build a virtual brick wall between you and the hackers out there (both on the Internet, and even within your local network). Follow these steps:

1. **Click the System Preferences icon on the Dock.**
2. **Click the Security icon.**
3. **Click the Firewall tab.**
4. **Click the Start button to activate your firewall.**
5. **Click the Advanced button.**
6. **Select the Automatically Allow Signed Software to Receive Incoming Connections check box.**
7. **Select the Enable Stealth Mode check box.**

    This is an important feature that prevents hackers from *trolling* for your iMac on the Internet — or, in normal-speak, searching for an unprotected computer — so it's much harder for them to attack you.

8. **Click OK.**
9. **Click the Close button to exit System Preferences.**

Snow Leopard even keeps track of the Internet traffic that you *do* want to reach your iMac, such as Web page requests and file sharing. When you activate one of the network features that I demonstrate in the preceding section,

Snow Leopard automatically opens a tiny hole (called a *port* by net-types) in your firewall to allow just that type of communication to your iMac. For example, if you decide to turn on Web Sharing (as I demonstrate earlier), Snow Leopard automatically allows incoming Web access.

You can also add ports for applications that aren't on the firewall's Allow list. This includes third-party Instant Messaging clients, multiplayer game servers, and the like. Depending on the type of connection, Snow Leopard will often automatically display a dialog prompting you for confirmation before allowing certain traffic, so most folks won't need to do anything manually.

However, you *can* add a program manually to your list of allowed (or blocked) Firewall ports. Follow these steps:

1. **Click the System Preferences icon on the Dock.**

2. **Click the Security icon.**

3. **Click the Firewall tab.**

4. **Click the Advanced button.**

5. **Click the Add button.**

   Snow Leopard displays a standard File browsing sheet.

6. **Browse to the application that requires access to the outside world — or the application that you want to block from outside communication — and click it to select it.**

7. **Click the Add button in the File sheet.**

   The application appears in the Firewall list. By default, it's set to Allow Incoming Connections.

8. **If you want to block any incoming communication to the application, click the Allow Incoming Connections pop-up menu and choose Block Incoming Connections instead.**

9. **Click the Close button to exit System Preferences.**

Part VI

The Necessary Evils: Troubleshooting, Upgrading, Maintaining

The 5th Wave   By Rich Tennant

"It all started when I began surfing the web for 'Baked Alaska' and frozen custards..."

In this part . . .

No computer is *completely* trouble-free — and if your iMac starts acting strangely, the troubleshooting tips you find in this part can help you get your favorite machine back to normal. I also provide you with all the guidance you need to maintain your iMac properly, and step-by-step instructions for upgrading your computer with goodies like additional RAM or external devices.

Chapter 22

It Just . . . Sits . . . There

1 wish you weren't reading this chapter.

Because you are, I can only surmise that you're having trouble with your iMac, and that it needs fixing. (The other possibility — that you just like reading about solving computer problems — is more attractive, but much more problematic.)

Consider this chapter a crash course in the logical puzzle that is computer *troubleshooting*: namely, the art of finding out What Needs Fixing. You also see what you can do when you just plain can't fix the problem by yourself.

Oh, and you're going to encounter a lot of Tips and Mark's Maxims in this chapter — all of them learned the hard way, so I recommend committing them to memory on the spot!

Can You Troubleshoot? Yes, You Can!

Anyone can troubleshoot. Put these common troubleshooting myths to rest:

✔ **It takes a college degree in computers to troubleshoot.** Tell that to my troubleshooting kids. They'll think it's a hoot because they have Apple computers of their own in their bedrooms. You can follow all the steps in this chapter without any special training.

✔ **I'm to blame.** Ever heard of viruses? Failing hardware? Buggy software? Any of those things can be causing the problem. Heck, even if you do something by accident, I'm willing to bet it wasn't on purpose. It's Mark's Maxim time:

Don't beat yourself up — your iMac can be fixed.

✔ **I need to buy expensive utility software.** Nope. You can certainly invest in a commercial testing and repair utility if you like. My favorite is TechTool Pro from Micromat (www.micromat.com), but a third-party utility isn't a requirement for troubleshooting. (I would, however, consider an antivirus application as a must-have, and you should have one already. Hint, hint.)

✔ **There's no hope if I can't fix it.** Sure, parts fail, and computers crash, but your Apple Service Center can repair just about any problem. And (ahem) if you backed up your iMac (like I preach throughout this book), you'll keep that important data (even if a new hard drive is in your future).

✔ **It takes forever.** Wait until you read the Number One Rule in the next section; the first step takes but 15 seconds and often solves the problem. Naturally, not all problems can be fixed so quickly, but if you follow the procedures in this chapter, you should fix your iMac (or at least know that the problem requires outside help) in a single afternoon.

With those myths banished for good, you can get down to business and start feeling better soon.

Basic Troubleshooting 101

In this section, I walk you through my Should-Be-Patented Troubleshooting Tree as well as the Snow Leopard built-in troubleshooting application, Disk Utility. I also introduce you to a number of keystrokes that can make your iMac jump through hoops.

The Number One Rule: Reboot!

Yep, it sounds silly, but the fact is that rebooting your iMac can often solve a number of problems. If you're encountering these types of strange behavior with your iMac, a reboot might be all you need to heal

✔ Intermittent problems communicating over a network

✔ A garbled screen, strange colors, or screwed-up fonts

✔ The Swirling Beach Ball of Doom that won't go away after several minutes

   ✔ An application that locks up

   ✔ An external device that seems to disappear or can't be opened

To put it succinctly, here's a modest Mark's Maxim:

Always try a reboot before beginning to worry. *Always.*

Try to save all your open documents before you reboot. That might not be possible, but try to save what you can.

If you need to force a *locked* application (one that's not responding) to quit so you can reboot, follow these steps to squash that locked application:

   1. Click the Apple (🍎) menu and choose Force Quit.

   The dialog that you see in Figure 22-1 appears on your screen.

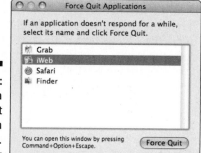

Figure 22-1:
Force a
recalcitrant
application
to take off.

   2. Click the offending application and then click the Force Quit button.

   If you can get everything to quit, you should be able to click the Apple menu and choose Shut Down (not Restart) without a problem.

If your iMac simply won't shut down (or you can't get the offending application to quit), then do what must be done:

   1. Press and hold your iMac Power button until it shuts itself off.

   You have to wait about four seconds for your iMac to turn itself off.

   2. Wait about ten seconds.

   3. Press the Power button again to restart the computer.

Note that you should not simply pull your iMac's power cord out of the AC socket (or turn off your power strip) to turn it off — pressing and holding the power switch on your iMac is a less destructive path to the same end.

After everything is back up, check whether the problem is still apparent. If you use your iMac for an hour or two and the problem doesn't reoccur, you likely fixed it!

Rebooting fixes problems because it resets *everything* — even your network connection. Rebooting also fixes problems due to brownouts or those notorious AC power flickerings that we all notice from time to time.

Special keys that can come in handy

A number of keys have special powers over your iMac. No, I'm not kidding! These keys affect how your iMac starts up, and they can really come in handy whilst troubleshooting.

Using Safe Boot mode

You can use Safe Boot mode to force Snow Leopard to run a directory check of your boot hard drive and disable any Login Items that might be interfering with Snow Leopard. Use the Shut Down menu item from the Apple ( ) menu to completely turn off your iMac, press the Power button to start the computer. Then press and hold down the Shift key immediately after you hear the startup tone. After Snow Leopard has completely booted, restart your iMac again (this time without the Shift key) to return to normal operation.

Startup keys

Table 22-1 provides the lowdown on startup keys. Hold the indicated key down either *when you push your iMac Power button* or *immediately after the screen blanks during a restart.* (As I just mentioned, the Shift key is the exception; it should be pressed and held down after you hear the startup tone.)

Danger, Will Robinson!

Many Disk Utility functions can actually **wipe your hard drives clean of data** instead of repairing them! These advanced functions aren't likely to help you with troubleshooting a problem with your existing volumes, anyway.

Remember: Don't use these Disk Utility functions unless an Apple technician *tells* you to use them:

✔ Partitioning and erasing drives

✔ Setting up RAID arrays

✔ Restoring files from disk images

Table 22-1	Startup Keys and Their Tricks
Key	**Effect on Your iMac**
C	Boots from the CD or DVD that's loaded in your optical drive
Media Eject	Ejects the CD or DVD in your optical drive
Option	Displays a system boot menu, allowing you to choose the operating system and startup volume
Shift	Prevents your Login Items from running; runs a directory check
T	Starts your iMac in FireWire Target Disk mode
⌘+V	Show Mac OS X Console messages
⌘+S	Starts your iMac in Single User mode
⌘+Option+P+R	Resets Parameter RAM (PRAM) and NVRAM

Some of the keys/combinations in Table 22-1 might never be necessary for your machine, but you might be instructed to use them by an Apple technician. I'll warrant that you'll use at least the C startup key fairly often.

All hail Disk Utility, the troubleshooter's friend

Snow Leopard's *Disk Utility* is a handy tool for troubleshooting and repairing your hard drive. You can find it in the Utilities folder within your Applications folder.

Fire up Disk Utility, click the volume and click the First Aid tab to bring up the rather powerful-looking window shown in Figure 22-2.

In the left column of the Disk Utility window, you can see

- ✔ The *physical* hard drives in your system (the actual hardware)
- ✔ The *volumes* (the data stored on the hard drives)

    You can always tell a volume because it's indented underneath the physical drive entry.

- ✔ Any CD or DVD loaded on your iMac
- ✔ Disk images you've mounted
- ✔ USB or FireWire Flash drives

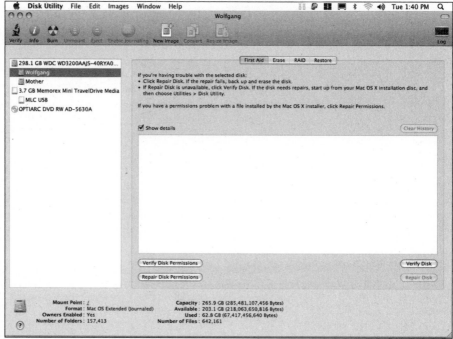

Figure 22-2:
The physician of hard drives — Snow Leopard's Disk Utility.

For example, in Figure 22-2, I have one hard drive (the 298.1GB entry) and one USB Flash drive (the 3.7GB entry). The hard drive has two volumes (Wolfgang and Mother), and the USB drive has one volume (MLC USB).

The information at the bottom of the Disk Utility window contains the specifications of the selected drive or volume . . . things like capacity, free space, and the number of files and folders for a volume, or connection type and total capacity for a drive.

Repairing disk permissions

Because Snow Leopard is built on a Unix base, lots of permissions can apply to the files on your drive — that is, who can open (or read or change) every application, folder, and document on your hard drive. Unfortunately, these permissions are often messed up by wayward applications or power glitches or application installers that do a sub-par job of cleaning up after themselves. And if the permissions on a file are changed, often applications lock up or refuse to run altogether.

I recommend repairing your disk permissions with Disk Utility once weekly. Figure 22-3 shows a permissions repair sweep on my internal hard drive's volume.

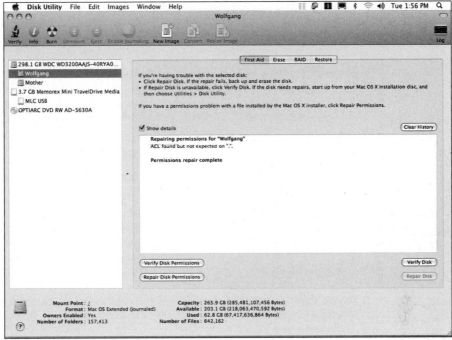

Figure 22-3:
A suc-
cessful
run, using
Repair Disk
Permissions.

Use these steps to repair permissions on your iMac's hard drive:

1. **Make sure that you're logged in with an admin account.**

2. **Save and close any open documents.**

   Chapter 20 shows you how to log in as an admin user.

3. **Double-click the Disk Utility icon in the Utilities folder.**

4. **Click the volume that you want to check.**

5. **Click the Repair Disk Permissions button.**

   I don't worry about verifying. If something's wrong, you end up clicking Repair Disk Permissions, anyway. Just click Repair Disk Permissions; if nothing pops up, that's fine.

6. **To finish the process, always reboot after repairing permissions.**

   This last step allows you to see whether a problem has been corrected!

Repairing disks

Disk Utility can check the format and health of both hard drives and volumes with Verify Disk — and, if the problem can be corrected, fix any error with Repair Disk.

Using Disk Utility to repair your hard drive carries a couple of caveats:

- ✔ **You can't verify or repair the boot disk or the boot volume.** This actually makes sense because you're using that disk and volume right now.

  To verify or repair your boot hard drive, you need to boot from your Mac OS X installation disc by using the C startup key. (Refer to Table 22-1 for keys that come in handy.) After your iMac boots from the Mac OS X installation disc, choose the Utilities menu and click Disk Utility.

  You should be able to select your boot hard drive or volume, and the Verify Disk and Repair Disk buttons should be enabled.

- ✔ **You can't repair CDs and DVDs.** CDs and DVDs are read-only media and thus can't be repaired at all (at least by Disk Utility).

  If your iMac is having trouble reading a CD or DVD, wipe the disc with a soft cloth to remove dust, oil, and fingerprints. Should that fail, invest in a disc-cleaning contrivance of some sort.

If you need to verify and repair a disk or volume, follow these steps:

1. **If you need to repair your *boot drive and volume,* save all your open documents and reboot from either *an external drive* or *your Mac OS X Installation disc.***

2. **Double-click the Disk Utility icon in the Utilities folder.**

3. **In the list at the left side of the Disk Utility window, click the disk or volume that you want to check.**

4. **Click the Repair Disk button.**

5. **If changes were made (or if you had to boot from a disc or external drive), reboot after repairing the disk or volume.**

Should I reinstall Mac OS X?

This question seems to get a lot of attention on Mac-related Internet discussion boards and Usenet newsgroups — and the answer is a definitive *perhaps.* (I know. That's really helpful.)

Here's the explanation. You *shouldn't* lose a single byte of data by reinstalling Mac OS X, so it's definitely okay to try it. However, reinstalling Mac OS X isn't a universal balm that fixes all hardware and software errors.

Follow the iMac Troubleshooting Tree all the way to the end before you consider reinstalling Snow Leopard. Contact an Apple support technician via the Apple Web site before you take this step.

Mark's iMac Troubleshooting Tree

As the hip-hop artists say, "Alright, kick it." And that's just what my iMac Troubleshooting Tree is here for. If rebooting your iMac hasn't solved the problem, follow these steps in order (until either the solution is found, or you run out of steps — more on that in the next section).

Step 1: Investigate recent changes

This is a simple step that many novice Mac owners forget. Simply retrace your steps and consider what changes you made recently to your system. Here are the most common culprits:

- ✔ **Did you just finish installing a new application?** Try uninstalling it by removing the application directory and any support files that it might have added to your system. (And keep your applications current with the most recent patches and updates from the developer's Web site.)

  From time to time, an application's *preference file* — which stores all the custom settings you make — can become corrupted. Although the application itself is okay, it might act strangely or refuse to launch. To check your preference files for signs of corruption, try scanning your iMac applications with Preferential Treatment, a freeware AppleScript utility by Jonathan Nathan, available from his Web site at `www.jonn8.com/html/pt.html`. (Preferential Treatment will flag any dicey preference files, setting them up for a quick trip to the Trash.)

- ✔ **Did you just apply an update or a patch to an application?** Uninstall the application and reinstall it without applying the patch. If your iMac suddenly works again, check the developer's Web site or contact its technical support department to report the problem.

- ✔ **Did you just update Snow Leopard by using Software Update?** Updating Snow Leopard can introduce problems within your applications that depend on specific routines and system files. Contact the developer of the application and look for updated patches that bring your software in line with the Snow Leopard updates. (And use Software Update in automatic mode to check for Mac OS X updates at least once weekly.)

- ✔ **Did you just make a change within System Preferences?** Return the options that you changed back to their original settings; then consult Chapter 6 for information on what might have gone wrong. (If the setting in question isn't in Chapter 6, consider searching Snow Leopard's online Help or the Apple support Web site for more clues.)

- ✔ **Did you just connect (or reconnect) an external device?** Try unplugging the device and then rebooting to see whether the problem disappears. Remember that many peripherals need software drivers to run — and without those drivers installed, they won't work correctly. (Not to mention that updated drivers may be available.) Check the device's manual or visit the company's Web site to search for software that you might need.

If you didn't make any significant changes to your system before you encountered the problem, proceed to the next step.

Step 2: Run Disk Utility

The preceding section shows how to repair disk permissions on your Snow Leopard boot drive.

If you're experiencing hard drive problems, consider booting from your Mac OS X Installation CD or DVD to run a full-blown Repair Disk checkup on your boot volume.

Step 3: Check your cables

Cables work themselves loose, and they fail from time to time. Check all your cables to your external devices — make sure that they're snug — and verify that everything's plugged in and turned on. (Oh, and don't forget to check for crimps in your cables or even Fluffy's teeth marks.)

If a FireWire or USB device acts up, swap cables around to find whether you have a bad one. A faulty cable can leave you pulling your hair out in no time.

Step 4: Check your Trash

Check the contents of your Trash to see whether you recently deleted files or folders by accident. Click the Trash icon on the Dock once to display the contents. If something's been deleted by mistake, drag it back to its original folder, and try running the application again.

I know this one from personal experience. A slight miscalculation while selecting files to delete made an application freeze every time I launched it.

Step 5: Check your Internet and network connections

Now that always-on DSL and cable modem connections to the Internet are common, don't forget an obvious problem: Your iMac can't reach the Internet because your ISP is down, or your network is no longer working!

A quick visual check of your DSL or cable modem will usually indicate whether there's a connection problem between your modem and your ISP — for example, my modem has a very informative activity light that I always glance at first. However, if your iMac is connected to the Internet through a larger home or office network and you can't check the modem visually, you can check your Internet connection by pinging www.apple.com, as shown in Figure 22-4.

1. **Open your Utilities folder (inside your Applications folder).**

2. **Double-click Network Utility.**

3. **Click the Ping button.**

4. **Enter** www.apple.com **in the Address box.**

5. **Click Ping.**

   You should see successful ping messages similar to those in Figure 22-4. If you don't get a successful ping *and* you can still reach other computers on your network, your ISP is likely experiencing problems. If you can't reach your network at all, then the problem lies in your network hardware or configuration.

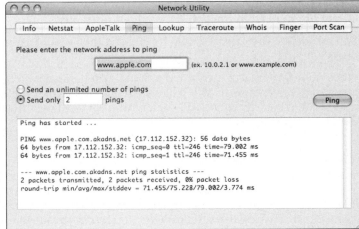

Figure 22-4:
Ping
apple.
com to
check your
Internet
connection.

Step 6: Think virus

If you made it to this point, it's time to run a full virus scan — and make sure that your antivirus application has the latest updated data files, too. My antivirus application of choice is Virus Barrier X from Intego (www.intego.com). (If a virus is detected and your antivirus application can't remove it, try *quarantining* it instead, which basically disables the virus-ridden application and prevents it from infecting other files.) I can also recommend ClamX AV, the antivirus application from www.clamxav.com (if you like ClamX AV, you can send a donation to the author).

Step 7: Disable your Login Items

Mac OS X might encounter problems with applications that you've marked as Login Items within System Preferences. In this step, I show you how to identify login problems and how to fix 'em.

Checking for problems

It's time to use another nifty startup key (refer to Table 22-1). This time, hold down Shift after you hear the startup tone.

This trick disables your account's Login Items, which are run automatically every time you log in to your iMac. If one of these Login Items is to blame, your iMac will simply encounter trouble every time you log in.

Finding the Login Item that's causing trouble

If your iMac works fine with your Login Items disabled, follow this procedure for each item in the Login Items list:

1. **Open System Preferences, click Accounts, and then click the Login Items button.**

2. **Delete the item from the list; then reboot normally.**

   You can delete the selected item by clicking the Delete button, which bears a minus sign.

   When your iMac starts up normally with Login Items enabled, you discovered the perpetrator. You'll likely need to delete that application and reinstall it. (Don't forget to add each of the *working* Login Items back to the Login Items list!)

Step 8: Turn off your screen saver

This is a long shot, but it isn't unheard of to discover that a faulty, bug-ridden screen saver has locked up your iMac. (If you aren't running one of the Apple-supplied screen savers and your computer never wakes up from Sleep mode or hangs while displaying the screen saver, you found your prime suspect.)

Open System Preferences, click Desktop & Screen Saver, click the Screen Saver button, and then either *switch to an Apple screen saver* or *drag the Start slider to Never.*

If this fixes the problem, you can probably remove the screen saver by deleting the application in the Screen Savers folder inside your Mac OS X Library folder. If you can't find the screen saver application, use Spotlight to search for it.

Step 9: Run System Profiler

Ouch. You reached Step 9, and you still haven't uncovered the culprit. At this point, you narrowed the possibilities to a serious problem, like bad hardware or corrupted files in your Mac OS X System Folder. Fortunately, Snow

Leopard provides System Profiler, which displays real-time information on the hardware in your system. Click the Apple menu and choose About This Mac; then click More Info. Figure 22-5 illustrates a typical healthy result from one of the Hardware categories, Disc Burning. Click each one of the Hardware categories in turn, double-checking to make sure that everything looks okay.

You don't have to understand all the technical hieroglyphics. If a Hardware category doesn't return what you expect or displays an error message, though, that's suspicious.

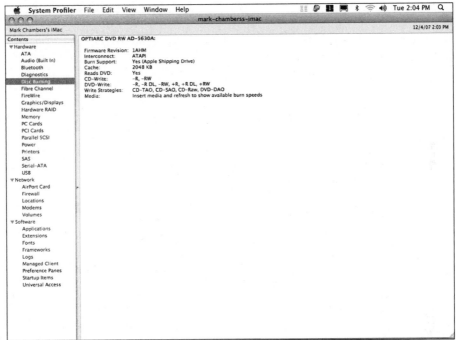

Figure 22-5:
Check your iMac hardware from System Profiler.

Okay, I Kicked It, and It Still Won't Work

Don't worry, friendly reader. Just because you've reached the end of my iMac tree doesn't mean you're out of luck. In this section, I discuss the online help available on the Apple Web site as well as local help in your own town.

Apple Help Online

If you haven't visited the Apple iMac Support site yet, run — don't walk — to www.apple.com/support/imac, where you can find

- ✔ **The iMac Troubleshooting Assistant,** which queries you on the symptoms being displayed by your iMac and offers possible solutions
- ✔ **The latest patches, updates, and how-to tutorials** for the iMac
- ✔ **iMac and Mac OS X discussion boards,** moderated by Apple
- ✔ **Tools** for ordering spare parts, checking on your remaining warranty coverage, and searching the Apple Knowledge Base
- ✔ **Do-it-yourself instructions** (PDF files) that you can follow to repair or upgrade your iMac

Local service, at your service

In case you need to take in your iMac for service, an Apple Store or Apple Authorized Service Provider is probably in your area. To find the closest service, launch Safari and visit

```
http://www.apple.com/buy/locator/service/
```

That's the Find Service page on the Apple Web site. You can search by city and state or ZIP code. The results are complete with the provider's mailing address, Web site address, telephone number, and even a map of the location!

Always call your Apple service provider before you lug your (albeit lightweight) iMac all the way to the shop. Make sure that you know *your iMac's serial number* (which you can display in System Profiler) and *which version of Mac OS X you're using.*

Chapter 23

I Want to Add Stuff

"*N*o iMac is an island." Somebody famous wrote that, I'm sure.

Without getting too philosophical — or invoking the all-powerful Internet yet again — the old saying really does make sense. All computer owners usually add at least one *peripheral* (external device), such as a printer, backup drive, joystick, iPod, or scanner. I talk about the ports on your iMac in Chapter 1. Those holes aren't there to just add visual interest to the back end of your treasured iMac. Therefore, I cover your USB and FireWire ports (and what you can plug in to them) in detail in this chapter.

Ah, but what about the stuff *inside* your aluminum supercomputer? That's where things get both interesting and scary at the same time. In this chapter, I describe what you can add to the innards of your computer as well as how to get inside there if you work up the courage to go exploring. (Don't tell your family or your friends, but adding memory to an aluminum iMac is as simple as loosening a screw and pulling on a plastic tab. There's actually nothing to fear whatsoever.)

Here's the trick: Just make it sound like an adventure from *Mission: Impossible,* and folks will crown you their new resident techno-wizard!

More Memory Will Help

Hey, wait a second. No *however* stuck on the end? You mean for once, there isn't an exception? Aren't all computers different? Hard as it is to believe, just keep in mind this Mark's Maxim:

More memory helps.

Period. End of statement. No matter what type of computer you own, how old it is, or what operating system you use, adding more memory to your system (to the maximum it supports) significantly improves the performance of your operating system (and practically every application that you run).

Memory maximizes the power of your computer: The more memory you have, the less data your iMac has to temporarily store on its hard drive. Without getting into virtual memory and other techno-gunk, just consider that extra memory as extra elbowroom for your applications and your documents. Believe me, both Mac OS X and Windows efficiently make use of every kilobyte of memory that you can provide.

Figuring out how much memory you have

To see how much memory you have in your computer, click the Apple menu (🍎) and choose About This Mac. Figure 23-1 shows the dialog.

The 4GB of memory supplied by Apple is plenty for running applications from the iLife and iWork suites as well as any of the applications bundled with Snow Leopard.

Figure 23-1:
Find out
how much
memory
your iMac
has.

At the time of this writing, the current crop of iMacs has sockets for four 1066 MHz PC3-8500 DDR3 SDRAM memory modules. (Don't fret over what those abbreviations mean. Rest assured that this memory type is fast.) Each module can range up to 4GB of memory, so you can install as much as 16GB of memory on your iMac.

How you plan memory upgrades depends on how much memory you want. If your iMac uses the two default 2GB modules supplied by Apple, you can add RAM by inserting memory modules in the empty slots. At the time of this writing, a 4GB memory module should set you back about $150 or so.

If your iMac already has all four memory slots filled and you'd still like to add more system RAM, it's time to remove one or all of the existing modules and replace them with full 4GB modules. With all four slots filled with 4GB modules, you'll have the coveted 16GB that marks you as one of the "In" People.

If your primary applications include video editing, game playing, or image editing, you can use all the memory your iMac can hold.

Unfortunately, Apple's prices for RAM are . . . well . . . *outrageous.* (As in, "Boy, howdy, I can't afford that!") Therefore, I can heartily recommend any one of these online sources that cater to Mac owners:

- ✔ MacMall (`www.macmall.com`)
- ✔ CDW (`www.cdw.com/content/brands/apple/default.aspx`)
- ✔ Crucial (`www.crucial.com`)
- ✔ SmallDog (`www.smalldog.com`)
- ✔ Newegg (`www.newegg.com`)

Getting inside your iMac

Apple designed the world's best all-in-one computer. That even includes making it EZ-Open. (Forgive me if your treasured work of art now reminds you of a longneck beer bottle. Come to think of it, the level of technical knowledge required to gain access to either one is about the same.)

Unlike earlier "picture frame" iMac models, however, you can't remove the back completely.

In fact, Apple allows the owner of an iMac to perform only one kind of upgrade, and there's only one opening you need to worry about. (***Note:*** You'll void your warranty by tinkering with anything other than your memory slots, so don't even think about it.) Naturally, an Apple repair technician can get deeper into the machine, but I hope that you never need aid from those folks.

Installing memory modules

I'm happy to report that adding extra memory to your system is one of the easiest internal upgrades that you can perform. Therefore, I recommend that you add memory yourself unless you simply don't want to mess with your iMac's internal organs. Your local Macintosh service specialist will be happy to install new RAM modules for you (for a price).

To add memory modules to an aluminum iMac, follow these steps:

1. **Get ready to operate.**

   a. *Spread a clean towel on a stable work surface, like your kitchen table.* The towel helps protect your screen from scratches.

   b. *Find a Phillips screwdriver.*

   c. *Shut down your iMac.*

   d. *Unplug all cables from the computer.*

2. **Tilt the computer over and lay the screen flat (face-down) on top of the towel.**

3. **Loosen the screw at the bottom of the computer's case.**

   Apple thought of everything! There's only one tiny screw, and you can't lose said screw because it's *captive.* It actually stays in the door, so don't try to remove it completely.

4. **Remove the RAM access door.**

5. **Stow the RAM access door safely out of reach of kids and cats.**

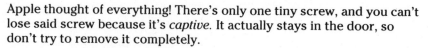

Let's get grounded!

Follow one cardinal rule when the unguarded insides of any computer are in easy reach: *Always ground yourself before you touch anything!* Your body can carry enough static electricity to damage the RAM you're installing or removing, and touching those modules without grounding yourself is an invitation for disaster.

Grounding yourself is easy to do: Just touch any metal surface around your work table, such as a chair leg or your local metal sink. After you ground yourself, you can then safely handle RAM chips that you remove (if any) as well as the new ones that you're installing.

If you walk anywhere in the room — say, hunting for a screwdriver, or taking a sip of liquid reinforcement that you stashed a comfortable and safe distance away — you *must* ground yourself again before you get back to work. *Remember:* You can actually pick up a static charge by simply walking. Go figure.

Tah-dah! That wasn't much of a challenge, was it? Here's your chance to gaze with rapt fascination at a small portion of the bare innards of your favorite computer.

1. ***Ground thyself!***

   Check out the sidebar, "Let's get grounded!".

2. **If you need to remove a module for your upgrade, untuck the tab over the existing module.**

3. **Gently pull on the tab to remove the module (as shown in Figure 23-2).**

   Save the old module in the static-free packaging that held the new module. Your old RAM (which you can now sell on eBay) will be protected from static electricity.

4. **Position the new module(s) in the socket(s).**

   a. *Line up the module's copper connectors toward the socket.*

   b. *Line up the notch in the module aligned with the matching spacer in the socket.* See what I mean in Figure 23-3.

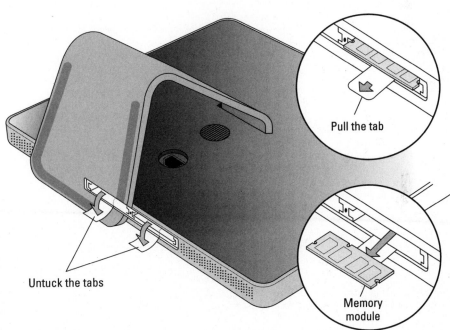

Pull the tab

Memory module

Untuck the tabs

Figure 23-2:
Remove
a memory
module
like a pro.

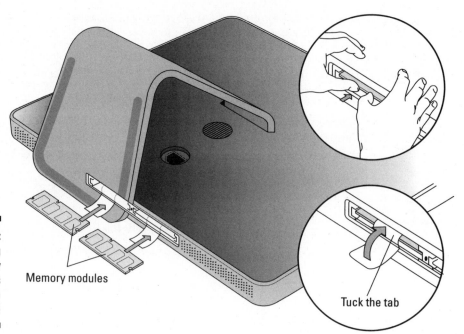

Figure 23-3:
Installing
the new
modules is
a snap (pun
intended)!

Memory modules

Tuck the tab

5. **Press gently (but firmly) on both ends of the module until the module's tabs click into place on both ends of the socket.**

6. **Tuck any loose tabs back into the body of your iMac.**

7. **Replace the RAM access door, reversing Steps 3–5 of the preceding step list.**

   Waxing nostalgic: This is rather like changing the oil on my Dad's 1970 Ford pickup truck.

Congratulations! You've done it — you're now an iMac memory guru! To verify that all is well with your iMac, boot the computer and once again click the Apple menu and choose About This Mac. Your iMac should report the additional memory.

Can I Upgrade My Hard Drive?

Asking whether you can upgrade your hard drive is a trick question. Yes, you certainly can upgrade your hard drive. But before you start cruisin' the Internet for a 2TB monster, though, I have two suggestions:

✔ **Be sure you really need a hard drive upgrade.**

Apple is pretty generous when configuring hard drive storage for its base systems. (Current models run with anywhere from a 500GB to a whopping 2TB drive — yep, that's 2 *terabytes*, or 2,000GB! Something tells me that your prized walnut brownie recipe will have plenty of elbow room on a 2TB drive, as will a huge amount of digital video.)

I'll be honest here: Most folks simply don't need more than 500GB of hard drive space. You're likely to find that you still have plenty of wide open spaces for a typical family's needs on your hard drive unless you're heavily into

- Digital video (DV)

- Cutting-edge video games

- Tons of high-quality digital audio

- Four generations of high-resolution digital photos of your family (hey, it's possible!)

✔ **If you decide that you do need to upgrade, don't install your internal hard drive yourself.**

Read more about this in the upcoming section, "Gotta have internal."

If you're short on hard drive space, clean up your existing hard drive by deleting all the crud you don't need, such as game and application demos, duplicate or "work" copies of images and documents, archived files you downloaded from the Internet, and the contents of your Trash. You can read how in Chapter 24.

Consider your external options

If you *do* need additional hard drive space, I recommend using an external drive. Use a high-speed FireWire or USB port to connect a second hard drive the quick and easy way.

Most of today's FireWire and USB peripherals don't even require the driver software that Mac old-timers remember with such hatred. You simply plug in a FireWire or USB device, and it works. You can move your external drive between different Macs with a minimum of fuss and bother.

An external hard drive can do anything that your internal hard drive can do. You can boot from it, for example, or install a different version of Mac OS X (great for beta testers like me).

Apple's Time Capsule unit is an external hard drive with a difference — it stores the huge Time Machine backup files created by the Macs running Snow Leopard on your network, and it uses a wireless connection to transfer data! (In fact, if you're thinking of adding a wireless base station to your wired network, your Time Capsule actually acts as a full AirPort Extreme base station, complete with USB port for connecting a USB printer.) At the time of this writing, Time Capsule is available with either a 1TB ($299) or 2TB ($499) drive.

Here's one problem with external drives: Data transfers more slowly this way than via an internal drive (even with a FireWire 800 connection). That's why most Mac owners use their external drives for storing backups and little-used documents and applications. Their favorite applications and often-used documents are housed on the internal drive.

Putting a port to work

An aluminum iMac carries two kinds of high-speed ports, either of which is a good match for connecting any external device.

USB 2.0

The USB standard is popular because it's just as common in the PC world as in the Mac world. (Most PCs don't have a FireWire port.) Your iMac carries its USB 2.0 ports on the back of the case. Hardware manufacturers can make one USB device that works on both types of computers.

I heartily recommend that you avoid using any USB 1.1 devices (except, perhaps, a USB 1.1 modem, keyboard or mouse). USB 1.1 is very slow compared with the USB 2.0 standard although you can connect a USB 1.1 device to a USB 2.0 port with no problem at all. You should buy only USB 2.0 external hard drives, CD/DVD recorders, or Flash drives. 'Nuff said.

FireWire 800

A FireWire 800 drive offers much better performance than either a FireWire 400 or a USB 2.0 drive, and today's FireWire 800 drives are getting cheaper every day. Your iMac proudly sports a FireWire 800 port on the back.

The physical FireWire 800 connector is shaped differently than an older FireWire 400 port, so don't try to force the wrong connector into the wrong port!

Connecting an external drive

With FireWire or USB, you can install an external hard drive without opening your iMac's case. With your iMac turned on and the external drive disconnected from the AC outlet, follow these steps:

1. **Connect the FireWire or USB cable betwixt the drive and your computer.**

2. **Plug the external drive into a convenient surge protector or UPS (uninterruptible power supply).**

3. **Switch on the external drive.**

4. **If the drive is unformatted (or formatted for use under Windows), partition and format the external drive.**

   The drive comes with instructions or software for you to do this. (Don't worry, external drives typically come from the factory completely empty, and you won't damage anything by formatting it. To be sure, check the drive's manual.) Partitioning divides the new drive into one (or more) volumes, each of which is displayed as a separate hard drive under Snow Leopard.

   If the drive comes preformatted for use with a Windows PC, I strongly suggest reformatting it for use with Mac OS X — this will result in faster performance and more efficient use of space.

After the drive is formatted and partitioned, it immediately appears on the Desktop. Shazam!

Gotta have internal

If you decide that you have to upgrade your existing internal hard drive — or if your internal drive fails and needs to be replaced — you must take your iMac to an authorized Apple service center and allow the techs there to sell you a drive and make the swap. Here are four darned good reasons why:

- ✔ **Warranty:** As I mention in the sidebar, "Getting inside your iMac," you're very likely to void your iMac's warranty by attempting a drive upgrade yourself.

- ✔ **Selection:** If you're worried about picking the proper drive, an Apple technician can order the right drive type and size for you . . . no worries.

- ✔ **Difficulty:** Swapping a hard drive in your iMac is nothing like adding RAM modules. It's complex and involves breaking into your iMac — not A Good Thing, even for the knowledgeable Mac guru.

- ✔ **Backup:** That very same Apple service technician can back up all the data on your existing drive and move it to the new drive, saving you from losing a single document. That will save you time and possible angst.

To those who *truly* won't be satisfied with their lives until they upgrade an internal drive in an iMac: Yes, I'm sure you can find a magazine article that purports to show you how. Even better, I've seen many how-to articles on the Web that will lead you down a rosy path to a hard drive upgrade. Here's my take on those savvy instructions: You're walking into a field of land mines with someone else's map, so you had better have *complete* faith in your tech skills. (And a darn good backup.)

Attractive Add-Ons

The USB and FireWire toys I cover in this section might add a cord or two to your collection at the back of your iMac, but they're well worth the investment. And they can really revolutionize how you look at technologies, such as television, digital audio, and computer gaming.

Game controllers

If you're ready to take a shot at the enemy — whether they be Nazi soldiers, chittering aliens, or the latest jet fighters — you'll likely find your keyboard and mouse somewhat lacking. (And if that enemy happens to be a friend of yours playing across the Internet, you'll be ruthlessly mocked while you're fumbling for the right key combination.) Instead, either pick up a USB joystick (for flying games) or a gamepad (for arcade and first-person shooting games)!

Video controllers

For armchair directors, specialized USB digital video controllers make editing easier. The ShuttleXpress from Contour Design (www.contourdesign.com) provides a five-button jog control that can be configured to match any DV editor. For around $40, you'll have the same type of editing controller as do those dedicated video-editing stations that cost several thousand dollars.

Audio hardware

Ready to put GarageBand to the test with your favorite version of *Chopsticks?* You need a USB piano keyboard, and I recommend the Keystation 61es from M-Audio (www.m-audio.com), which retails for a mere $200. It provides 61 keys and uses a USB connection.

Chapter 24

Tackling the Housekeeping

*N*othing runs better than a well-oiled machine, and your iMac is no exception. In this chapter, I demonstrate how you can make good use of every byte of storage space provided by your hard drive.

With a little Snow Leopard maintenance, such as Time Machine (for backing up and restoring your hard drive), and frequent scans of your hard drive for permissions errors, you can ensure that your iMac is performing as efficiently as possible. Automator allows your iMac to perform tasks automatically that used to require your attention. In addition, configuring Software Update to run automatically can allow you to live life free and easy, watching your favorite soaps and eating ice cream (or yogurt — your pick).

Cleaning Unseemly Data Deposits

Criminy! Where does all this stuff *come* from? Suddenly that spacious 500GB hard drive has 19GB left, and you start feeling pinched.

Before you consider buying a new internal or external hard drive (which you can read about in Chapter 23), take the smart step: "Sweep" your hard drive clean of unnecessary and space-hogging software.

Getting dirty (or, cleaning things the manual way)

If you're willing to dig into your data a little, there's no reason to buy additional software to help you clean up your hard drive. All you really need is the willpower to announce, "I simply don't need this application any longer." (And, sometimes, that's tougher than it might seem.)

Unnecessary files and unneeded folders

Consider all the stuff that you probably don't really need:

- Game demos and shareware that you no longer play (or even remember)
- Movie trailers and other QuickTime video files that have long since passed into obscurity
- Temporary files that you created and promptly forgot
- Log files that chronicle application installations and errors
- StuffIt archives that you downloaded and no longer covet
- iTunes music that no longer appeals to your ear

How hard is it to clean this stuff off your drive? Easier than you might think!

- You can easily delete files.
- You can get rid of at least the lion's share of any application (often the whole application) by deleting its application folder that was created during the installation process.

Removing an application or file from your hard drive is usually two simple steps:

1. **Display the file or application folder in a Finder window.**

2. **Delete the file or folder with one of these steps:**

    - Drag the icon to the Trash.
    - Press ⌘+Delete.
    - Right-click the icon and choose Move to Trash.
    - Select the icon and click the Delete button on the Finder toolbar (if you added one).

Truly, no big whoop.

Mac owners like you and me can once again feel superior to the Windows folks because most Mac OS X applications don't need a separate, silly "uninstall" program. In fact, Macintosh software developers have always followed a simple general rule: All (or virtually all) of an application's support data should reside in a single folder.

Don't forget to actually *empty* the Trash, or you'll wonder why you aren't regaining any hard drive space. (Snow Leopard works hard to store the contents of the Trash until you manually delete it, just in case you want to undelete something.) To get rid of that stuff permanently and reclaim the space, do the following:

1. **Click the Trash icon on the Dock and hold down the mouse button — or right-click — until the pop-up menu appears.**

2. **Choose Empty Trash.**

Associated files in other folders

Some applications install files in different locations across your hard drive. (Applications in this category include the Microsoft Office suite and Photoshop.) How can you clear out these "orphan" files after you delete the application folder?

The process is a little more involved than deleting a single folder, but it's still no big whoop. Here's the procedure:

1. **Click the Search text box in a Finder window.**

   You can read more about Search and Finder windows in Chapter 7.

2. **Type the name of the application in the Search text box.**

   Figure 24-1 shows this search. I want to remove Toast Titanium, so I search for every file with the word *toast* in its name.

3. **Decide which of these files belong to the to-be-deleted application.**

   Be sure that the files you choose to delete are part of the deleted application. For example, a text file with the name *Instructions on Making a Perfect Piece of Toast* might not be part of Toast Titanium.

   Many associated files either

   • Have the same icon as the parent application

   • Are in the Preferences, Caches, or Application Support folders

4. **In the Search Results window, click the associated file(s) that you want to delete and just drag them to the Trash.**

   Don't empty the Trash immediately after you delete these files. Wait a few hours or a day. That way, if you realize that you deleted a file that you truly need, you can easily restore it from the Trash.

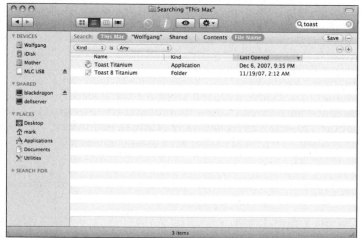

Figure 24-1:
Mine your
hard drive
for addi-
tional files
to delete.

Using a commercial cleanup tool

If you'd rather use a commercial application to help you clean up your hard drive, a number of them are available, but most are shareware applications that perform only one task. For example, Tidy Up! from Hyperbolic Software (www.hyperbolicsoftware.com) does one thing, but it does it well. It finds duplicate files on your hard drive, matching by criteria such as file-name, size, and extension. It's a good tool at $30.

For a truly comprehensive cleanup utility, I recommend Spring Cleaning, from Smith Micro Software (my.smithmicro.com), the same company that produces the archiving utility StuffIt. Spring Cleaning sells for $50. Not much crud squeaks by all those search routines, including duplicates, orphan preference files, and log files. Spring Cleaning even includes a separate feature called MacUninstaller that can help automate the steps that I cover in the preceding section.

Backing Up Your Treasure

Do it.

I'm not going to lecture you about backing up your hard drive . . . well, perhaps just for a moment. Imagine what it feels like to lose *everything* — names, numbers, letters, reports, presentations, saved games, photographs, and music. Then ask yourself, "Self, isn't all that irreplaceable stuff worth just a couple of hours every month?"

Time for a Mark's Maxim:

***Back up.* On a regular basis. Then store those DVDs or that external backup device somewhere safe, away from calamities.**

Take my word for it — you will thank me some day!

You can back up your files either by saving them to external media or by using Snow Leopard's awesome Time Machine feature.

Saving Files

The simplest method of backing up files is simply to copy the files and folders to an external hard drive or a CD or DVD. Nothing fancy, but it works.

Backing up to an external hard drive

If you have an external hard drive on your iMac, you can easily drag backup files to it from your internal hard drive (I cover external hard drives in Chapter 23):

1. **Open separate Finder windows for**
   - The external hard drive
   - The internal hard drive
2. **Select the desired files that you want to back up from your internal drive.**
3. **Drag the selected files to the external drive window.**

Backing up to CD and DVD

You can burn backup files to a recordable CD or DVD.

Burning backups from the Finder

To use the Finder's Burn feature with a CD or DVD, follow these steps:

1. **Load a blank disc into your iMac's optical drive.**

   If you're using the default settings in the CDs & DVDs pane in System Preferences, a dialog asks you for a disc name.

2. **Into the disc's Finder window, drag the files and folders that you want to back up.**

   They can be organized any way you like. Don't forget that the total amount of data shouldn't exceed 4GB or so (on a standard recordable DVD) or 8GB (on a dual-layer recordable DVD). You can see how much free space remains on the disc at the bottom of the disc's Finder window.

3. **Click File and then choose Burn Disc from the menu.**

   You can also click the Burn button on the Recordable DVD bar — it appears at the top of the disc's Finder window.

4. **Choose the fastest recording speed possible.**

5. **Click Burn.**

Burning backups from other recording applications

If you've invested in Toast Titanium from Roxio (www.roxio.com) or another CD/DVD recording application, you can create a new disc layout to burn your backup disc. (Think of a layout as a "road map" indicating which files and folders Toast should store on the backup.)

You can save that disc layout and use it again. This simplifies the process of backing up the same files in the future (if you don't move folders or files from their current spot).

Putting Things Right with Time Machine

If you enable backups via Snow Leopard's Time Machine feature, you can literally move backward through the contents of your iMac's hard drive, selecting and restoring all sorts of data. Files and folders are ridiculously easy to restore — and I mean easier than *any* restore you've ever performed, no matter what the operating system or backup program. Time Machine can even handle such deleted items as Address Book entries or photos you sent to the Trash from iPhoto!

Because Time Machine should be an important and integral part of every Mac owner's existence, the Time Machine icon is included on the Dock. (Apple is not messing around!)

Apple's Time Capsule device is designed as a wireless storage drive for your Time Machine backup files — if you're interested in a single Time Machine backup location for multiple Macs across your wireless network, Time Capsule is a great addition to your home or office.

Before you can use Time Machine, it must be enabled within the Time Machine pane in System Preferences. I cover the Time Machine configuration settings (and how to turn the feature on) in more detail in Chapter 6.

Here's how you can turn back time, step by step, to restore a file that you deleted or replaced in a folder.

1. **Open the folder that contained the file you want to restore.**

2. **In a separate window, open your Applications folder and launch the Time Machine application, or click the Time Machine icon on the Dock (which bears a clock with a counter-clockwise arrow).**

   The oh-so-ultra-cool Time Machine background appears behind your folder, complete with its own set of buttons at the bottom of the screen (as shown in Figure 24-2). On the right, you see a timeline that corresponds to the different days and months included in the backups that Snow Leopard has made.

3. **Click within the timeline to jump directly to a date (displaying the folder's contents on that date).**

   Alternatively, use the Forward and Back arrows at the right to move through the folder's contents through time. (You should see the faces of Windows users when you "riffle" through your folders to locate something you deleted several weeks ago!)

   The backup date of the items you're viewing appears in the button bar at the bottom of the screen.

4. **After you locate the file you want to restore, click it to select it.**

5. **Click the Restore button at the right side of the Time Machine button bar.**

   If you want to restore all the contents of the folder, click the Restore All button instead.

Time Machine returns you to the Finder, with the newly restored file now appearing in the folder. Out-*standing!*

To restore specific data from your Address Book or images from iPhoto, launch the desired application first and then launch Time Machine. Instead of riffling through a Finder window, you can move through time within the application window.

For simple backup and restore protection, Time Machine is all that a typical Mac owner at home is likely to ever need. Therefore, a very easy Mark's Maxim to predict:

Get an external hard drive, connect it and turn on Time Machine. *Do it now*. Don't make a humongous mistake.

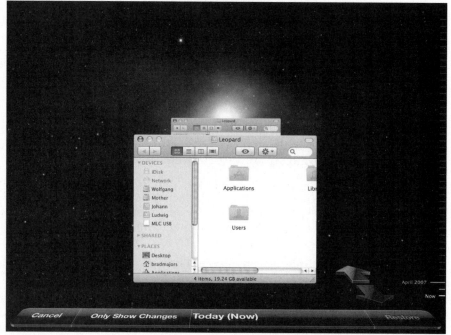

Figure 24-2:
Yes, Time
Machine
really *does*
look like
this!

Maintaining Hard Drive Health

Shifty-eyed, sneaky, irritating little problems can bother your hard drive: *permissions errors.* Incorrect disk and file permissions can

- ✔ Make your iMac lock up
- ✔ Make applications act screwy (or refuse to run at all)
- ✔ Cause weird behavior within a Finder window or System Preferences

To keep Snow Leopard running at its best, I recommend that you fix permissions errors at least once per week. Follow these steps:

1. **Open a Finder window, click Applications, and then click Utilities.**

2. **Double-click the Disk Utility icon.**

3. **Click the volume at the left that you want to check. (*Volume* is just computer-speak for a named partition, like Macintosh HD, which appears under your physical hard drive.)**

4. **Click the Repair Disk Permissions button.**

   Disk Utility does the rest and then displays a message about whatever it has to fix. (When will someone invent a *car* with a Repair Me button?)

Automating Those Mundane Chores

One popular feature in Snow Leopard — Automator — has generated a lot of excitement. You use Automator (as shown in Figure 24-3) to create customized tools that automate repetitive tasks.

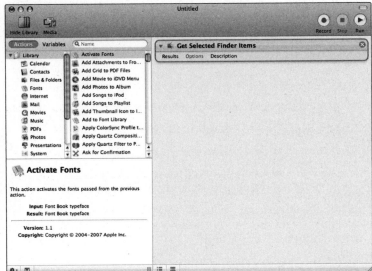

Figure 24-3: Automator is a dream come true for those who hate repetitive tasks.

You can also create *workflows,* which are sequential (and repeatable) operations that are performed on the same files or data, and then your Automator application can automatically launch whatever applications are necessary to get the job done.

Here's a great example: You work with a service bureau that sends you a CD every week with new product shots for your company's marketing department. Unfortunately, these images are flat-out *huge* — taken with a 12-megapixel camera — and they're always in the wrong orientation. Before you move them to the Marketing folder on your server, you have to use Preview to laboriously resize each image and rotate it, and then use the Finder window to save the smaller version.

With help from Automator, you can build a custom application that automatically reads each image in the folder, resizes it, rotates it, generates a thumbnail image, prints the image, and then moves the massaged images to the proper folder. You'll find Automator in your Applications folder. Currently, Automator can handle specific tasks within about 30 or 40 applications (including the Finder), but both Apple and third-party developers are busy adding new Automator task support to all sorts of new and existing applications.

Creating an application in Automator

To create a simple application with Automator, launch the application and follow these steps:

1. **Select Custom and click Choose.**

2. **Click the desired item in the Library list.**

   Automator displays the actions available for the item you've selected. Some of these items are media files, while others include Address Book contacts, files and folders in the Finder, PDF documents and even Apple Mail messages.

3. **Drag the desired action from the Library pane to the workflow pane.**

4. **Modify any specific settings provided for the action you chose.**

5. **Repeat Steps 1–3 to complete the workflow.**

6. **Click Run (upper right) to test your application.**

   Use sample files while you're fine-tuning your application, lest you accidentally do something deleterious to an original (and irreplaceable) file!

   Figure 24-4 illustrates an application that will take care of the earlier example — resizing and rotating a folder full of images, and then moving them to the Pictures folder.

7. **When the application is working as you like, press ⌘+Shift+S to save it.**

Figure 24-4: Now you can handle 10 or 1,000 images in a folder — your application does the work!

8. **In the Save As dialog that appears, type a name for your new application.**

9. **Click the Where pop-up menu and specify a location where the file should be saved.**

10. **Click the File Format pop-up menu and choose Application.**

11. **Click Save.**

    Your new Automator application icon appears, sporting an Automator robot standing on a document.

    If you're going to use your new Automator application often, you can drag the application icon to your Dock or to your desktop.

 To find all the actions of a certain type within the Library list, click in the Search box at the bottom of the Library pane and type in a keyword, such as **save** or **burn**. You don't even need to press Return!

Running applications at start up

If your Automator application should run every time you log in, follow these steps to set it up as a Login Item:

1. **Open System Preferences.**

2. **Display the Accounts pane.**

3. **Click the Login Items button.**

4. **Click the plus button at the bottom of the list.**

5. **Navigate to the location of your new Automator application.**

6. **Click Add.**

    Now your Automator application is *really* automatic.

 Many third-party applications have their own Automator actions. Check the developer's Web site often to see whether additional Automator applications have been added that you can download.

Updating Mac OS X Automatically

I prefer my iMac to take care of cleaning up after itself, so updating Snow Leopard should be automatic as well. In Mac OS X Snow Leopard, operating system updates are performed by the Software Update application.

Software Update uses the Internet, so you need an Internet connection to shake hands with the Apple server and download any updates.

Software Update can be found in two convenient spots:

- **The Apple menu:** Click the Apple menu (🍎) and then click Software Update, which displays the Update dialog and alerts you to anything new that's available.

- **System Preferences:** Click the Software Update icon to display the Software Update pane that you see in Figure 24-5.

  If you take the System Preferences route, you can set Software Update to check for updates automatically:

  a. *Mark the Check for Updates check box to enable it.*

  b. *Choose the time period from the Check for Updates pop-up menu.*

  Software Update covers every Apple application, so I usually check once daily just to make sure that I don't miss anything.

  If something needs to be updated, the program alerts you, either automatically downloading the update(s) or displaying a dialog letting you know what you can update (depending on the settings you choose in the System Preferences Software Update pane).

You can even check for updates immediately from System Preferences. That, dear reader, is just plain thoughtful design.

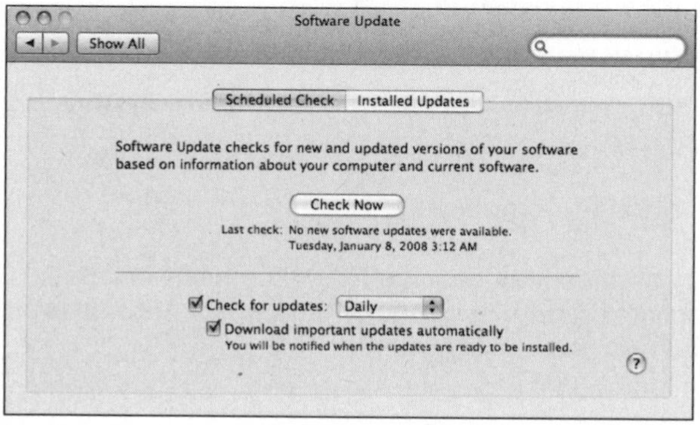

Figure 24-5:
Setting up
Software
Update
to launch
itself, all by
itself.

Software Update

Show All

Scheduled Check | Installed Updates

Software Update checks for new and updated versions of your software based on information about your computer and current software.

Check Now

Last check: No new software updates were available.
Tuesday, January 8, 2008 3:12 AM

☑ Check for updates: Daily

☑ Download important updates automatically
You will be notified when the updates are ready to be installed.

Part VII
The Part of Tens

The 5th Wave   By Rich Tennant

In this part . . .

Ah, what book in the *For Dummies* series is truly complete without the infamous Part of Tens? Here you
find lots of this author's raw opinion on things like tips for
boosting your computer's performance and Ten Things to
Avoid Like the Plague.

Chapter 25

Ten Ways to Speed Up Your iMac

*E*ven an iMac with an Intel Quad-Core i7 processor can always go just a bit faster . . . or *can* it? There's actually a pretty short list of tweaks that you can apply to your iMac's hardware to speed it up, and these suggestions are covered in this chapter.

You can also work considerably faster within Snow Leopard by customizing your Desktop and your Finder windows, which makes it easier to spot and use your files, folders, and applications. That's in this Part of Tens chapter, too.

Finally, you can enhance your efficiency and make yourself a power user by tweaking yourself. (Sounds a bit tawdry or even painful, but bear with me, and you'll understand.)

Nothing Works Like a Shot of Memory

Okay, maybe *shot* is the wrong word, but adding additional memory to your iMac (by either replacing or adding a memory module) is the single surefire way to speed up the performance of your entire system. That includes every application as well as Snow Leopard itself.

With more memory, your iMac can hold more of your documents and data in memory, and thus has to store less data temporarily on your hard drive. It takes your iMac much less time to store, retrieve, and work with data when that data is in RAM (short for *random access memory*) rather than on your hard drive. That's why your system runs faster when you can fit an entire image in Photoshop in your iMac's system memory.

Hold a Conversation with Your iMac

Many Mac owners will attest that you *can* significantly increase your own efficiency by using the Speakable Items feature, which allows you to speak common commands within applications and Finder windows. Your voice is indeed faster than either your mouse or your fingers! Common commands in the Speakable Items folder include "Log me out" and "Get my mail."

To enable Speakable Items, choose System Preferences⇨Speech and then select the On radio button next to Speakable Items to enable speech recognition. Remember, by default, that the speech recognition system is active only when you press and hold the Esc key.

Vamoose, Unwanted Fragments!

Apple would probably prefer that I not mention disk fragmentation because Snow Leopard doesn't come with a built-in defragmenting application. (Go figure.) A disk-defragmenting application reads all the files on your drive and rewrites them as continuous, contiguous files, which your machine can read significantly faster.

To keep your hard drive running as speedily as possible, I recommend defragmenting at least once monthly. You can use third-party applications like Micromat's TechTool Pro (www.micromat.com) to defragment your drive.

Keep Your Desktop Background Simple

It's funny that I still include this tip in a chapter dedicated to improving performance. After all, I recommended using a solid color background in my first books on Mac OS 8 and Windows 98! Just goes to show you that some things never change.

If you're interested in running your system as fast as it will go, choose a solid-color background from the Desktop & Screen Saver pane in System Preferences. (In fact, there's even a separate category that you can pick called Solid Colors.)

Column Mode Is for Power Users

One of my favorite features of Mac OS X is the ability to display files and folders in column view mode. Just click the Column button in the standard Finder window toolbar, and the contents of the window automatically align in well-ordered columns.

Other file display options require you to drill through several layers of folders to get to a specific location on your hard drive — for example, `Users/mark/Music/iTunes/iTunes Music`, which I visit on a regular basis. In column mode, however, a single click drills a level deeper, and often you won't even have to use the Finder window's scroll bars to see what you're looking for. Files and folders appear in a logical order. Plus, it's much easier to move a file (by dragging it from one location on your hard drive to another) in column mode.

Make the Dock Do Your Bidding

Just about every Mac owner considers the Mac OS X Dock a good friend. But when's the last time you customized it — or have you ever made a change to it at all?

You can drag files and folders to the Dock, as well as Web URLs, applications, and network servers. You can also remove applications and Web URLs just as easily by dragging the icon from the Dock and releasing it on your Desktop.

I find that I make a significant change to my Dock icons at least once every week. I find nothing more convenient than placing a folder for each of my current projects on the Dock or adding applications to the Dock that I might be researching for a book or demonstrating in a chapter.

You can position the Dock at either side of the Desktop or even hide the Dock from sight entirely to give yourself an extra strip of space on your Desktop for application windows.

It All Started with Keyboard Shortcuts

Heck, keyboard shortcuts have been around since the days of WordStar and VisiCalc, back when a mouse was still a living rodent. If you add up all those seconds of mouse-handling that you save by using keyboard shortcuts, you'll see that you can save hours of productive time every year.

You're likely already using some keyboard shortcuts, like the common editing shortcuts ⌘+C (Copy) and ⌘+V (Paste). When I'm learning a new application, I often search through the application's online help to find a keyboard shortcut table and then print out that table as a quick reference. Naturally, you can also view keyboard shortcuts by clicking each of the major menu groups within an application. Shortcuts are usually displayed alongside the corresponding menu items.

Hey, You Tweaked Your Finder!

Here's another speed enhancer along the same lines as my earlier tip about customizing your Dock: You can also reconfigure your Finder windows to present you with just the tools and locations that you actually use (rather than what Apple *figures* you'll use).

For example, you can right-click the toolbar in any Finder window and choose Customize Toolbar. By default, Snow Leopard's Finder toolbar includes only the default icon set that you see at the bottom of the sheet, but you can drag and drop all sorts of useful command icons onto the toolbar. You can save space by displaying small-sized icons, too.

The Sidebar — which hangs out at the left side of the Finder window — is a healthy, no-nonsense repository for those locations that you constantly visit throughout a computing session. For example, I have both a Games folder and a Book Chapters folder that I use countless times every day — it's important to balance work with pleasure, you know — and I've dragged both of those folders to the Sidebar.

Keep in Touch with Your Recent Past

Click that Apple menu (🍎) and use that Recent Items menu! I know that sounds a little *too* simple, but I meet many new Apple computer owners every year who either don't know that the Recent Items menu exists or forget to use it. You can access both applications and documents that you've used within the last few days. Consider the Dock and Finder Sidebar as permanent or semipermanent solutions, and the Recent Items menu as more of a temporary solution to finding the stuff that you're working on right now.

Go Where the Going Is Good

To round out this Part of Tens chapter, I recommend another little-known (and under-appreciated) Finder menu feature (at least among Macintosh novices): the Go menu, which is located on the Finder menu.

The Go menu is really a catchall, combining the most important locations on your system (like your Home folder and your iDisk) with folders that you've used recently. Plus, the Go menu is the place where you can connect to servers or shared folders across your local network or across the Internet.

Pull down the Go menu today — and don't forget to try out those spiffy keyboard shortcuts you see listed next to the command names. (For example, press ⌘+Shift+H to immediately go to your Home folder.) And if a Finder window isn't open at the moment, a new window opens automatically — such convenience is hard to resist!

Chapter 26

Ten Things to Avoid Like the Plague

If you've read other books that I've written in the *For Dummies* series, you might recognize the title of this chapter: It's a favorite Part of Tens subject of mine that appears often in my work. I don't like to see any computer owner fall prey to pitfalls. Some of these pitfalls are minor — like being less than diligent about keeping your iMac clean — but others are downright catastrophic, like providing valuable information over the Internet to persons unknown.

All these potential mistakes, however, share one thing in common: They're *easily prevented* with a little common sense — as long as you're aware of them. That's my job. In this chapter, I fill in what you need to know. Consider these pages as experience gained easily!

Man, That Is the Definition of Sluggish

Let's see, what could I be talking about? Oh, yes . . . **only** a USB 1.1 external hard drive, Flash drive or CD-ROM drive could be as slow as a turtle on narcotics.

Unfortunately, you'll still find countless examples of USB 1.1 storage hardware hanging around. The auction site, eBay, is stuffed to the gills with USB 1.1 hard drives. A USB 1.1 hard drive is simply a slow-as-maple-syrup-in-January embarrassment. If a peripheral's job is to store or move data *quickly* — I'm talking hard drives, network connections, CD-ROM drives, and USB Flash drives — opt for a USB 2.0 or FireWire device.

Phishing Is No Phun

Phishing refers to an attempt by unsavory characters to illegally obtain your personal information. If that sounds like an invitation to identity theft, it is — and thousands of sites have defrauded individuals like you and me (along with banks and credit card companies) out of billions of dollars.

A phishing scam works like this: You get an e-mail purporting to be from a major company or business, such as eBay, a government agency, a social networking site, or a major credit card company. The message warns you that you have to update your login or financial information to keep it current, or that you have to validate your information every so often — and even provides you with a link to an official-looking Web page (although sometimes full of spelling errors, and always with a bogus address). After you enter information on that bogus page, it's piped directly to the bad guys, and they're off to the races.

Here's a Mark's Maxim that every Internet user should take to heart:

No *legitimate* company or agency will solicit your personal information through an e-mail message!

Never respond to these messages. Don't use the link provided in the phishing e-mail! If you smell something phishy, open your Web browser and visit the company's site (the *real* one) by typing in the address directly; then contact the company's customer support department to report the scam.

In fact, sending any valuable financial information through unencrypted e-mail — even to those whom you know and trust — is a bad idea. E-mail messages can be intercepted or can be read from any e-mail server that stores your message.

Put Floppy Disks to Rest

Did you know that the iMac was the first model produced by a major computer manufacturer that didn't include a floppy drive? Apple always looks ahead five years when it develops a new computer model, and the good folks in Cupertino accurately predicted the demise of the stodgy 1.44MB floppy disk.

If you still need a portable storage bin of some sort to carry from computer to computer, I heartily recommend that you pick up a USB Flash drive. These drives hold anywhere from 2 to 256GB, and they work in any USB port. (And they're downright warp-drive fast when compared with a floppy disk, especially the USB 2.0 variety.)

Do You Really Want a Submerged Keyboard?

Your answer should be an unequivocal "No!" — and that's why everyone should make it a rule to keep all beverages well out of range of keyboards, speakers, mice, backup drives, and any other piece of external hardware. Especially when kids or cats are in close proximity to your iMac.

Cleaning up a hazardous soda spill is hard enough in the clear, but if that liquid comes in contact with your hardware, you're likely to be visited with intermittent keyboard problems (or, in the worst-case scenario, a short in an external peripheral or your iMac's motherboard).

Suffice it to say that 12 inches of open space can make the difference between a simple cleanup and an expensive replacement!

Don't Use Antiquated Utility Software

If you're using Snow Leopard you should upgrade your older utility programs. These older disk utility applications can actually do more damage than good to a hard drive under Mac OS X Snow Leopard. A number of things changed when Apple made the leap to Snow Leopard, including subtle changes to disk formats and memory management within applications. With an out-of-date utility, you could find yourself with corrupted data.

Make sure that you diagnose and repair disk and file errors by using only a utility application that's specifically designed to run in Snow Leopard, like TechTool Pro from Micromat (www.micromat.com). Your iMac's hard drive will definitely thank you.

(Oh, and while you're at it, don't forget to check the manufacturer's Web site for any updates to drivers or application software for your third-party external hardware! 'Nuff said.)

Don't Endorse Software Piracy

This one's a real no-brainer — remember, Apple's overall market share among worldwide computer users currently weighs in at little more than 12 percent. Software developers know this, and they have to expect (and *receive*) a return on their investment, or they're going to find something more lucrative to do with their time. As a shareware author, I can attest to this fact firsthand.

An iMac is a great machine, and Snow Leopard is a great operating system, but even the best hardware and the sexiest desktop won't make up for an absence of good applications. Pay for what you use, and everyone benefits.

Call It the Forbidden Account

You might never have encountered the *root*, or *System Administrator*, account within Mac OS X — and that's always A Good Thing. Note that I'm not talking about a standard administrator (or admin) account here. Every iMac needs at least one admin account (in fact, it might be the only visible account on your computer), and any standard user account can be toggled between standard and admin status with no trouble at all (by another admin account).

The root account, though, is a different beast altogether, and that's why it's disabled by default. All Unix systems have a root account; because Snow Leopard is based on a Unix foundation, it has one, too. Anyone logging in with the root account can do *anything* on your system, including deleting or modifying files in the System folder (which no other account can access). Believe me: Deliberately formatting your hard drive is about the only thing worse than screwing up the files in your System folder.

Luckily, no one can accidentally access the root/System Administrator account. In fact, you can't assign the root account with System Preferences; you must use the Terminal application in Utilities (within your Applications folder). Unless an Apple support technician tells you to enable and use it, you should promptly forget that the root account even exists.

Don't Settle for a Surge Suppressor

Technically, there's nothing wrong with using a surge suppressor to feed power to your iMac and all your external peripherals, but it doesn't do the *entire* job. Your system is still wide open to problems caused by momentary brownouts, not to mention the occasional full-fledged blackout. Losing power in the middle of a computing session will likely lead to lost documents and might even result in disk or file errors later. With an uninterruptible power supply (UPS), you can rest easy knowing that your iMac will have a few minutes more of "ilife."

Most Mac owners know about the backup battery power that a UPS provides, but they don't know about the extra work performed by most UPS units: namely, filtering your AC current. A filtering UPS prevents electronic noise (think about a vacuum being used next to a TV set) and momentary current spikes. These days, you'll find good UPS models for under $100.

Refurbished Hardware Is No Deal at All

Boy, howdy, do I hate refurbished stuff. To quote someone famous, "If the deal sounds too good to be true, it probably is."

Examine what you get when you buy a refurbished external hard drive. It's likely that the drive was returned as defective, of course, and was then sent back to the factory. There, the manufacturer probably performed the most cursory of repairs, perhaps tested the unit for a few seconds, and then packed it back up again. (I should, however, note that Apple sells refurbished Macs, and generally has a good reputation for value on these computers.)

Before you spend a dime on a bargain that's *remanufactured* — I can't get over that term — make sure that you find out how long a warranty you'll receive, if any.

If at all possible, I recommend spending the extra cash on trouble-free, brand-new hardware that has a full warranty.

iMacs Appreciate Cleanliness

Clean your machine. Even though your iMac has a fan, dust is an insidious enemy within the confines of your computer's case. I know Mac owners who celebrate each passing year by opening up their machines to blow them clean of dust bunnies with a can of compressed air. (I'm one of them, as a matter of fact.)

If you're adding memory to your aluminum iMac, as I demonstrate in Chapter 23, take advantage of the chance and use that trusty can of compressed air to clean up.

Your screen should be cleaned at least once every two or three days. Never spray anything — cleaners, water, **anything!** — directly on your screen or your iMac's case. I highly recommend using premoistened LCD cleaning wipes to safely clean your iMac monitor.

Your iMac case needs only a thorough wiping job with a soft cloth should stay spotless. Don't forget to turn off your Aluminum Supercomputer.

Index

• **E** •

• Z •